Welcome to

W9-AVN-756

THESE HANDY, PORTABLE BOOKS are designed to be the perfect traveling companions. Whether you're traveling within a tight family budget or feeling the urge to splurge, you will find all you need to create a memorable family vacation.

Use these books to plan your trips, and then take them along with you for easy reference. Does Jimmy want to go sailing? Or maybe Jane wants to go to the local hobby shop. *The Everything® Family Guides* offer many ways to entertain kids of all ages while also ensuring you get the most out of your time away from home.

Review this book cover to cover to give you great ideas before you travel, and stick it in your backpack or diaper bag to use as a quick reference guide for activities, attractions, and excursions you want to experience. Let *The Everything® Family Guides* help you travel the world, and you'll discover that vacationing with the whole family can be filled with fun and exciting adventures.

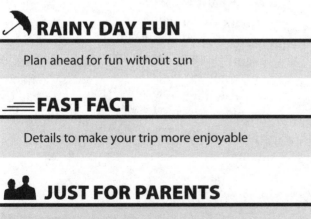

TRAVEL TIP

Quick, handy tips

RAINY DAY FUN

Plan ahead for fun without sun

FAST FACT

Details to make your trip more enjoyable

JUST FOR PARENTS

Appealing information for moms and dads

THE
EVERYTHING®
— Family Guides —
Washington D.C.

Dear Reader,

You are about to have the time of your family's life. Among the world's cities, Washington is unique in its openness and user-friendliness. Other cities may accommodate visitors, but our nation's capital exists because of them. We feel at home here because, no matter where we come from, it is every American's home town. The city houses our government and our representatives, a piece of us. It is supported by our tax money. It exists to welcome us and show where we have come from and what we have accomplished.

I have lived a good portion of my adult life in the Washington D.C., metropolitan area, as well as other cities here and abroad. And there is no place that comes even close to making its guests feel as cared for and welcome. Here, we are all "fellow Americans," it is a remarkable truth found in no other city in the country. Washington is our heritage, our birthright. What happens here touches all of our lives to the tiniest degree. Its monuments are instantly recognized. Its historic soul is our past as well.

For all that, Washington is a modern, dynamic city. It is cosmopolitan yet manageable and will fill your needs whatever they might be. So enjoy your second home, learn a little more about your country and yourself, but most of all have a good time!

Jesse Leaf

THE
EVERYTHING
FAMILY GUIDE TO
WASHINGTON D.C.
3rd Edition

All the best hotels,
restaurants, sites, and attractions

Jesse Leaf

Adams Media
Avon, Massachusetts

To my wife, Mindy, and children, Joanna, Jason, and Alison, who never ceased to remind me how boring my choice of "exciting" things to do were, and brought me back to the world of the teenager and child.

• • •

Publisher: Gary M. Krebs
Managing Editor: Laura M. Daly
Associate Copy Chief: Sheila Zwiebel
Acquisitions Editor: Lisa Laing
Development Editor: Brett Palana-Shanahan
Associate Production Editor: Casey Ebert

Director of Manufacturing: Susan Beale
Associate Director of Production:
Michelle Roy Kelly
Prepress: Erick DaCosta, Matt LeBlanc
Design and Layout: Heather Barrett,
Brewster Brownville, Colleen
Cunningham, Jennifer Oliveira

• • •

An Everything® Series Book.
Everything® and everything.com® are registered trademarks of F+W Publications, Inc.

Published by Adams Media, an F+W Publications Company
57 Littlefield Street, Avon, MA 02322 U.S.A.
www.adamsmedia.com

ISBN 10: 1-59869-287-9
ISBN 13: 978-1-59869-287-7

Printed in Canada.

J I H G F E D C B

Library of Congress Cataloging-in-Publication Data
Leaf, Jesse.
The everything family guide to Washington D.C. / Jesse Leaf. — 3rd ed.
p. cm. — (An everything series book)
Includes bibliographical references and index.
ISBN-13: 978-1-59869-287-7
ISBN-10: 1-59869-287-9
1. Washington (D.C.)—Guidebooks. 2. Family recreation—Washington (D.C.)—
Guidebooks. 3. Children—Travel—Washington (D.C.)—Guidebooks. I. Title.
F192.3.L43 2007
917.5304'42—dc22
2006036472

This publication is designed to provide accurate and authoritative information with regard to the subject matter covered. It is sold with the understanding that the publisher is not engaged in rendering legal, accounting, or other professional advice. If legal advice or other expert assistance is required, the services of a competent professional person should be sought.
　　　　—From a *Declaration of Principles* jointly adopted by a Committee of the American Bar Association and a Committee of Publishers and Associations

Many of the designations used by manufacturers and sellers to distinguish their products are claimed as trademarks. Where those designations appear in this book and Adams Media was aware of a trademark claim, the designations have been printed with initial capital letters.

This book is available at quantity discounts for bulk purchases.
For information, please call 1-800-289-0963.

Visit the entire Everything® series at *www.everything.com*

Contents

Top Ten Things to Do in D.C.

1. Spend a special holiday: Memorial Day ceremonies, July 4th fireworks (then a visit to the Archives), Halloween at the Zoo, and the winter holiday season.

2. Shake the hand of your senator or representative.

3. See Tai Shan, the cute little panda bear at the National Zoo.

4. Take a Segway tour of the city.

5. See all the money being printed at the Bureau of Engraving and Printing.

6. Climb inside the International Space Station with your kids and join them on a ride on the flight simulator at the awesome Air and Space Museum.

7. In the wintertime, ice skate in the outdoor sculpture garden of the National Gallery of Art.

8. In the springtime, stroll through the cherry blossoms in full bloom.

9. Take the D.C. Duck Tour with kids, and let them blow those duck bills until you hear them in your sleep.

10. Eat as many of Ben's chili dogs as you can and then go to Cake Love for buttercream-frosted cupcakes.

Acknowledgments

The hundreds of revisions made to this edition were made possible only with the help of scores of people—too numerous to mention individually—behind the reception and manager's desks of hotels, restaurants, attractions, and retail stores around the city. Special thanks, however, are due to the patient and giving experts at the Smithsonian Institution and the Washington Metropolitan Area Transit Authority. I also want to single out "Miller," the ebullient guard at the Petersen House, and Gary and Barbara Nooger, who extended my eyes and ears into Northern Virginia and nearby Maryland. Also thanks to Lisa Laing of Adams Media and June Clark of the Peter Rubie Literary Agency, two people who prove that professionalism and huge workloads don't preclude a human touch to their jobs and decent treatment of writers of travel guides.

Introduction

Washington D.C. is one of the world's most popular tourist destinations. More than 30 million people a year visit this city of 600,000. Some are drawn by the mystique of government and the sheer beauty of this showplace city, but most have an understandable feeling of belonging, of coming home, and they are welcomed as such.

If you have never visited the capital, you may be in for a surprise. Far from being a marble-clad and dusty repository of the past or a bastion of the elite, Washington D.C. is a vibrant, dynamic, and accessible city. In the past, the city depended on its position as our nation's capital to "automatically" draw tourists. Today, a new city administration has drastically "kicked it up a notch." They have taken a cue from European tourist centers such as Monaco, and a new energy level and creativity have reformed the city's tourist industry. Festivals, theme "months" and "weeks," specialized tours, and events have turbocharged the hospitality industry, and it has responded with a rash of new hotels and services (including theme packages and discounted dates).

One example is The District's famed cherry blossoms. People were once content to stroll around the Tidal Basin to welcome spring by viewing the flowers. Now the blooming of the cherry blossoms has become a mega-event involving scores of restaurants (cherry-theme food), hotels (special package deals), and city services (a parade and fireworks show).

In the short time since the second edition of *The Everything® Family Guide to Washington D.C.* was published, many new hotels have been built and old standbys extensively renovated (the Park Hyatt Washington, Hotel Palomar, Marriott M Street, Westin Arlington Gateway, Residence Inn Capitol, Hampton Inn, Four Seasons). The city's big news is the reopening, after six years, of the Donald W. Reynolds Center for American Art & Portraiture, formerly the Smithsonian American Art Museum and National Portrait Gallery. Many new tours have been added, some with ethnic themes—for example, the Bilingual Heritage Trail in the Adams Morgan neighborhood. Some other major additions to the D.C. scene are the National Marathon race and the Capitol Visitors Center with its huge cafeteria, perfect for families.

The increase in visitors has prompted expanded airline service and the construction, albeit only for a set number of years, of City Center Parking. The Metro continues its outstanding service to the city, and there are several intracity shuttles to take you where you want to go.

Of course, this dynamic scene has necessitated a thorough revision of *The Everything® Family Guide to Washington D.C.* Many hundreds of changes were made and new features added. With this current edition, it will be easier for visitors to navigate the city because destinations now have the nearest Metro station and line color listed up front. Also, every listing has a telephone number and Web site (when present) so you can call ahead or preview information online, allowing you to buy and print out savings coupons and tickets, scan menus, and make reservations before you even leave home.

Washington D.C. is a multifaceted city that will offer whatever it is you seek, no matter what age groups your family members fall into. It is not only the seat of our government but a major art and museum center, college town, entertainment and sports venue, shopping resource, and restaurant destination. Washington D.C. is at once fun, solemn, educational, and exciting.

D.C. is one of the most fun and educational places you can visit with your kids. The city is like an interactive American history lesson and playground. Aside from the most obvious kid-pleasing attractions (the National Zoo, the Air and Space Museum, and the Museum of Natural History), there are many other one-of-a-kind kid-pleasing experiences, from the International Spy Museum to the Bureau of Engraving and Printing—and what kid (no matter what age) doesn't love seeing money printed and shredded? The National Geographic Explorer's Hall has interactive exhibits and a giant dinosaur-egg fossil, and the National Museum of Health and Medicine has the most astounding display of gross medical artifacts in the country.

For those interested in American history and how our government works, the city offers the White House; the Capitol; the Pentagon; the National Archives; the Supreme Court; and the Jefferson, Lincoln, Roosevelt, Vietnam, Korean, and World War II War Memorials, as well as a treasure trove of historic homes and monuments.

The Smithsonian Institution itself is like an American theme park. Its most popular museums are the National Air and Space Museum (with planes and interactive exhibits from the Wright Brothers' 1903 *Flyer* to space exploration), the Udvar-Hazy Center (where you can see up close the *Enola Gay* and the space shuttle *Enterprise*, as well as the most popular treasures of the closed-for-renovation National Museum of American History like the ruby slippers Judy Garland wore in *The Wizard of Oz*), and the Museum of Natural History (with the cursed Hope Diamond and the dramatic Hall of Mammals, as well as all those dinosaur fossils and bones). The Smithsonian collection also encompasses museums on arts and industries, African and Asian art, decorative arts, American art, great portraits, and modern art.

And that's not all! There's plenty of shopping to do in the museum shops, specialty stores, and even outlet centers outside of town, not to mention eating in a huge selection of restaurants of every possible description!

Because of all this, you will want to return often, revisiting favorites, exploring things you missed. Many people make Washington a rotating spot on a variable list of vacation places and see a different side of the city each time they visit. So read through these pages and plan one of the best vacations you and your family will ever have!

CHAPTER 1

Welcome to Washington D.C.

WASHINGTON D.C., THE CAPITAL of the United States, is one of the leading vacation destinations for American and foreign tourists every year. It is a showcase city, full of attractions and rich with history. From its birth as a compromise site between the northern and southern states and up to the present day, this city has remained the symbolic center of our country and the center of our federal government. In this chapter, you'll get an introduction to D.C.'s history and the details about traveling there.

A City Is Born

Most students of American history know that D.C. was not the first choice for the nation's capital. Both New York City and Philadelphia were considered and given trial runs as the nation's capital. A decision was soon made that the capital should be centrally located between the northern and southern states, but at the time no such city existed. Maryland and Virginia both donated some of their land around the Potomac River to form the federal district, the District of Columbia (D.C.). George Washington played an important role in planning the city, and he entrusted Charles L'Enfant, a French engineer, with designing many of the city's major structures and monuments. A year after George Washington's death in 1799, Congress passed the law that formally moved the U.S. capital from Philadelphia to Washington D.C.

Naming the city after our first president was Congress's way of honoring George Washington for all that he had done for our country.

A Turbulent Beginning

Just over a decade after its establishment, D.C. came under attack. During the War of 1812, the Americans fought the British, who were determined to recapture their former colonies. (The War of 1812 is the only international war fought on American soil after the Revolution.) In the summer of 1814, the British defeated American troops at the Battle of Bladensburg and entered the American capital. Their goal was to burn the city as a symbolic act showing their victory over the Americans. The British set the White House on fire and also torched the Capitol building, the Library of Congress, and several military sites. Fortunately, because of heavy rains, the fire subsided without harming much of the city.

≡FAST FACT

Dolley Madison, who was first lady at the time of the 1814 fire, is remembered for rescuing the life-size Gilbert Stuart portrait of George Washington and other artifacts of the presidential building before evacuation. After the fire subsided and the building was renovated with white paint, it became known as the White House.

Washington During the Civil War

The city recovered from the War of 1812 and thrived again, but it soon found itself in the middle of another war—the Civil War. Although no battles were fought in Washington D.C., the city became a virtual military camp, with armed troops housed everywhere from the White House to the alleys of the Foggy Bottom neighborhood, which was referred to as "camptown." D.C. was the main storage area for military supplies for the Union Army, as well as a medical center. Many of the city's buildings, such as the U.S. Patent Building (now the Donald W. Reynolds Center for American Art and Portraiture), were transformed into makeshift hospitals.

As a result, the population of the city swelled from 60,000 to 120,000 almost overnight. Many of the new residents were freed slaves who came to the city for protection; many of them made their home on the grounds of the Arlington House, where they formed their own town, known as the Freedman's Village.

The Assassination of President Lincoln

Five days after the city celebrated the end of the Civil War, President Lincoln was assassinated while at a performance at Ford's Theatre. As a result the country went into a state of mourning. Washington D.C. was in chaos, from both the overburdening of its resources with so many new residents and the political upheaval. Many of the city's slums formed during this time, and those neighborhoods remained in poor condition until well into the twentieth century.

Nevertheless, the government pulled through, and it made rebuilding the city one of the first orders of business. Washington D.C. became a mecca for freed slaves and a true seat of government. Federal funding literally rebuilt the city in the nineteenth and early twentieth centuries, giving us the marvelous monuments, museums, and parks we have today.

≡ FAST FACT

The tradition of rallies and protests that make our capital the political entity it is today started after the Civil War and increased through the 1960s, when anti–Vietnam War protests and civil rights demonstrations were held almost daily on the Mall. It was there that Martin Luther King Jr. made his "I Have a Dream" speech, written at the nearby Willard Hotel.

D.C. Today

Today, Washington D.C. is a beautiful city with fine dining and excellent art, theater, music, and entertainment that rivals the world's leading hot spots. It's a great place to visit year-round, with many wonderful seasonal attractions such as the famous cherry trees that blossom in the early spring or the candlelight tours of the White House during the winter holiday season. Many people come for the solemn and touching Memorial Day ceremonies at the Vietnam Veterans Memorial and Arlington National Cemetery, for the fabulous fireworks display over the National Mall on the Fourth of July, or for the annual black family reunion weekend on the Mall the first weekend of September.

TRAVEL TIP

Before you go, do some research online. Even if you don't have a computer, most public libraries offer free Internet access and can help you take advantage of it. Once you are on the Internet, choose a search engine and search the words "Washington D.C." This will bring hundreds of listings, everything from event calendars to sports listings.

Because the climate is relatively mild for three of the four seasons, there is never a bad time to visit the nation's capital, which means that it is a city that regularly receives and accommodates tourists. However, this also means that the many sites and attractions are often crowded, which can translate into long lines to get into popular sites or no entry at all.

Best Times to Visit D.C.

If you're not sure what the best time is for you to visit D.C., there's a lot to consider. If you're worried about the crowds, autumn and winter are preferable, but in these seasons Congress is in session, so hotel rates are higher than in the summer.

Autumn

Washington D.C. and the adjacent states of Virginia and Maryland are beautiful in the fall. The city and the surrounding countryside are filled with trees and parklands that offer a wonderful display of fall foliage. Mount Vernon is especially scenic this time of year. The tourist crowds are sparse, except over three-day weekends that mark national holidays like Columbus Day and Veterans Day.

Winter

Winter is also a good time to visit the capital. There are many special events planned around the holidays, and most of the museums and historic houses offer special Christmas displays. While the winter in D.C. is milder than in the Northeast, it still snows in the capital.

TRAVEL TIP

Christmas in Washington is delightful. The White House features its tree-lighting ceremony; Ford's Theatre has an annual performance of Charles Dickens' *A Christmas Carol*; and Mount Vernon and the Pope-Leighey House are festooned with seasonal ornaments.

Spring

Spring in the capital city is spectacular. The District has a wealth of public gardens and greenery, as well as the annual Easter-egg roll on the White House lawn. When the cherry trees along the Tidal Basin near the Jefferson Memorial are in bloom in the early spring, D.C. is at its finest in a sea of pink. For this two-week period in late March or early April, there are constant festivities, marked by a parade at the end of the cherry blossom season. The 3,700 cherry trees were a gift to the United States from Japan in 1912. The first two trees were planted by First Lady Mrs. William Howard Taft and Viscountess Chinda of Japan, the Japanese ambassador's wife. Those two trees are still standing today, near the statue of John Paul Jones on 17th Street.

As the weather grows warmer, more and more tourists arrive to tour the capital. Many schools plan organized trips for this time of the year, so museums and historical sites are generally crowded in the later part of the spring.

TRAVEL TIP

The two busiest tourist weekends in D.C. are the Fourth of July and Memorial Day. So if you are planning on visiting then, make your hotel, transportation, and touring arrangements as early as possible.

Summer

Summer is the city's busiest tourist season, with tourists outnumbering residents by twelve to one. The National Air and Space Museum and the National Museum of Natural History receive at least a million visitors each during the months of July and August. From Memorial Day through Labor Day all the sites are crowded, and you will need tickets for all major attractions this time of year.

But the good news is that the city is well aware of the volume of visitors it receives, so many of the nation's leading attractions are open late during the summer. You can pack more into a summer visit than any other time of the year. There are also free concerts and outdoor activities throughout the city all summer long.

Summer in D.C. can be brutally hot, but everything is well air-conditioned, from the museums to the Metro to the lobbies of buildings.

What to Pack

Washington D.C. is a fairly laid-back city. If you plan on visiting the tourist sites, comfort should be your priority: jeans (or shorts in the summer) and sneakers or comfortable walking shoes. If you're visiting a lot of museums and plan to shop, bring an empty backpack, or you'll be carrying around shopping bags loaded with souvenirs all day. Be prepared to check your backpack at the door of every attraction and to have your belongings screened by security.

If you know you will be attending an arena event, an outdoor concert, or parade, you might want to pack binoculars. Also, don't forget your camera and/or video camera.

Spring and late summer are often rainy, so pack a collapsible umbrella or a rain poncho and put it in that knapsack. In the summer, pack a bathing suit. Many of the hotels have pools, and you'll want to cool off.

JUST FOR PARENTS

If you are planning on going to the theater, the Kennedy Center, or some of the better restaurants, plan to dress up a bit. But even the most stylish of places accept "business casual."

Plan Ahead

It is possible to visit Washington D.C., and wing it, but there are so many must-see things to do that require tickets (both free and paid) that it is really in your interest to plan ahead, especially if you are going for a short visit or vacationing during the holidays or the peak travel season.

Almost all the government tours require tickets, and some of these tours have very limited windows of opportunity, especially after the terrorist attacks of September 11. For instance, the White

House was closed to tours by the general public for over two years and reopened with a much more limited public touring policy. It is now possible to have a guided tour only through your member of congress. These self-guided tours of ten people may visit the national residence between 7:30 A.M. and 12:30 P.M., Tuesday through Saturday, excluding Federal holidays. However, there is an ongoing process trying to open the White House to more public access, so call the White House information line at 202-456-7041 or check its Web site at *www.whitehouse.gov* to see if any more tickets have been added or if the hours have been expanded.

To plan a trip through your member of congress, it is now suggested that you call your representative's or senator's local office six months before your trip. You can find the phone numbers in your local phone book, call information, or search on the Web for his or her Web site. You can also write to him or her at the following address:

Name of Representative House of Representatives Washington D.C. 20515	Name of Senator U.S. Senate Washington D.C. 20510

Write the words "Advance Tickets" on the envelope. If you're short on time, it might be worth your while to call the Washington office and fax your letter. You may also be able to apply for tickets online through your representative's office.

In addition to the White House tour, government tours and sites that require tickets include:

- The Washington Monument
- The Bureau of Engraving and Printing
- The Capitol
- The Supreme Court
- The State Department
- The Treasury Department
- The Kennedy Center

Getting Your Tickets Online

Some of the more popular attractions also require tickets. Waiting in line for a ticket can waste a lot of your day, but you can call a ticket service and get advance tickets for a small service charge. Tickets.com will supply you with up to four tickets for a varying nominal service charge and overall processing charge on the whole order.

Tickets.com

✆ 1-800-400-9373 (10 A.M. to 9 P.M.)

✉ *www.tickets.com*

For instance, Tickets.com offers tickets to the Holocaust Museum, and if you purchase them online or by phone, tickets will be waiting for you inside the museum at the pass desk. If you use Tickets.com to book a Ford's Theatre tour, tickets can be picked up at the will-call desk.

▣ TRAVEL TIP

The National Parks Service offers tickets to the Washington Monument for a charge of $1.50, plus an overall order charge of fifty cents. To contact this service, call 1-800-967-2283, or visit its Web site at *http://reservations.nps.gov.*

Events and Performances

Washington D.C. has a number of terrific theatrical and musical venues, some of which are free. Before your trip, it might be a good idea to find out what events and performances are coming up while you are in town. *The Washington Post* publishes an excellent weekend guide every Friday, so if you have a friend in the city, make sure he or she saves a copy for you. If you don't, visit the *Post*'s Web site at *www.washingtonpost.com* and go to the entertainment listings of your choice. The following are major cultural venues in Washington.

John F. Kennedy Center for the Performing Arts

The Center hosts free concerts most evenings at 6 P.M., as well as paid performances of theater, dance, music, and more. Call 1-800-444-1324 for information or visit the Web site at *www.kennedy-center.org*.

Verizon Center

The Verizon Center is the venue for sports and concerts in D.C. For more information and to order tickets, call 1-800-551-7328 or 202-397-7328, or visit their Web site at *www.verizoncenter.com*.

Wolf Trap Theatre

This is an outdoor venue where you can catch wonderful performances—operas, classical music concerts, and more. Call 703-255-1868 or visit the site at *www.wolftrap.org*.

☂ RAINY DAY FUN

If you decide you want to see a performance the day of the show, you might be able to get half-price tickets. You can call TICKETplace at 202-842-5387, (*www.ticketplace.org*) the night before or the day of the show. Tickets may be purchased online or directly at TICKETplace at 407 7th St. NW, between D & E Sts. Metro: Gallery Pl. (Red, Yellow, or Green Line).

National Shakespeare Company

The National Shakespeare Company presents classical theater productions. Call 413-637-1199 or visit it online at *www.shakespeare dc.org*.

Ford's Theatre

The theater where President Lincoln was assassinated is still an active theater. Call 202-347-4833 for information about performances.

CHAPTER 2

Must-See Attractions

THERE IS SO MUCH to do in Washington D.C. that you could spend a month in the city and still not have seen the whole town. There are some forty museums, regular concerts, and performances (some of which are free). There are also many events every weekend, in addition to incredible restaurants offering high cuisine and one-of-a-kind dining experiences. But there are some D.C.-based attractions and events that define a trip to the nation's capital, and these should be on every first-time visitor's agenda.

The Smithsonian Institution

The Smithsonian is composed of nineteen museums and galleries dedicated to preserving our nation's history, art, and culture, as well as the art and culture of other countries. There is nothing else in the world like this museum's collection, a true one-of-a-kind gem that we, as a nation, should be very proud of. (The individual museums are covered in detail in Chapters 5 and 6.)

It would be impossible to see all the Smithsonian museums in one day or even a few days. Some of them are simply too large, and others don't enjoy a convenient location, but most visitors to the city make time for the impressive and fun National Air and Space Museum, as well as the National Museum of Natural History (which may still be undergoing renovation when you read this) and the National

Museum of American History. Visiting these three museums in one day is an accomplishment, really possible only during the summer months, when the museums are often open late. Along with seven others, these museums are all located on the Mall, between 4th and 14th Streets and Constitution and Independence Avenues.

The National Air and Space Museum

This is the most popular of the Smithsonian museums, getting close to 8 million visitors a year. That means it is often crowded. Get there early, and plan on spending at least three hours there.

RAINY DAY FUN

Catch one of the wonderful IMAX movies or let the kids explore the new flight-simulator rides at the Air and Space Museum. Many of these rides are replicas of the planes on display.

The museum is huge. It now has a sister, the Steven F. Udvar-Hazy Center, in the D.C. suburbs (the *Enola Gay* is there), because the airplanes and spacecraft themselves are so large.

Some of the wonderful objects and exhibits in the main museum include the following:

- The Wright brothers' *Flyer*
- Charles Lindbergh's *Spirit of St. Louis*
- Amelia Earhart's airplane
- The airplane in which Chuck Yeager broke the speed of sound
- *Apollo II*, with space suits
- A lunar rock
- The Hubble space telescope
- The space shuttle *Columbia*

In addition, there's an IMAX theater with some wonderful films about space exploration and the history of flight, as well as interactive games in which you can pilot a plane or spacecraft, some of which are on display in the museum. When you've had enough museum sights there's an expansive remodeled food court that offers fast food from Mezza Café, Boston Market, Donato's Pizza, and McDonald's.

The National Museum of Natural History

This museum has something for everyone in the family. Many women love the exhibit of gems—especially the legendary cursed Hope diamond (a replica of which can be purchased in the Smithsonian gift shop). And kids love the dinosaurs and the lifelike animals in the Hall of Mammals. There's also one of the few preserved specimens of the giant squid and the wonderfully creepy Orkin Insect Zoo, where some of the live specimens can be touched. In the spring and summer, the museum hosts a butterfly garden.

The IMAX theater on the premises has spectacular 3D films about dinosaurs, fossils, and bugs, and special movies that are often linked to an exhibit. The Albert Einstein Planetarium features new technology that actually makes you feel the sensation of flying through the universe. Two cafeterias offer a full selection of salads, sandwiches, and hot dishes.

There is a lot to do and see at the National Museum of Natural History. Plan on spending at least two to three hours here.

≡FAST FACT

The mammal wing of the National Museum of Natural History has a number of hands-on (interactive, in modern vernacular) displays for kids, where tiny hands (well, those under twelve) can touch fossilized bones and examine the skull of an extinct bear up close to get a real "feel" for how familiar animals have evolved.

The National Museum of American History

The Museum of American History is an absolute must-see on any visit to D.C., but you'll have to wait until major renovations are completed in 2008. It is a smorgasbord of American history starting with the Revolution. Also, you shouldn't leave the city without looking at the exhibit of the first ladies' inaugural gowns or Judy Garland's ruby slippers from *The Wizard of Oz*.

Among the many must-see items that were on display at this museum, most of which are relocated at other museums around town, are the original star-spangled banner (the one that inspired the national anthem), and various exhibits on the development of technology, featuring such artifacts as Foucault's pendulum, Edison's light bulb, and an early Model T Ford, as well as a very interactive exhibit on transportation. This exhibit was located in the wing on the history of transportation, which featured compelling looks into the making of the New York City subway system and Route 66. If this is not your first trip to this museum, and it's reopened when you visit, go to this exhibit first and stay a while. There's plenty for kids to explore.

This museum takes about two and a half hours to see properly, and when you are done touring, plans are to retain the old-fashioned replica of an ice cream parlor on the first floor with its wonderful pastries, coffee, and ice cream.

The White House

This is a truly American experience but one you will really have to plan. After the terrorist attacks of September 11, 2001, the White House was closed to public touring, and it has only recently reopened for very limited touring. You have to request a tour through your congressperson, and it is suggested that you do this six months before your trip. Tours are given only Tuesday through Saturday, 7:30 to 11:30 A.M.

Should you be lucky enough to tour the White House, seven rooms and the public halls are open to viewing, including the China Room, where pieces of china from every presidency are on display, as well as the library and the Map Room.

🧳 TRAVEL TIP

There are no bathrooms or phones available to the public in the White House, so make sure you make a stop at the Visitors' Center before you go through the security check. Also, all cell phones must be turned off.

There is also a White House Visitors' Center on the southeast corner of 15th and E Streets, where there is an exhibit of White House history, furniture, architecture, and first family artifacts.

The International Spy Museum

This is a relatively new museum to the city (opened in 2003), but it is utterly charming and entertaining. It takes somewhere between two and three hours to see and is like no other museum. You are given an alias when you enter the museum to tour through the history of spying, with an emphasis on American spying activities during the twentieth century. James Bond's Aston Martin is here, as well as an extensive display on female spies, a duct tunnel your children can crawl through, and some good exhibits on famous spies of World War II and the infamous Cold War. In short, the International Spy Museum is wonderfully interactive. The museum also hosts a great gift shop and a nice cafeteria where you can buy "killer sandwiches."

≡FAST FACT

What do chef Julia Child, director John Ford, actress Marlene Dietrich, and dancer Josephine Baker have in common? They all merit write-ups in the celebrity section of the International Spy Museum. Find out why when you visit the museum.

The Washington Monument

Due to the terrorist attacks of September 11, access to the Washington Monument has changed. The monument itself is open, but the grounds are closed for security reasons.

To visit the monument, you'll need to get tickets. You can get them through the National Park Reservation Service (NPRS) over the phone by calling 1-800-967-2283, or online at the Web site at *http://reservations.nps.gov* (at a $1.50 fee per ticket). Free tickets are given out at the kiosk on the grounds of the monument from 8 A.M. until 4:30 P.M, but in the summer months they are often gone by noon or earlier. Purchasing the tickets in advance is definitely worth it.

A restoration of the monument was completed in 2000, and as a result the observation deck now has air-conditioning along with its unparalleled vistas of the city. There is also a newly revised interpretive exhibit area and a new elevator with glass doors so you can view the commemorative stones in the stairwell.

The Vietnam Veterans Memorial

How could something so simple have such power? The Vietnam Veterans Memorial is one of those brilliant pieces of public art that captures the right emotions and serves its purpose of commemorating the American soldiers who lost their lives in the conflict. The big black granite wall of the memorial is etched with the names of the 58,249 soldiers who died or are missing in action. The effect is solemn and powerful. Every day, friends and family of the deceased can be seen making a charcoal rubbing of a name or leaving letters or mementos.

▮ TRAVEL TIP

If possible, try to visit the Vietnam Veterans Memorial in the daytime and again at night—the effect is very different. It is open from 8 A.M. until midnight. If you go just before dusk, you can experience both at one time.

The Lincoln and Jefferson Memorials

Both the Lincoln and the Jefferson Memorials are open late (the Lincoln until 11:30 P.M., the Jeff until midnight) and are brilliantly lit up in the evening. If you have a car or can take an evening tour of the memorials by bus or trolley, that is the time to visit, because their stature is at its best.

The Lincoln Memorial was designed to resemble a Greek temple, with the seated president overlooking a reflecting pool. His writings appear on the wall behind him. There's an exhibit area where you will find excerpts from Lincoln's speeches as well as a changing display of photographs.

The Jefferson Memorial with its domed rotunda overlooks the Tidal Basin. The memorial features a bronze statue of Jefferson as well as a sampling of his writing. Although the two presidents lived almost a century apart, their two memorials were completed within thirty years of each other, and Lincoln's was erected first.

The National Zoo

No trip to the nation's capital is complete without a trip to the zoo, where you can see the pair of pandas on loan from China and their adorable new cub, Tai Shan; the tropical rain forest; a white tiger, and one of the few Komodo dragons bred in captivity. There are two restaurants and a number of gift shops, as well as some terrific spots for family photos.

CHAPTER 3

Getting There

WASHINGTON D.C. IS A full-access city, with many routes of transportation available. It has access to three international airports, has a very comfortable and safe combination train and bus station, and offers highways that are fairly easy to navigate.

Many visitors to the city drive in, but you do not need a car once you are there. The city's Metro system is as good as Paris's or New York's—actually better, because it's newer and completely air-conditioned—and taxis are affordable, whereas parking downtown is hard to come by and very expensive. Because of the number of rallies, demonstrations, and political activities, as well as a fair amount of tourist traffic, it is often impossible to reach the downtown streets close to tourist attractions by car.

Take an Airplane

The three airports serving Washington D.C. have all been recently modernized and are still undergoing expansion. Two of them are accessible by Metro, and you can get to and from the third via Amtrak, making it very easy and affordable to get from the airport to your hotel.

Ronald Reagan Washington National Airport (DCA)

Known until 1998 as National Airport, Reagan National (DCA) is the airport closest to downtown Washington. Situated just across the Potomac River from D.C., it is a short cab ride (about twenty minutes) or an easy Metro ride from the heart of the city. The Metro system's Blue and Yellow Lines (National Airport) can take you to or from Reagan National.

The airport is served by fifteen airlines, none of which flies direct international flights (except to and from Canada, and a flight to El Salvador that stops in Atlanta), as it is required by law that no Reagan National flight can exceed 12,500 miles. Even with this restriction, it is one of the busiest airports in the nation.

TRAVEL TIP

There is a kids' playground in Baltimore-Washington International Airport. In the play area is a Youth Art Gallery hung with works from children around the state. It is located adjacent to the Observation Gallery (which the kids will also love) near Concourse B.

With the presidential-name change came a rehab and new terminal. If you have some free time at the airport, look for the artwork displayed there. The various concourses also feature a Smithsonian and National Geographic shop (just in case you forgot to buy something during your visit), and a selection of quick-serve (fast-food), sit-down, and take-out restaurants, ATM machines to get money to pay for them, and currency exchange.

Washington Dulles International Airport (IAD)

One of two international airports serving the city, Dulles is twenty-six miles from downtown in Dulles, Virginia. By car, it is a thirty-five-to-forty-minute ride without rush-hour traffic. Most travelers take a cab from the airport, which runs about $50 to $60. However, there are many private shuttle services you can take. The Washington Flyer shuttle (703-661-6655) serves the airport, connecting with the Orange Line of the Metro system (Metro: West Falls Church). The bus ride takes thirty minutes ($8 one way, $14 round trip), and then it's another ten to twenty minutes by subway. Or take Metrobus 5A from the Metrorail stops at Metro: L'Enfant Plaza (Red, Blue, Yellow, or Green Line) or Metro: Rosslyn (Red or Blue Line).

The various concourses feature a wealth of news and bookstores, as well as coffee shops and restaurants, ATMs, and foreign currency exchange. The airport is undergoing a ten-year expansion that will double its capacity by the year 2010. The Web site is *www.bwiairport.com.*

Baltimore-Washington International Airport (BWI)

This is a smaller airport than either Reagan National or Dulles. It is easier to book because most people go to the large airports. It is forty-five minutes from downtown by car, just a few miles outside Baltimore.

Its main terminal offers several eateries, shops, and a kid's playground. You can catch Amtrak and be in Washington's Union Station in thirty minutes, or hop the Metrobus service that takes about twenty minutes to get to D.C. Metro's Green Line. Most of the food and shopping is in the airport's five concourses. The grand new Concourse A/B has a full spectrum of establishments in state-of-the-art surroundings.

Domestic and International Carriers

Almost every major airline flies into Washington D.C. Eighteen domestic airlines and twenty-one foreign ones serve the capital.

DOMESTIC CARRIERS

AirTran Airways (DCA, IAD, BWI)	☎1-800-247-8726 ✈*www.airtran.com*
Alaska Airlines (DCA)	☎1-800-252-7522 ✈*www.alaskaair.com*
American Airlines (DCA, IAD, BWI)	☎1-800-433-7300 ✈*www.aa.com*
ATA (DCA)	☎1-800-435-9282 ✈*www.ata.com*
Continental (DCA, IAD, BWI)	☎1-800-525-0280 ✈*www.continental.com*
Delta (DCA, IAD, BWI)	☎1-800-221-1212 ✈*www.delta.com*
Frontier Airlines (DCA, BWI)	☎1-800-432-1359 ✈*www.frontierairlines.com*
JetBlue (IAD)	☎1-800-538-2583 ✈*www.jetblue.com*
Maxjet (IAD)	☎1-888-435-9629 ✈*www.maxjet.com*
Midwest Express (DCA, BWI)	☎1-800-452-2022 ✈*www.midwestexpress.com*
North American Airlines (BWI)	☎1-800-359-6222 ✈*www.northamericanair.com*
Northwest Airlines (DCA, IAD, BWI)	☎1-800-225-2525 ✈*www.nwa.com*
Southwest Airlines (BWI)	☎1-800-435-9792 ✈*www.southwest.com*
Spirit Airlines (DCA)	☎1-800-772-7117 ✈*www.spiritair.com*
Sun Country (IAD)	*S1-800-359-6786* ✈*www.suncountry.com*
United Airlines (DCA, IAD, BWI)	☎1-800-241-6522 ✈*www.ual.com*
USA 3000 (BWI)	☎1-877-872-3000 ✈*www.usa3000.com*
US Airways (DCA, IAD, BWI)	☎1-800-428-4322 ✈*www.usairways.com*

👥 JUST FOR PARENTS

Meals aboard have become a casualty of economics, but if you are flying a distance and your flight has meal service, you can call ahead and request a "child's meal" on the flight. You can also ask if they have any special features for kids. Cockpit visits are now strictly forbidden, but some airlines still give out wings and small toys.

Shuttle Services from New York City and Boston

If you live in the New York City or Boston areas, you can take a U.S. Airways, American Eagle, or Delta shuttle to D.C.'s Reagan National Airport.

U.S. Airways' shuttle service flies from New York's LaGuardia Airport and Boston's Logan Airport to Reagan National. Hourly flights from New York run 6 A.M. to 8 P.M. on weekdays (plus a 5:30 P.M. flight); and 9 A.M. to 9 P.M. Saturday and Sunday.

American Eagle flies its shuttle service to D.C. from JFK in New York and Logan in Boston. There are at least ten daily flights offered.

Delta runs an hourly shuttle flight between New York's LaGuardia Airport and Reagan National Airport on the half hour, from 6:30 A.M. until 8:30 P.M. on weeknights, with a last flight at 9 P.M. The shuttle flies from 7:30 A.M. to 8:30 P.M. on Saturday and from 8:30 A.M. till 9 P.M. on Sunday.

If you're flying into Washington D.C., from overseas, you might take one of the following international carriers.

INTERNATIONAL CARRIERS	
Aeroflot (Dulles)	☏1-888-686-4949 ✉ www.aeroflot.org
Air Canada (DCA, Dulles, BWI)	☏1-888-247-2262 ✉ www.aircanada.com

Air France (IAD)	☎1-800-321-4538 🖅 *www.airfrance.com*
Air Jamaica (BWI)	☎1-800-523-5585 🖅 *www.airjamaica.com*
Alitalia (IAD)	☎1-800-223-5730 🖅 *www.alitaliausa.com*
ANA (IAD)	☎1-800-235-9262 🖅 *www.ana.co.jp/eng*
Austrian Airlines (IAD)	☎1-800-843-0002 🖅 *www.aua.com*
British Airways (IAD, BWI)	☎1-800-247-9297 🖅 *www.ba.com*
BWIA International Airway	☎1-800-538-2942 🖅 *www.bwee.com*
Ethiopian Airlines (IAD)	☎1-800-445-2733 🖅 *www.flyethiopian.com*
Icelandair (BWI)	☎1-800-223-5500 🖅 *www.icelandair.com*
KLM Royal Dutch Airlines (IAD)	☎1-800-225-2525 🖅 *www.klm.com*
Korean Air (IAD)	☎1-800-438-5000 🖅 *www.koreanair.com*
LAB (Lloyd Aero Boliviano) (IAD)	🖅 *www.boliviacontact.com*
Lufthansa (IAD)	☎1-800-645-3880 🖅 *www.lufthansa.com*
Mexicana (BWI)	☎1-800-531-7921 🖅 *www.mexicana.com*
SAS Scandinavian Airlines (IAD)	☎1-800-221-2350 🖅 *www.scandinavian.net*
Saudi Arabian Airlines (IAD)	☎1-800-472-8342 🖅 *www.saudiairlines.com*
South African Airways (IAD)	☎1-800-722-9675 🖅 *www.flysaa.com*
TACA Airlines (IAD)	☎1-800-535-8780 🖅 *www.taca.com*
Virgin Atlantic (IAD)	☎1-800-862-8621 🖅 *www.virgin-atlantic.com*

In and Out of the Airport

Travel to and from any of the D.C. airports is easy. Your best options are to take the Metro or a taxi.

Reagan National Airport

If you arrive at the Ronald Reagan National Airport and you don't have a lot of luggage, the fastest and cheapest way to get to your hotel is the Metro system. Reagan National Airport connects directly with the Blue and Yellow Metro Lines. The cost of a ride is $1.35 during nonrush hours and rises during rush hours (if you arrive during rush hours, you might want to take an alternate method of transportation because the trains get very crowded at this time). You can also take a Metrobus from the airport.

A taxi from Reagan National Airport to downtown should cost you between $15 and $20. D.C. cabs are run on a zone and passenger number system, so it should be straightforward and affordable, but some cab drivers try to gouge tourists (especially if they think you don't know the city), so ask about the price before you get going.

Dulles International Airport

A Metrobus takes passengers to an Orange Line Metro station (with a bus transfer, the two rides cost only an additional twenty-five cents). *The Washington Flyer* bus will take you to the Metro station for $8.00. It takes about an hour to get downtown. A cab ride from Dulles to downtown Washington will run you between $50 and $60.

Baltimore-Washington International Airport

There are a number of easy ways to get from BWI to the District. The SuperShuttle runs a regular service; see its listing on the next page. Amtrak and the Maryland Rural Commuter System (MARC) have train service to Union Station from BWI; information is given in the following Travel Tip. If you prefer to take a cab, the fare would be about $55 to $70 to downtown D.C. You can take the B30 Metrobus express from the BWI to the Metro: Greenbelt Station, which will run into D.C.'s Green Metro Line, for $3.00 per trip. Buses come every forty minutes, seven days a week. There are twenty-five buses a day on weekdays, twenty-one a day on weekends. Call 202-637-7000, or go to *www.wmata.com.*

▎📖 TRAVEL TIP

If you'd like to take Amtrak between BWI and Union Station, fares run from $11 to $21 per person. You can pay on the train, and the trip takes about half an hour. Another option is the Maryland Rural Commuter System (MARC). During the week, commuter trains will take you from the BWI train station to Union Station for $6 per person.

Private Transportation Services

There are many private transportation services that will pick you up and drive you to your hotel (and vice versa on the way back). Sightseeing brochures, the Internet, and the Yellow Pages will give you a wide choice of services, from buses to limousines. Here are a few.

Super Shuttle
✆ 1-800-258-3826
✆ 202-296-6662
✉ www.supershuttle.com

This is a seven-passenger, shared-ride van service that is easily recognizable by its blue color. It provides service twenty-four hours a day, seven days a week, and serves all three airports. Fares are based on zip code. A ride from Reagan National runs about $12, from Dulles about $26, and from BWI about $31. There are reduced rates for additional persons traveling to the same destination.

Washington Flyer
✆ 1-888-WASH-FLY
✉ www.washfly.com

This bus service runs between Dulles and Reagan National Airports, as well as to Union Station downtown and to the Metro station at West Church Falls. The ride to the Metro station is $9 one way or $16 round-trip to Reagan National, and there is a family fare for up to three members. Children under six ride free.

Go Airports Transportation
✆ 1-800-741-9049
✉ www.goairportshuttle.com

This is a twenty-four-hour-service that goes from all three airports to the District. The rate from BWI is $65, but call for fares from DCA or IAD. There is a surcharge for pickups before 7 A.M. and after 9 P.M.

Getting to D.C. by Train

Amtrak goes directly into D.C.'s remodeled Union Station, with daily service from Boston, Chicago, New York, and Los Angeles, and many stops in between. From New York to Washington D.C., there are Metroliner trains that make the trip in less than three hours, which competes with the airline shuttle services now that you have to get to the airport earlier due to security measures.

Amtrak fares to the same destination vary depending on what day and what time of the day you leave. Special fares for students, seniors, veterans, military, and AAA members are available, and other discounts may apply. For more information, call 1-800-USA-RAIL (1-800-872-7245), or log on to *www.amtrak.com*.

👥 JUST FOR PARENTS

Amtrak has a half-price program for children traveling with adults, so check before you buy your tickets to see if it is still running that promotion.

It is a pleasure to disembark at Union Station. The station has three levels of shops, good upscale restaurants, and an entire food court offering a wide variety of fast food from sushi to sauerbraten. It also features a nine-screen movie theater, which means it is bustling with locals, as well as travelers, at all times. See page 198 for more details.

Union Station is a stop on the Red Line of the Metro system, so if you pack light, this is a quick and convenient way to get to your hotel. Outside the station is a taxi stand where you will never have to wait for a cab. Most cab rides to downtown hotels cost only $6.50 (one zone fare) but will charge an additional fee per person.

≡FAST FACT

Greyhound (1-800-231-2222, *www.greyhound.com*) serves Washington D.C. from almost anywhere in the country. Buses arrive at a station four blocks from Metro: Union Station (Red Line, which is the closest Metro station), so if you arrive after dark, plan to take a cab to your destination because the neighborhood is often desolate. Greyhound offers many kinds of discounts, including for children.

Make It a Road Trip

Washington D.C. is accessible from a number of major highways, and the ride is straightforward. From the north you can take I-270, I-95, or I-295; from the south, you can take Route 1 or Route 301; from the east you can take Route 50/301 or Route 450; and from the west, you can take Route 50/I-66 or Route 29/211.

Once you hit the city proper, you will have to navigate the fabled beltway (I-95 and I-495). This 66-mile highway circles the city and is usually crowded, especially during the morning and evening rush hours.

Signage is not perfect in the city, so make sure you consult your map and know exactly where you are going. The city also has an enormous number of one-way streets and traffic circles, so go to *www.expedia.com*, *www.google.com*, *www.mapquest.com*, or *www.yahoo.com* and print out directions before you leave home (as well as reverse directions, although most hotel staff are gifted at getting you onto the highways). Without directions you could lose half an hour (and your cool) going in circles on one-way streets. If you are traveling during rush hour, you might want to tune your car radio to one of the city's all-news stations, which offer periodic traffic reports. WTOP-FM is at 820 AM and 103.5 FM.

Renting a Car

You don't need a car in D.C. itself, but if you have business or vacation plans in the surrounding areas of Virginia and Maryland (for instance, you plan to visit Mount Vernon), having a car is your best bet.

Car rentals are available at all three airports as well as at Union Station. Most, but not all, of the major car-rental chains have offices in the city.

Alamo Rent a Car	☎1-800-462-5266 ✍*www.alamo.com*
Avis	☎1-800-331-1212 ✍*www.avis.com*
Budget Car Rental	☎1-800-527-0700 ✍*www.budget.com*
Dollar Rent a Car	☎1-800-800-3665 ✍*www.dollarcar.com*
Enterprise Rent-a-Car	☎1-800-261-7331 ✍*www.enterprise.com*
Hertz	☎1-800-654-3131 ✍*www.hertz.com*
National Car Rental	☎1-800-227-7368 ✍*www.nationalcar.com*
Thrifty Car Rental	☎1-800-367-2277 ✍*www.thrifty.com*

Car rentals at the airports are often more expensive than at other locations, so be sure you price your package. Also ask about local taxes and surcharges.

🧳 TRAVEL TIP

If you are flying or taking Amtrak, inquire about fly/drive and fly/drive/hotel packages when you purchase your ticket because they often can give you a good package deal.

Parking in D.C.

Whether you arrive in your car or rent one during some part of your stay in the District, you should consider leaving your car at a parking garage as you go and see the sights inside city limits. Most visitors park their cars in the hotel's parking lot for an additional fee of up to $25 a day. Or you may choose to take advantage of the services provided by the twenty-four-hour parking lot at Union Station (30 Massachusetts Ave. NE, 202-898-1950, *www.unionstationdc.com*), since it offers cheaper rates than hotel parking. Maximum extended daily rate is $15. Entrances are on H Street between N. Capitol and 2nd Sts. NE; and on Massachusetts Ave. at Columbus Circle.

There is metered parking downtown (free from 6:30 to 10:30 P.M. in Georgetown—and on weekends), but you can get ticketed if you run over-meter or park in the wrong place. The amount varies with the severity of your misconduct and location. If your car is towed (and it won't be unless it constitutes a public danger), it will be taken to a tow pound. To retrieve your car, call 202-541-6078, and they will tell you where and how to retrieve it. You'll also get a ticket if you speed on Washington D.C. streets, which are patrolled by robot cameras. And they *will* find you. Check out the cameras at *http://app .ddot.dc.gov/services_dsf/traffic_cameras*. Eliminate all this worry by reading the well-posted traffic rules on signs and meters.

CHAPTER 4

Discover the City

WASHINGTON D.C. IS A city that's perfect for tourists. Its layout is planned according to an easily grasped system of letters and numbers; its neighborhoods are accessible; and you've got lots of options for public transportation to go from one place to the next. To familiarize yourself with D.C., review this chapter, then take a tour that will give you an overview of the city and its major attractions before you move on to more specific plans.

The D.C. Street System

Because Washington D.C. was designed before building ever began, its layout makes perfect sense. East-west streets use the letters of the alphabet (A Street, B Street, and so on) and north-south streets are numbered (First Street, Second Street). When all the letters have been used, the east-west streets continue alphabetically with two-syllable names—Adams, Belmont—and then move on to three-syllable ones. Diagonal avenues named after various states intersect the grid and form several traffic circles.

The city is divided into four quadrants—northwest, northeast, southwest, and southeast—with the U.S. Capitol more or less at the center. These quadrant locators are important when writing to someone in the city or when you give cab drivers the address of your destination.

≡FAST FACT

Here are a few terms that will help you get around Washington D.C. "The Hill" (Capitol Hill) is the area immediately surrounding the U.S. Capitol. "The Mall" is the downtown area where you will find most of the Smithsonian museums and several of the city's major sightseeing attractions. "The Metro" is the city's underground mass transit system (subway).

While this design is quite wonderful, it is meaningless when you are trying to find a movie theater in the Adams Morgan neighborhood using only a subway map, which has no street names—just Metro station names and routes in bright colors. Therefore, one of the first things you need to do when you get to your hotel room (or on your way to the city) is orient yourself with the dozen or so neighborhoods that make up the city, as well as the distance from your hotel to your destination. This will help you in planning Metro trips, as well as judging how expensive a cab ride will be. We also give you the nearest Metro station and line in the listings.

Overview of the Neighborhoods

The following sections should suffice as a good introduction to D.C.'s neighborhoods. We'll begin with the three most frequented areas (downtown, the Mall, and Capitol Hill) and then go on to other neighborhoods in alphabetical order.

Most of the hotels in Washington D.C., both upscale and budget, are located in what is called the downtown area, so this will most likely be your first stop from the airport. Downtown is also the location of many of the city's finest tourist sites that lie outside the Mall.

Downtown

This is a fifteen-block area between 7th and 22nd Streets along Pennsylvania Avenue. The downtown area has undergone a major renovation in the past decade. Almost every block has already been renewed or is scheduled to be undergoing construction.

Many of the city's tourist attractions are located in this neighborhood, including the following:

- National Aquarium
- Ford's Theatre
- Petersen House
- Verizon Center
- Old Post Office Pavilion
- National Museum of Women in the Arts
- National Museum of American Art
- International Spy Museum
- Washington D.C. Convention Center
- White House
- National Archives

These are only the standouts in a very concentrated area of things to see. If you have comfortable walking shoes, you can walk throughout the downtown area, but you don't have to because there are frequent Metro stops along the way. Most of them are not named after the nearest street—for example, they include Federal Triangle, Metro Center, National Archives/Navy Memorial, and the far exit of the Gallery Place/Chinatown station. This means you have to carry two maps with you at all times—a street map and a Metro map. There are various maps of the District and a Metro map in Appendix C.

The downtown neighborhood offers plenty to do. There are many fabulous restaurants for every budget and occasion. A strip on 7th Street that's lined with art galleries has become one of the best places to view local art. There's plenty of nightlife in the downtown area, too.

💼 TRAVEL TIP

When you exit the Gallery Place–Chinatown Metro Station (Yellow, Green, or Red Line) at 7th and H Streets, you will see a gilded arch of gold and red that marks the entrance to Washington's small China-town. This, the world's largest Chinese arch, was given to the District by its sister city, Beijing, and is referred to as the Chinese Friendship Archway. During the Chinese New Year celebration, the archway is lit up and topped with 300 painted dragons.

The National Mall

Everyone who comes to D.C. heads to the Mall at some point during his or her stay. Ten of the nineteen Smithsonian museums and galleries are here; so are most of the monuments and memorials. It is easy to find on most street maps, for it is defined by 2½ miles of parkland between Constitution and Independence Avenues from the Capitol to the Lincoln Memorial. Popular sites in this area include:

- Smithsonian Castle
- National Air and Space Museum
- National Museum of Natural History
- National Museum of American History
- Hirshhorn Museum and Sculpture Garden
- National Gallery of Art
- Freer Gallery of Art and Arthur M. Sackler Gallery
- National Museum of African Art
- Arts and Industries Building (currently closed)
- Washington Monument
- U.S. Holocaust Museum
- Korean War Veterans Memorial
- Vietnam Veterans Memorial
- National World War II Memorial
- Lincoln Memorial

There are few restaurants in this area other than those in the museums. The Smithsonian Metro stop (Orange and Blue Line) will bring you to the middle of the Mall.

Capitol Hill

Even though the Capitol and a number of heavily visited sites are in this neighborhood, Capitol Hill is mainly residential, with many apartment buildings and neighborhood restaurants. Consequently, the food is good and less expensive than in other parts of the city. It is also the location of the city's famed Eastern Market (at 7th and C Streets SE), which has been a site of free-for-all commerce since the Victorian days, with vendors selling everything from crafts to produce on a daily basis. It's especially bustling on weekends.

Other sites in the Capitol Hill area include the following:

- Library of Congress
- Folger Shakespeare Library
- National Postal Museum
- Union Station
- United States Botanic Garden
- Supreme Court Building

Metro stops in this area are Eastern Market or Capital South (Orange or Blue Line), and Judiciary Square or Union Station (Red Line).

Adams Morgan and Kalorama

Centered on 18th Street and Columbia Road (NW), Adams Morgan is a slightly off-the-beaten-track neighborhood that features a wealth of ethnic restaurants, cafes, nightclubs, bookstores, and the National Zoo. The Kalorama district (*kalorama* is a Greek word for "beautiful view") runs from Adams Morgan to North Dupont Circle and showcases beautiful homes and apartment buildings. To get to Adams Morgan and Kalorama, take the Metro to Woodley Park Zoo (Red Line), or walk up from Dupont Circle.

Dupont Circle

You just might find yourself returning to Dupont Circle over and over again, even though it is a relatively small part of the city. It has wonderful restaurants of all varieties, bookstores, art galleries, movie theaters, and a thriving nightlife. The Circle is also the center of the District's gay nightlife, with several gay bars within walking distance of one another. Tourist sites in this area include the Heurich and Woodrow Wilson Houses, the Textile Museum, and the Phillips Collection. The Metro stop is Dupont Circle (Red Line).

≡FAST FACT

Dupont Circle is named after Samuel F. Dupont, of New Jersey, a commander in the Navy during the Civil War who captured the Confederate site of Port Royal, South Carolina. A statue of Dupont stands in the center of the circle.

Foggy Bottom

This neighborhood was the industrial area of the city in the late eighteenth and early nineteenth centuries. In the summertime, the area was marshy and infested with mosquitoes, which is how it got its name. Before it got that nickname, it had been known as Funkstown, named after Jacob Funk, the owner of a particularly nasty local factory. Of course, Foggy Bottom has since been drained and spiffed up.

Foggy Bottom lies just southwest of the downtown tourist district and northwest of Georgetown. Tourist sites in this neighborhood include the U.S. State Department, The John F. Kennedy Center for the Performing Arts, and the luxurious (and notorious) Watergate complex. The closest Metro stops are Foggy Bottom and Farragut North (Orange or Blue Line).

≡FAST FACT

Foggy Bottom was the industrial center of the city even before the American Revolution. In 1765, Jacob Funk, a German immigrant, bought 130 acres of land, where he placed his factories. The neighborhood also became the home of two universities by the early 1800s—a theological seminary and The Columbian College, which later became George Washington University. After the Civil War, Catholic University was added to the mix.

Georgetown

Georgetown is one of the oldest Colonial townships in the country and has some of the oldest homes in the city. One of its prime tourist sites is the Old Stone House, which was built before the Revolutionary War.

Georgetown was already an independent town when Washington D.C. was in the process of being designed. While it is now part of the city, Georgetown does keep its distance from the heart of downtown by being nearly inaccessible without a car and by having some of the highest-priced homes in the region.

Georgetown is a bit easier to get to since the recent inauguration of the D.C. Circulator. The bus connects Union Station, Georgetown, and many other places in between. Definitely worth visiting, it's one of the most charming parts of the city; many visitors enjoy strolling about to see its historic homes, such as Dumbarton Oaks. Because Georgetown is home to Georgetown University, it is packed with interesting, youth-oriented shops, as well as many restaurants and pubs and a co-op of art galleries. It is also one of the city's nightlife centers, especially on weekends. To reach Georgetown, you can take the Metro to the Foggy Bottom (Orange or Blue Line) stop, but it's a long walk. A cab ride from downtown may be a better option—the fare should be less than $10—and Georgetown is always full of cabs.

Glover Park

This is the residential neighborhood bordering the Washington National Cathedral. There are a number of good restaurants and movie theaters in this area. The former mansions and now embassies that make up Embassy Row (a must-see walk or drive) are located between Glover Park and Woodley Park.

In the midst of Embassy Row lies the Naval Observatory, where the nation's master clocks are set. Next door to the Observatory is the vice president's mansion, which is so far off the road that it can hardly be seen from the street. Across from the British Embassy, you'll find an idyllic park featuring a statue of the Persian poet Kahlil Gibran.

The nearest Metro station is Tenleytown (Red Line), but it's a ten-minute walk to the National Cathedral, so take a bus transfer when you exit the train station and you can hop on any bus for thirty-five cents.

≣FAST FACT

Washington's Embassy Row is an entire neighborhood devoted to the city's diplomatic community. It houses fifty-eight different embassies along Massachusetts and New Hampshire Avenues. Many of the embassies and ambassadors' residences are restored mansions. For instance, General Patton's home is now the home of the Australian ambassador. Other ambassadors have commissioned fabulous (and quirky) buildings and homes.

Woodley Park

This is a beautiful residential neighborhood that grew up around Martin Van Buren's and Grover Cleveland's summer homes. It borders the Adams Morgan neighborhood and starts at the National Zoo. There are a number of good restaurants in the area. Its largest landmark is the Washington Marriott Wardman Park, and it is also home to the Omni Shoreham, another large hotel. Cleveland Park or Woodley Park–Zoo (Red Line) are the closest Metro stops.

☂ RAINY DAY FUN

Pay a visit to the U Street Corridor for some culinary treasures. Ben's Chili Bowl, a neighborhood institution for more than fifty years, is world-renowned after being featured on *The Cosby Show* in the 1990s. Oprah Winfrey's raves about the Love Café; its homemade cakes have put this restaurant on the map.

U Street Corridor

This stretch of the city between 12th and 16th Streets on U Street NW was once the center of African-American nightlife in the city (known as "Black Broadway"), where such luminaries as Duke Ellington and Cab Calloway performed when they were in town. It still retains its reputation for nightlife, with a number of jazz and rock nightclubs, and now features the Lincoln Theater, recently restored to its 1920s splendor, a cultural landmark for music, dance, theater, and cinema. Metro stops include U Street–Cardozo or Shaw–Howard University (Green Line).

Tyson's Corner, Virginia

Though not technically a D.C. neighborhood, Tyson's Corner is a shopping hotspot and a bargain-shopping mecca for tourists and residents alike. It is one of the largest U.S. retail centers outside New York City.

The name comes from two of the malls—Tyson's Corner Center and Tyson's Galleria—which together feature a total of eight major department stores, including Bloomingdale's and Nordstrom's, as well as more than 400 shops and restaurants. Tyson's Corner isn't on the Metro. If you have a car available, take Route 7.

Getting Around Town

Once you know where you are and where you want to go, Washington D.C. is a very easy city to navigate. The Metro system is safe, convenient, affordable, and fairly extensive throughout downtown. If the Metro doesn't go somewhere, the Metrobus system probably does, but it takes much longer, and buses do not run as frequently. Taxis are abundant and usually quite affordable.

Take the Metro

The Metrorail system is run by Washington Metropolitan Area Transit Authority, which began in 1973. The Metro system now includes eighty-six stops and 106 miles of track.

The system runs efficiently throughout the downtown area (where most of the tourist sites are located) and to specific destinations in suburban Maryland and northern Virginia. If the Metro system can get you where you need to go, it is the best way to travel in the nation's capital.

Kids love the Metro; it's often an attraction in itself for them. Many of the stations (such as Dupont Circle) are deep below the ground, with long escalators and high, domed ceilings.

Each Metro station is marked with a brown obelisk with the capital letter M at the top. Every station has a station-manager kiosk on the premises, and you can usually ask them questions and for directions. Note that eating and drinking on the Metro system is strictly prohibited.

≡FAST FACT

The deepest station is at Forest Glen on the Red Line, which is 196 feet below ground (twenty-one stories). The longest escalator is at Wheaton Station (also on the Red Line)—at 230 feet, it is the longest escalator in the Western Hemisphere.

Purchasing Tickets

Once you enter a Metro station, you have to buy a ticket at an automated machine. A chart shows you how much the fare is from your starting station to your destination. Currently, regular fare is $1.35 minimum, $3.90 maximum, from opening to 9:30 A.M., 3 to 7 P.M., and 2 A.M. to closing. Other hours, a $1.85 midrange fare is added, and the maximum is reduced to $2.35. Seniors and disabled fare is half-price. The machines take coins as well as bills of up to $20, but they will give you only up to $5 in change.

You can buy a round-trip ticket or a $6.50 one-day fare. If you plan your trips around a central location and use a combination of the Metro system, the bus system, and walking, it's unlikely that you'll spend $6.50 on the Metro in one day. A round-trip ticket is probably all you'll need.

≡FAST FACT

Because it is a relatively new system, Metrorail has a science-fiction feel to it. It is a popular urban myth that it was designed by Disney architects, because it reminds people of Space Mountain or the monorail. The Metro's media department wouldn't corroborate this story, but it's been around ever since the Metro became operational in 1976, so you be the judge.

There are special discount passes as well. A full week's worth of Metro riding can be purchased for $22, which could certainly be a wise choice if you will be visiting the different neighborhoods of the city. However, there's a slight catch. Should any individual trip cost more than $2.20, you will be required to pay the additional amount before exiting the station. There is also a $32.50 seven-day card, if you know you'll be visiting the stations that require additional fees.

Once you have walked through the entrance turnstile, your ticket will pop back out at you. You must retain it and put it in the exit turnstile at your destination station. If you lose your ticket, you can buy another one inside the station to exit.

The Metro Network

There are five lines in the D.C. Metro system: Red, Orange, Green, Yellow, and Blue. The Metro Center Station (in downtown Washington) connects three of them (Red, Blue, and Orange), and the next stop, Gallery Place–Chinatown, links the other two (Yellow and Green), so it is very easy to change trains. There are pocket Metro maps available in six languages outside most of these kiosks.

If you know you are going to take a bus later in the day (or you think you may get tired walking from one tourist site to another), look for the bus-ticket machine inside the station (before you exit) and take a transfer ticket. This will enable you to take a Metrobus for a 35-cent fee—otherwise, you would have to pay $1.25. There is no transfer from the bus to the train.

≡ FAST FACT

It took four decades of planning to create the Washington D.C. mass transit system. Congress authorized the creation of a planning commission to study mass transit in 1952, but the first Metro station didn't open until 1976. On the first day of service in March 1976, there were 19,913 passengers. In August 1988, the Metrorail carried its billionth rider.

Hours of Operation

The Metro system opens at 5:30 A.M. on weekdays and 7 A.M. on weekends. It closes at midnight Sunday through Thursday, and at 3 A.M. Friday and Saturday. But check the last train departure time posted in every station. It may leave before these hours. For Metro's holiday schedule, refer to the Web site.

For more information on the Metro system call 202-962-1234 or visit the Web site at *www.wmata.com*. There is a search engine on the Web site that will plot your route for you if you type in your starting point and destination.

Take the Bus

The city's surface transit system is also extensive (over 15,000 stops) and works wonderfully, either in conjunction with the Metro system or for short rides when your feet give out on you. You can usually catch a bus within five to ten minutes of waiting, and most stops include a bus shelter where you can wait for the next bus.

You will need a Metrobus card or exact change for the bus, because the driver cannot give change, but the bus does take dollar bills. Rides are $1.25, and transfers are free. If you have a transfer from Metrorail, the fare is only 35 cents.

Take a Taxi

Instead of a meter system, taxis in D.C. run on a zone system, which is posted in every cab. Most rides in the downtown area, or from downtown to Georgetown, are one fare zone, which is $6.50 for one person and $1.50 extra for each additional person. There is a dollar surcharge for rush-hour traffic. Of course, you have to tip the driver—between 10 and 15 percent.

If you ask a cab to take you outside the city, you will be charged by the mile, which is how the airport fares are calculated. This fare system starts at $3.25 for the first half mile and adds 90 cents for each half mile after that.

The D.C. Taxi Commission Web site (*www.dctaxi.dc.gov/dctaxi*) has a taxi fare calculator, which you can use to get a specific idea of how much your trip should cost. You can also call 202-331-1671 to find out the fare between locations within the city.

You can hail a cab on the street or call a cab service, which will cost you an additional $2. There are a gazillion cab companies available for radio service; a few are Diamond, 202-387-6200, Capitol, 202-636-1600, and Yellow Cab, 202-544-1212.

Make sure you pay attention to the driver's license number and the cab number when you get in the taxi. If you have a complaint about a driver, you can call the Taxi Commission at 202-645-6005 to report the problem.

Guided Tours

Washington D.C. offers an unusual number of options to tour the city, from faux trolley cars to buses to boat tours, and even mobility scooters, Segways, and amphibious vehicles. These tours offer an easy way for you to get oriented in the city. Be aware, though, that many of these tours are closed during the winter months and depend on the weather or health of the tour guide, so always call ahead to confirm availability.

Walking Tours

Walking tours aren't just walking tours anymore. On some you don't even walk! Washington D.C. has a wide variety of walking tours that you can take, some of which last an entire day and others that are just a few hours long. There is a lot to choose from here, from the offbeat (such as Talking Streets or Scandal Tours) to more traditional historic tours.

Washington Walks
✆ 202-484-1565
✉ www.washingtonwalks.com

This young touring company has some terrific off-the-beaten-track routes, including the "White House Un-Tour" every Tuesday through Saturday and a tour of Haunted Washington every Wednesday. Recommended family walks are "Good Night, Mr. Lincoln," "In Fala's Footsteps," and the White House Un-Tour. Tickets are $10 per person. Walks last approximately two hours (the three recommended family tours above are only one hour long); groups meet outside a Metro station.

Celebrity Tours

📞 301-762-3049

💻 www.dcregistry.com/users/celebrity/index.html

Of course, many rich and famous people live in Washington D.C. or at least have residences here; for instance, Arnold Schwarzenegger and Elizabeth Taylor both owned homes in Georgetown. If you enjoy seeing how celebrities live, you can join Jan Pottker, author of *Celebrity Washington*, on a guided tour of the city's famous past and present residences, watering holes, and movie locations. Tours are given Thursday, Friday, and Saturday, 10 A.M. to noon, and meet at the upstairs café at Barnes & Noble, 3040 M. St. NW in Georgetown. Cost is $15. As usual, call to make sure the tour will be run.

☂ RAINY DAY FUN

The embassies and mansions of Embassy Row house some incredible art and culture from the various countries represented, but you can't just go up to a door and go in to view it. There used to be organized Embassy Row guided tours, but the events of September 11 put an end to the tradition. Many embassies offer tours with prior notification.

Scandal Tours

📞 202-783-7212

💻 www.gnpcomedy.com

Costumed members of the Washington comedy group Gross National Product impersonate political figures and offer a humor-filled tour of the city's most notorious history, from the Watergate to the Tidal Basin to Gary Hart's townhouse and the White House itself. Tours start at 15th & F Streets, NW (Metro Center station Red Line) Saturday at 1 P.M., and run from April Fool's Day (of course) to Labor Day.

Talking Street
✆ 202-396-TOUR (8687)
✎ www.talkingstreet.com

Those people you see walking along with their cell phones to their ears might just be taking a tour! Talking Street delivers a walking tour of the Mall's most famous sites via your own cell phone. You can choose your own schedule at your own pace, even over several days. Larry King narrates, with music, interviews, and dramatic readings to round out the experience. Cost is $5.95 for fifteen sites, about three minutes a site. You can charge your cell phone account, use a credit card, or prepay. A map is downloadable from the Web site, where you can listen to a sample. The service runs 24/7.

Georgetown Walking Tour
✆ 301-588-8999

Mary Kay Ricks offers a variety of tours of Georgetown, as well as a tour of Oak Hill Cemetery and a ride on the Underground Railroad with a look at Georgetown during the Civil War. She was booking only private walks at the time of this publication but may return to public touring. Call for details.

Site Seeing Tours, Inc.
✆ 301-445-2098
✎ www.siteseeingtoursinc.com

These African-American-tour specialists offer a variety of tour choices at different times. There are two walk-in tours given on different Saturdays, no appointment necessary: the Black History Tour and "Walk in the Footsteps of Martin Luther King, Jr." Other tours include Duck Ellington's Jazz, U Street, and Arlington County. Call for schedules and information. Tours usually start at 10 A.M. at different locations. Adults: $12; seniors and children under twelve, $5; a portion is donated to charity.

Washington Photo Safari
✉ 4545 Connecticut Ave. NW #620
✆ 1-877-512-5969
✆ 202-537-0937
🖝 www.washingtonphotosafari.com

A unique experience. Tour and learn travel photography at the same time. Safaris cover a number of themes, but start with the half-day Monuments and Memorials ($69) as an introduction. Other safaris start at $49.

JUST FOR PARENTS

You can lose the kids for a couple of hours with Washington Photo Safari's "Just for Kids" tour. Drop them off at 2:30 P.M. and it will do the rest, which means a fun trip and photography lessons for $39. Pickup is at 4 P.M. Seasonal; call for availability.

Motorized Tours

City Segway Tours
✆ 1-877-734-8687
🖝 www.citysegwaytours.com

Technology marches on, or rather rolls on the Segway. This is the first of three new companies making use of the far-out motorized vehicles you've read so much about. After a forty-minute orientation and practice session, the company takes you on a four-hour tour of the top tourist attractions, offering both day tours and an evening tour. Tours leave at 9:30 A.M., 2 P.M., and 6:30 P.M. from April 1 to November 30. You have to be sixteen years old or older to take the tour, and leave a refundable $499.95 deposit on the Segway (which is returned without being processed when you get back). Tours are $70.

Segs in the City

✉ Old Post Office Pavilion
   1100 Pennsylvania Ave., NW

☎ 410-263-2344

☎ 800-SEGS393 (800-734-7393)

✍ www.segsinthecity.com

This is another company that has you moving along comfortably on a Segway while the world trudges by with hot feet and hurting shoes. They have shorter tours: two hours for $70, one hour for $35, and a two-hour C&E Safari (Cathedral and Embassy Row) for $70. Fee includes training, a license, and a bottle of water. Tour times and schedules are on the Web site. You must be at least sixteen and weigh less than 260 pounds. Segs in the City also rents Segways and runs tours in Maryland and Pennsylvania (where the age minimum is fourteen).

🧳 TRAVEL TIP

Parents with younger kids may have a problem if they want to Segway, but Capital Segway has solved the problem. They offer the "SegShaw," which totes behind the Segway. Rental is $35. Capital Segway is at 1350 I St., 202-682-1980, www.capitalsegway.com. Tours are $65.

City Tours

☎ 301-294-9514

✍ www.dcsightseeing.com

Washington author and tour guide Anthony S. Pitch offers private-group, anecdotal history tours of Washington D.C. on any topic or area you choose, or leave it up to him. His three-hour tours cover the most important highlights of the city; his five-hour tours tell you just about everything you want to know about the town. There is no minimum or maximum number of people required, and his tours are very family-friendly. The fee is $100 an hour, with a three-hour minimum. Transportation is extra depending on the mode you choose, from sedan to luxury bus. Occasional public tours are listed on his Web site.

Old Town Trolley
202-832-9800
www.historictours.com

This is a narrated two-hour tour on an orange-and-green open-air trolley. Its nineteen stops include most of the downtown sites, as well as Arlington National Cemetery, Georgetown, Embassy Row, and the National Cathedral. You can get off and on throughout the day by showing the bus driver your ticket stub or a sticker they give you to wear (trolleys come around every thirty minutes). They also have printed flyers of walking tours of Georgetown and the Mall. There's a map of tour stops, which features a number of discounts on food and shopping if you show the establishment your ticket.

Tours start at 9 A.M. and end at 4:30 P.M. in the fall and winter, an hour later in spring and summer. You may be able to buy a ticket at your hotel gift shop or concierge (and therefore charge it to your room), or you can pay on the trolley or buy a ticket at the counter in Union Station (which is the first stop). Tickets are $32 for adults, $16 for children ages four to twelve.

Old Town Trolley also offers a Monuments by Moonlight after-hours tour. This two-and-a-half-hour narrated night tour features stories and views of the city's monuments. Tours start at 6:30 P.M. in the fall and winter, 7:30 P.M. in spring and summer. Tickets are $32 for adults and $26 for children. These tours are often sold out before noon during the busy season, so call early for reservations. You can also buy your tickets online for a 10 percent savings.

Tourmobile
📞 1-888-868-7707
📞 202-554-5100
✍ www.tourmobile.com

The blue-and-white Tourmobile travels to many of the same locations as the Old Town Trolley, but it does not go to Georgetown or the National Cathedral. It is, however, the only vehicle allowed to tour inside Arlington National Cemetery (authorized to do so by the National Park Service). Instead of trudging up the green hills on foot, you can sit as the trolley takes you by the Kennedy graves, the Tomb of the Unknown Soldier, Arlington House, and the Women in Service Memorial on the cemetery grounds. This is a definite consideration if you have young children or visitors who have a hard time walking long distances. You can buy Tourmobile tickets to tour just the cemetery, which cost $6 for adults, $5 for seniors, and $3 for children three to eleven and can be purchased at the cemetery's visitors' center.

You can board the Tourmobile at any of its nineteen stops and pay the driver when you get on. As with Old Town Trolley, you can get on and off the Tourmobile at any stop and reboard later (with ticket). Tourmobiles come around every twenty minutes. On-demand service is available to those who are mobility impaired. Call 703-979-0690 between 8 A.M. and 5 P.M. daily except December 25.

The cost of the Tourmobile is $20 for adults and $10 for children. The Tourmobile operates from 9:30 A.M. to 5:30 P.M. It is available all year long, except December 25 and January 1, when most national and government sites are also closed.

Tourmobile also offers a Washington by Night tour, which is a three-and-a-half-hour narrated tour of the Jefferson, Roosevelt, Lincoln, Korean, Vietnam, and World War II Memorials (where you can disembark for visits). It departs from Union Station and is $20 for adults and $10 for children three to eleven. Reservations are suggested for Washington by Night tours.

There are combination two-day packages for various tours such as Arlington Cemetery, Washington D.C., Mount Vernon, and/or

Cedar Hill. Call or visit the Tourmobile Web site for prices and more information; these tours are not always available.

You can also purchase tickets at TicketMaster by calling 1-800-551-SEAT, but there is a small fee for this service.

RAINY DAY FUN

If you want to treat yourself and your family to a taste of the good life, you can hire a luxury limo and do a tour. Several companies will be glad to accommodate: American Eagle (703-550-7200, 800-730-7878, *www.americaneaglelimo.com*); All Events/Majestic (703-273-4222, *www.majesticlimoservice.com*); and National Transportation (202-232-1000).

Gold Line/Gray Line
✆ 1-800-862-1400
✆ 301-386-8300
✉ www.graylinedc.com

This tour company offers a wide variety of narrated tours of the city, both on land and sea. The motorcoach will leave from Union Station or pick you up and drop you off at your hotel. You can pay for tours by credit card. The After Dark Tour leaves Union Station at 7:45 P.M. and drops you off at your hotel about four hours later. An all-day Mt. Vernon/D.C. after-dark combo runs from June to October; the price is $62 for adults, $31 for children, dinner not included.

On Location Tours
✆ 1-800-979-3370
✆ 1-212-209-3370
✉ www.screentours.com

Movie and television buffs will love this bus tour of thirty locations used in TV shows and movies that were shot in Washington, DC. Shop in the mall where *No Way Out* and *True Lies* were filmed; stand on the steps of the house used in *The Exorcist*; visit the bar from

St. Elmo's Fire and the park used in *The Sentinel*; and see locations from *The Wedding Crashers, Thank You for Smoking, Election, X Files, Independence Day, Forrest Gump,* and many others.

The three-hour guided tour takes place on luxury coach buses and is led by actors and actresses who share inside industry information. Clips from the movies shot at the locations enhance the overall experience.

Tours run Friday, Saturday, and Sunday at 2 P.M. and depart from Union Station. Price: $34 for adults; $17 for children ten and under.

Water Tours

If you and your family are feeling adventurous, you might consider seeing Washington D.C. on a water tour. There are lots of ways to get a new perspective on Washington—do-it-yourself kayaking or canoeing, or enjoy being a passenger and cruise the river.

Atlantic Kayak
✆ 301-292-6455
✍ www.atlantickayak.com

This offers short and long tours. Short tours are recommended for newbies and view Georgetown ($44) and Piscataway Creek ($54). There are also sunset, midnight, and overnight tours. Call for information and reservations. Guides paddle alongside tourists in small groups of boats. Children must be twelve years old or older to paddle their own kayak; children over five may sit in a parent's kayak. The tour operators state that no experience is necessary.

Capital River Cruises
🚇 Metro: Waterfront (Green Line)
✆ 1-800-405-5511
✆ 301-460-7447
✍ www.capitolrivercruises.com

This fifty-minute, narrated tour of the Potomac on a sixty-five-foot riverboat departs from Washington Harbor, Georgetown, and circles the city, offering views of the Kennedy Center, the various monuments, and the Capitol building. Tours leave hourly from noon until 7 P.M. Monday to Friday, and noon to 9 P.M. Saturday and Sunday. Tickets are $12 for adults and $6 for children; under three go free. A small discount is available on the Internet. Seasonal snack bar and restrooms are on board.

D.C. Ducks
✆ 202-832-9800
✍ *www.dcducks.com*

Is this a water tour or a land tour? Surprise, it's both, and it's a terrific tour for families. This famous tour uses white amphibious vehicles (boats on wheels)—which were built for the U.S. Army during World War II to transport troops (and are fully restored and U.S. Coast Guard approved)—to provide tourists a one-hour tour of the city on the ground followed by a half-hour tour ride on the Potomac. Tours with a wise-quacking guide leave from Union Station from 10 A.M. to 4 P.M. from mid-March through late October (call to make sure, of course). No reservations are needed. Tickets are $26 for adults and $13 for children.

Spirit Cruises
✆ 1-866-211-3811
✆ 202-554-8000
✍ *www.spiritofwashington.com*

The *Spirit of Washington* climate-controlled riverboat offers a sumptuous buffet as part of its lunch, early dinner, evening, and midnight moonlight cruises. Call for schedule and pricing. The *Spirit of Washington II* cruises to Mount Vernon, boarding at 8:15 A.M. Round-trip fares include the admission to Mount Vernon and are $38 for adults, $36 for seniors, and $31 for children. You can purchase breakfast and lunch on board. Reservations are recommended.

🧳 TRAVEL TIP

There are two other cruise lines that lend the taste of class to your touring. Both offer deluxe European-like river cruising for moderate prices. Dandy Restaurant Cruise Ships, 703-683-6076, *www.dandy dinnerboat.com*; and Odyssey, 1-888-741-0281, *www.odysseycruises .com*, are both worth exploring.

C&O Canal Barge Rides
☎ 202-653-5190

Travel back to the 1870s with this mule-drawn canal ride along the C&O Canal. Commentary by costumed park rangers describes what life was like for the families who lived and worked on the canal. The one-hour trip costs $8 for adults, $6 for seniors, and $5 for children. The replica canal boats depart from Georgetown and operate from April through October, so be sure to call and get the current schedule.

Bicycle Tours

If you want a change of pace and a little exercise on your vacation, hop on a bike and take a tour. None of these is strenuous, and all cater to families.

Bike the Sites Tour
✉ Old Post Office Pavilion
   1100 Pennsylvania Ave., NW
☎ 202-842-BIKE (2453)
🖳 *www.bikethesites.com*

The Bike the Sites tour group offers three three-hour guided bicycle tours and three biking and walking Family Bike Adventures.

All are easy. The Capital Sites Tour is 7 to 8 miles long, The Sites @ Nite and the Monuments Tour are both 4 miles in length. There is a seasonal Cherry Blossom Festival tour as well. The tours are $40 for adults and $30 for kids under twelve. "Family Bike Adventures" are two-and-a-half hours long and cost $35 for adults and $25 for children under twelve. All tours include bicycle rental, a helmet, a licensed guide, bottled water, and a snack.

JUST FOR PARENTS

If the grandparents are along, or the family is just too tuckered to tour, hop on a mobility scooter and see the sites on a four-wheel cart. City Scooter Tours runs a three-hour tour of the Mall and Tidal Basin, with commentary via electronic earphones. Even kids over thirteen can drive along. Cost is $75. Tours are run Wednesdays, 1 P.M. to 4 P.M., and Sundays 10 A.M. to 1 P.M. Old Post Office Pavilion, 888-441-7575, *www.cityscootertours.com.*

DC Tours
888-878-9870
www.dctours.us

This multifaceted company offers a huge array of tours, but we'll concentrate on their bicycle forays here. There are three tours offered: Capital Monuments, Capital Sites, and Capital Evening Sites. Each runs about three hours, and the price includes a guide, bike, helmet (mandatory), and bottled water. In addition, trailer carriages or tandems are available. The tours are run at a relaxing pace for the "occasional" exerciser. Fees for the Capital Monuments and Capital Evening tours are $47.95, minus a $5 discount via Internet, children under twelve pay $31.95. The Capital Monument tour is $42.95, minus a $5 Internet discount; kids pay $26.95. Tours are conducted from March 25 through November 11, 10 A.M. daily in the summer, no tours on Wednesday spring and fall. Evening tours start at 7 P.M. Monday to Saturday in the summer and 6:30 P.M. Tuesday, Friday, and Saturday in the spring and fall.

CHAPTER 5

Introduction to the Smithsonian

YOU CAN'T VISIT WASHINGTON D.C. without seeing some of the Smithsonian Institution's nineteen museums and galleries. They are the jewels in the crown of this town. If you have the luxury of being able to explore all or most of the Smithsonian branches in D.C., you will see a breadth of art, history, science, and culture unparalleled anywhere in the world. (If you have time only for the top three Smithsonians, they are covered in the next chapter.) The museums are open every day except December 25, and they are all free.

The History of the Smithsonian Institution

The story of the Smithsonian Institution is fascinating. The Smithsonian exists because James Smithson, a wealthy English scientist, thought the principles of our nation and the scientific discoveries that were being produced here in the nineteenth century were so amazing that he wanted to found "an establishment for the increase and diffusion of knowledge among men" in the United States.

Upon his death in Italy in 1829, he willed his fortune to his nephew and stipulated that should his nephew die without heirs, the entire Smithson fortune, which was worth about half a million dollars (an enormous amount of money in those days, which eventually came to the United States in bags of gold sovereigns) would be given to the United States to fund such an institution.

Smithsonian Made into Law

It took eight years of discussion in Congress before the Smithson gift was accepted and then another nine years before the Smithsonian Institution became a reality, with President Andrew Polk signing an act of Congress that established the Smithsonian Institution.

Since then, a trust has been established to oversee the Institution; this trust receives private funds and donations as well as more than $620 million in government funding a year. This funding is how the museums are able to function without charging entrance fees.

The Smithsonian Today

In the century and a half since the Smithsonian was founded, it has grown from a one-building science center to nineteen museums and galleries—one in New York—the National Zoo, numerous research facilities, and 138 affiliates nationwide and in Panama and Puerto Rico. The collection contains more than 200 million objects and keeps growing daily.

Major donations still enrich the institution. Recently, a noted collector of Asian art, Dr. Paul Singer, donated art to complement the existing collection in the Arthur M. Sackler Gallery. And billionaire Steven F. Udvar-Hazy donated $60 million to create a spectacular sister museum, the Air and Space Museum at Dulles Airport, which displays 180 airplanes and spacecraft, including the space shuttle *Enterprise.*

In 2004, the Smithsonian also saw the addition of a new building that houses a new museum—the National Museum of the American Indian, located on the Mall. Furthermore, the renovated and restored National Museum of American Art and the National Portrait Gallery reopened in 2006. Also undergoing extensive renovation are the Arts and Industries building and the National Museum of American History, which will make the star-spangled banner the Museum's central icon. It should reopen in 2008.

The Castle

⊠ 1000 Jefferson Dr. SW
🚇 Metro: Smithsonian (Orange or Blue Line)
✆ 202-633-1000
⌨ *www.si.edu*

The Smithsonian Institution Building, also known as the Castle, is home to the Information Center and the offices of the Smithsonian Institution. When you get to the Mall, you'll be sure to spot it—look for the red sandstone building that looks like a castle. Though not a museum itself, this is the headquarters of the Institution, where all its main offices are located.

The Norman-style castle (a combination of twelfth-century Romanesque and Gothic architectural styles) was designed in 1855 by noted architect James Renwick, who also designed St. Patrick's Cathedral in New York and the Renwick Gallery. It has become the symbol of the Smithsonian over the years; you can find it on key chains and Christmas ornaments in any of the museum's shops.

Think of the Castle as your gateway to the Smithsonian theme park. There is a visitor's information desk where you can ask questions and get directions. You can also see models of the museums on the Mall and watch interactive videos. There is a twenty-four-minute film on the history of the Institution, as well as an overview of the museums and galleries that runs continuously throughout the day. Information on special exhibits and events is also available at the Castle.

Location and Hours

The Castle is located on the Mall, accessible from the Smithsonian Metro station. The Information Center is open from 8:30 A.M. until 5:30 P.M., sometimes later in the summer (call for hours).

☂ RAINY DAY FUN

You may be able to visit the Smithsonian in your own community. How? The organization has affiliated with about 140 museums in 28 states, Puerto Rico, and Panama. It supplies artifacts from the collection, sometimes for extended periods of time, and works with the curatorial staff in presenting exhibitions. Find out if your hometown has an affiliate institution at *www.affiliations.si.edu*.

A Haunting at the Smithsonian?

The marble sarcophagus of James Smithson, the founder of the Institution, is also housed in this building in its own room behind the information desk, and to the right (in a former guardroom) you will find a piece of smithsonite, a zinc carbonite he discovered that was named after him.

Believe it or not, Smithson never actually visited the United States when he was alive (and never even corresponded with any Americans that we know of). His bones were brought over to the United States at the turn of the twentieth century when an Italian marble drilling company bought the cemetery in Genoa where Smithson was buried. His crypt was set up in a former guardroom in the Smithsonian Castle.

In the 1970s, guards and Castle workers started to comment on weird occurrences in the Castle, such as alarms going off without cause and the ancient elevator jamming for no reason. Books were being pulled out and abandoned in the Woodrow Wilson Library, and many late-night workers complained of feeling that someone was watching them. This went on for about a decade. Then, in the late 1970s, Smithson's sarcophagus was opened during a renovation. Inside was a tin box with Smithson's bones inside, haphazardly mixed together with fragments of his original coffin. Ever since the bones were realigned properly and the sarcophagus resealed, the Castle has remained quiet.

The Freer Gallery of Art

✉ Jefferson Dr. at 12th St. SW
🚇 Metro: Smithsonian (Orange or Blue Line)
✆ 202-633-1000
🖥 *www.asia.si.edu*

This museum, admittedly smaller than some of the giants like the National Air and Space Museum, is a real find. Its home is an Italian Renaissance–style building originally designed to hold the National Museum of Fine Arts.

The Freer Gallery is named after its donor, Charles Lang Freer, a Detroit industrialist who collected Asian art and nineteenth- and twentieth-century American works. He donated 7,500 pieces of art to the gallery, as well as the money to build the gallery; another 20,000 pieces have been donated or acquired since 1923, making it one of the world's most extensive collections of ancient and modern Asian and Asian-inspired art.

Since the collection is so extensive, pieces are shown on a rotating schedule, but there are some permanent features on view. These include the largest collection of Whistler's paintings in the Western world; a wing on Japanese art that features some incredible painted wooden screens; Korean ceramics; Chinese paintings and ancient art; Buddhist art; South Asian art; Islamic art—Freer was especially fond of Persian painting from the sixteenth century; Egyptian glass; and the Luxury Arts of the Silk Route Empires exhibit. The Freer Gallery's museum shop offers many beautiful and unusual items from around the world. The kids will be enthralled with Chinese brush painting kits and origami kits, as well as haiku writing guides, books, and Asian music CDs. Adults will find jewelry, music, artwork, and Japanese tea items, as well as books about Asian art that are unique to this gift shop.

The Peacock Room

The epitome of Freer's vision is the restored Peacock Room, designed and painted by James McNeill Whistler. This room is a one-of-a-kind visual experience that is spectacular to behold more than 100 years after it was painted. When the museum is open late on summer evenings, or in the early morning hours, you may be able to sit alone here for a while and take in the all-encompassing splendor of it.

The Peacock Room was once the dining room of one of Whistler's London patrons, who had an interior architect design a room to hold his Chinese porcelain collection and his prized Whistler painting, *The Princess from the Land of Porcelain,* which was displayed above the fireplace. The architect consulted Whistler on the color of the room, and while the patron was away on a business trip Whistler took over the design of the room, having the ceiling covered in gold leaf, over which he painted a pattern of peacock feathers. He echoed that pattern in four painted wooden panels of peacocks on wooden shutters.

Whistler had done all this interior design without his patron's permission, and when the patron was presented with the bill, he was not amused and refused to pay the full price. Whistler got back at him by painting a confrontational scene of two peacocks fighting, which he titled *Art and Money; or The Story of the Room.*

The room was purchased by Freer in 1904 and dismantled and brought to his home. It was willed to the gallery in 1919. The Peacock Room has been restored twice since it was installed in the Freer, the most recent installation having revealed the blue, green, and gold peacock feather pattern on the ceiling and the gold paint on the wainscoting. It is indeed an inspired home for *The Princess from the Land of Porcelain.*

👥 JUST FOR PARENTS

The Peacock Room is so serene and peaceful that you might want to ask your spouse to take the kids for a run through the nearby Enid Haupt garden outside the Smithsonian Castle while you sit for a few quiet minutes, contemplating how this fabulous piece of art history made it intact into our national heritage.

Location and Hours

The Freer Gallery is located on the Mall, accessible from the Smithsonian Metro station (Orange or Blue Line). It is open from 10 A.M. to 5:30 P.M., later on some summer evenings.

The Arthur M. Sackler Gallery

✉ 1050 Independence Ave. SW
🚊 Metro: Smithsonian (Orange or Blue Line)
✆ 202-633-1000
✍ *www.asia.si.edu*

This gallery, housed underground, is dedicated to the history of the artistic development of Asian and Near Eastern art from ancient times to the present. Shows of contemporary Asian artists are often on view here, as well as traveling exhibits from major museums. Some exhibits offer the visitor the chance to touch objects to feel their weight and texture. In the Japanese porcelain exhibit, there are shards of porcelain for viewers to handle.

Like the Freer Gallery, the Sackler has an extensive collection shown on a rotating schedule. Permanent exhibits include:

- **"The Arts of China"** (from Dr. Sackler's own collection)
- **"Fountains of Light: Islamic Metalwork"**
- **"Luxury Arts of the Silk Route Empires"** (which it shares with the Freer Gallery of Art)
- **"Sculpture of South & Southeast Asia"**

The gallery runs a program called ImaginAsia for children six to fourteen years old and accompanied by an adult. Starting in the classroom on the second floor, they use an activity book to explore the collection and create an art project they can take home.

Guided tours are conducted daily at 12:15 P.M. except Wednesdays and public holidays. The museum gift shops mirrors the collection with a wide variety of prints, books, and porcelain available for purchase.

💼 TRAVEL TIP

If you plan on making purchases at any Smithsonian gift shop, you might be interested to know that the merchandise is tax free. That's because the Smithsonian is run by the government.

Location and Hours

The Arthur M. Sackler Gallery is adjacent to the Freer Gallery. It is located on the Mall and is accessible from the Smithsonian Metro station (Orange or Blue Line). Hours of operation are from 10 A.M. to 5:30 P.M., later on some summer evenings.

The Hirshhorn Museum and Sculpture Garden

✉ Independence Ave. at 7th St. SW
🚆 Metro: L'Enfant Plaza (Orange, Blue, Yellow, or Green Line)
📞 202-633-1000
🖰 *www.hirshhorn.si.edu*

The Hirshhorn is one of the leading museums of contemporary art in America, comparable with New York's Museum of Modern Art and the Guggenheim, and it's something no visitor interested in modern art should miss. It has an extensive collection of twentieth-century art, from a room full of Picassos to the latest controversial works by the likes of Britain's bad-boy artist Damian Hirst (the only one of his works on permanent display in the United States). Popular favorites include the Calder mobiles, Nam June Paik's video American flag made out of television screens, and the various icons from the 1960s Pop Art movement.

The sunken outdoor sculpture garden reveals a marvelous collection of important modern sculpture, from pivotal works by Rodin to unusual three-dimensional work by de Kooning.

≡FAST FACT

The Hirshhorn is named after Latvian-born mining entrepreneur, philanthropist, and art collector Joseph Hirshhorn (1889–1981). He gave the Smithsonian more than 6,000 pieces (think of it!) of modern art, and these formed the nucleus of the museum's collection, which opened in 1974.

The museum itself is a work of art, echoing the spiraling interior design of New York's Guggenheim Museum so that each floor is a self-contained circle around a courtyard with floor-to-ceiling windows that make use of natural light. Some have commented that the museum, designed by Gordon Bunshaft, looks like a giant doughnut or drum.

Lay of the Land

On the lobby level, you have the option to view a continuously shown twenty-minute film that discusses the art on display in the museum, as well as an overview of modern art and suggestions on how to experience the works. The lobby level also houses special exhibitions and the museum's gift store, which has a quirky collection of art knickknacks, as well as a good selection of books and posters. There is also a kid's corner with toys, puzzles, and project books.

The second floor has a series of galleries that present recent acquisitions and an impressive display of abstract expressionist works from the permanent collection, which might include Jackson Pollock, Barnett Newman's *Stations of the Cross*, and 1960s pop icons such as Claes Oldenburg's *7-UP* and Andy Warhol's *Marilyn Monroe's Lips.*

The galleries on the third level concentrate on the work of individual artists. You'll see Alexander Calder's colorful mobiles, and the wildly expressionist painting of Willem de Kooning. The kids will like Nam June Paik's *Video Flag*, a seven-by-twelve-foot bank of seventy video monitors that takes the form of the American flag while flashing images of American politics and technological advances. Other stars of the collection are the post-1960 representational paintings of James Rosenquist, Alex Katz, Tom Wesselman, and Eric Fischl.

On the lower level there are galleries showing contemporary art from the collection and two small spaces that continuously show film and video. The Black Box Theater shows new video work and is a nice place to rest and cool off or warm up, depending on the season.

Sculptures are located in the interior galleries of the first three floors, overlooking the courtyard, and these galleries chronicle the spatial developments of the last century with works by Degas, Picasso, Giacometti, and Matisse. You'll find a rare wooden sculpture by Gauguin, as well as a clever piece by Man Ray, all of which culminates in the powerful Robert Arneson giant bust called *General Nuke.*

Circling the museum are a number of recent sculpture acquisitions. You can sit in a tree-lined area while eating self-service from the Full Circle Café, which is open from May until September.

Location and Hours

The Hirshhorn Museum and Sculpture Garden is located on the Mall, accessible from the L'Enfant Plaza Metro station (Orange, Blue, Yellow, or Green Line). The museum is open from 10 A.M. to 5:30 P.M., and often later in the summer; the Plaza is open 7:30 A.M. to 5:30 P.M.; the sculpture garden is open from 7:30 A.M. until dusk. Guided tours are available on weekdays at noon, and there's an additional tour at 2:30 P.M. on Sunday. Sculpture Garden tours are held weekdays from June 1 to September 30 at 10:30 A.M., with a Sunday tour at 12:15 added.

The National Museum of African Art

✉ 950 Independence Ave. SW
🚇 Metro: Smithsonian (Orange or Blue Line)
✆ 202-633-1000
🖰 *http://africa.si.edu*

This museum, with its ground floor and underground galleries, is one of the country's few museums dedicated solely to African art, with more than 7,000 items in the collection. Included in its holdings are traditional pieces as well as contemporary works.

The museum welcomes you with African music and an introductory film. There are also computer stations that offer information about the exhibits, programs, and collections of the museum. The museum is built below ground level, and most of the exhibits are on Level 1, with a large exhibition gallery, lecture hall, and workshop on Level 2, and a gallery on Level 3. The permanent collection includes a marvelous show, "Art of the Personal Object," with more than 100 utilitarian items on view, such as chairs, stools, pipes, drinking horns, baskets, bowls, and cups, principally from eastern and southern Africa. Level 3 is the place to see the permanent exhibit on African ceramics, which displays more than 140 bowls and figures.

The gift shop is on the first level and offers a selection of African crafts and jewelry, as well as books and posters.

Location and Hours

The National Museum of African Art is located on the Mall, accessible from the Smithsonian Metro station (Orange or Blue Line). It is open from 10 A.M. to 5:30 P.M. Walk-in tours may be given depending on staff availability.

The National Postal Museum

✉ 2 Massachusetts Ave. at First St. NE
🚇 Metro: Union Station (Red Line)
✍ www.postalmuseum.si.edu

This surprisingly entertaining, family-oriented museum is dedicated to the history of postal service and stamps in this country. And you don't have to be a philatelist to love it. The exhibits on the Pony Express and airmail are particularly interesting, especially to children, but there is truly something here for everyone. Visitors get a chance to sort the mail, create their own mail routes over land and sea, ride a stagecoach, land an airmail biplane via a computer game (it's quite difficult), drive a Freightliner big-rig, and create their own postal imprint on a postcard, which they can mail to friends and family, and it's all for free.

In addition, there are extensive exhibits on the printing and history of stamps, rotating displays of the world's great collections, and the role the mail and its transportation had in binding the nation together. The museum also features an exhibit, "War Letters: Lost and Found," which showcases letters thrown away and later found by strangers written to and from American troops from the Civil War through Vietnam. Art lovers will appreciate the exhibition of the history of migratory hunting stamps, possibly the most beautiful nonpostage stamps ever produced. Also on view are a number of vehicles used to deliver the mail, from 1911 biplanes based on the designs of the Wright Brothers to a 1931 Ford Model A mail truck to that Freightliner semi.

☔ RAINY DAY FUN

What a surprisingly engaging museum the National Postal Museum is! Though seemingly geared toward children and stamp collectors, the museum exhibits operate on many levels, and the philosophically inclined may ruminate on the political, economic, and social importance of the U.S. Mail Service.

There are two gift shops on the premises. One offers posters, T-shirts, and various items from the general Smithsonian collection. In the stamp store across the hall, you can buy stamps for the postcards you create in the museum, as well as rare and special-edition stamps.

Location and Hours
The National Postal Museum is located in the Washington City Post Office Building, next to Union Station. It is open from 10 A.M. to 5:30 P.M. Guided tour times are variable; call 202-633-5535 for dates and times. Self-guided tours may be taken at any time. Get a brochure at the museum or download it from the Web site. The museum is wheelchair accessible.

The Renwick Gallery of the Smithsonian American Art Museum

✉ Pennsylvania Ave. at 17th St. NW
🚇 Metro: Farragut West (Orange or Blue Line)
   or Farragut North (Red Line)
✆ 202-633-1000
🖱 www.americanart.si.edu

This museum is situated in an Empire-style mansion (designed by James Renwick and begun in 1859) near the White House and not far from the Corcoran Gallery. The building itself was once the site of the Corcoran Gallery, and the exterior features the inscription "Dedicated to Art" and an etched portrait of Corcoran. Later, it was used as a courthouse until Jackie Kennedy convinced the Smithsonian Institution to take it over. The museum is a branch of the Smithsonian American Art Museum, and it highlights craft and design from the nineteenth to the twentieth century.

When you enter its lush interior, restored in late nineteenth-century grandeur, you'll find yourself in the Grand Salon, which features mauve walls, carved wainscoting, and a large skylight that makes you feel as if you've stepped back in time to the Victorian era. The Grand Salon is home to a number of paintings by minor nineteenth- and twentieth-century painters and two colossal Centennial urns on top of the plush velvet banquettes.

Across the hall from the Grand Salon is an archway that was built to showcase Hiram Powers's highly controversial sculpture *Greek Slave*, a nude woman in chains considered so scandalous in the nineteenth century that it was shown to groups of men and women on different days of the week. Now Wendal Castle's trompe l'oeil *Ghost Clock* is displayed in this space (with the *Greek Slave* on display in the Corcoran Gallery of Art), and it too is a masterpiece, its brilliantly carved wood painted white to resemble a sheet draped over a grandfather clock.

Other rooms in the museum feature outstandingly quirky pieces of American craft and design such as Larry Fuente's *Game Fish*, made from bright pieces of beads, buttons, coins, game pieces, blocks, magnetized letters, light bulbs, paintbrushes, and even a yo-yo.

The Renwick Gallery is an unexpectedly fun museum in an exquisite setting. Its gift shop features a rich selection of scarves and glass pieces, as well as unique jewelry.

Location and Hours

The Renwick Gallery is located one block west of the White House. It is accessible from the Farragut West (Orange or Blue Line) or Farragut North (Red Line) Metro station. Hours of operation are

10 A.M. to 5:30 P.M. Tours are offered weekdays at noon, and on weekends at 1 P.M.

The National Zoological Park

✉ 3001 Connecticut Ave. NW
🚇 Metro: Woodley Park–Zoo/Adams Morgan
 or Cleveland Park (Red Line)
☎ 202-633-4800
🖥 www.nationalzoo.si.edu

This 163-acre zoo features what seems like almost every creature known to man, with 2,400 animals representing 400 species, 20 percent of which are endangered or threatened. The zoo was designed by Frederick Law Olmsted, the ingenious landscape architect who also designed New York's Central Park and Boston's Public Gardens.

This zoo has so many highlights, it is difficult to narrow them down. Without a doubt, the current star of the zoo is the little panda bear Tai Shan, born at the zoo in 2005. The kids will also love the antics at the monkey house, the Amazonian tropical rain forest, the Kids' Farm, and the seals. There are also lions, tigers, bears, elephants, hippos, snakes, and a wonderful aviary. Children find the exhibit of mole rats in the small-mammals building particularly fascinating. The National Zoo is also the home of one of the few Komodo dragons ever bred in captivity. To see everything, you'll have to walk around, so be sure everyone wears comfortable shoes! It will take you a minimum of four hours to do the zoo justice.

Exhibits at a Glance

During the summer months, four exhibits are often crowded: Amazonia, the invertebrate exhibit, the Reptile Discovery Center, and especially the giant panda exhibit. Amazonia, the zoo's largest exhibit, features a steamy habitat for free-roaming amphibians, small mammals, and birds, as well as an aquarium to hold tropical fish. The Reptile Discovery Center has a number of interactive exhibit areas for children to learn about the biology of reptiles and amphibians.

The invertebrate exhibit features a giant octopus, which is fed several times a day. The museum director claims that the octopus has been able to open a screw-top jar with a shrimp inside all by itself! The Pollinarium, a glass-enclosed addition, illustrates the mechanics of pollination and the role insects play.

The giant panda exhibit features baby Tai Shan ("Peaceful Mountain") and his parents Mei Xiang (the mommy) and Tian Tian (good old dad). Although the baby was born here, he will probably be returned to China soon to become part of the breeding population. The older pandas are here on a ten-year loan from China, where there are only about 1,000 giant pandas left. Only twenty of those live outside China, which is why this family is so popular with American visitors. The older pandas are due to return home in 2010, but experts expect them to breed again before that. In the winter months the pandas may be indoors, but in the summer they can be seen through glass walls strolling through their outdoor yard. You'll have to get free, timed tickets to view Tai Shan. It's best to get them in advance, although a limited number of same-day tickets may also be available.

≡FAST FACT

When President Nixon opened diplomatic relations with China in 1971, the nations exchanged gifts. China gave the United States two giant pandas. Ling-Ling ("Darling Little Girl") and Hsing-Hsing ("Shining Star"), two of the four giant pandas then living outside China. Ling-Ling died at age 23 in 1992, and Hsing-Hsing died in 1999.

Other exhibits at the museum include the recently renovated monkey house that features the Think Tank, where orangutans play on computers. In addition to housing giraffes, rhinos, and hippos, the elephant house has a wonderful indoor exhibit on the anatomy of the elephant in comparison to dinosaurs that will leave any child fascinated. The small-mammal house features everything from small cats to mongooses. The Indoor Flight Room and the Outdoor Flight Cage combine to make a wonderful aviary with 150 species of birds. The outdoor cage is particularly well done, like the neighboring exhibit on the wetlands, which contains five wading pools featuring waterfowl and wading birds. The lion and tiger exhibit is also quite interactive, with many displays for children to learn about these animals' jungle instincts and preservation of the species.

Other exhibits include Beaver Valley, a fun-to-watch habitat when the animals (especially the otters) are active and viewable behind a glass wall, and the new Asia Trail.

Food and Shops

There are several places to eat on the premises. The full-scale Mane restaurant is located on Lion/Tiger Hill, and the Panda Café is near the Fujifilm Giant Panda Habitat. Express Grill is at Panda Plaza, and Popstop (seasonal) is across from the small-mammal house. There are snack stands and picnic areas (you may bring your own food) scattered throughout the park. Three fabulous gift shops (at Panda Plaza, Lion/Tiger Hill, and the Visitors' Center) feature all sorts of zoo-related toys, books, plates, scarves, and jewelry with an animal motif. If you forget to buy something here, there are Smithsonian stores at Union Station and Reagan National Airport.

Location and Hours

The National Zoo is located on the 3000 block of Connecticut Avenue, between Cathedral Avenue and Devonshire Place, and is accessible from the Woodley Park/Zoo or Cleveland Park Metro station (Red Line)—a ten-minute walk will get you from the station to the zoo. From April 2 to October 28, the grounds are open from 6 A.M. until 8 P.M.; the buildings from 10 A.M. to 6 P.M. From October 29 to April 1, the grounds are open from 6 A.M. to 6 P.M.; the buildings from 10 A.M. to 4:30 P.M. There is limited pay parking on the zoo grounds, which fills up in the summer by 10 A.M. Stroller rentals are available.

Other Galleries and Museums

The following offers brief reviews of the rest of the museums and galleries of the Smithsonian currently located in the nation's capital.

The Anacostia Museum & Center for Afro-American History & Culture

✉ 1901 Fort Place SE

🚇 Metro: Anacostia (Green Line)

✆ 202-633-1000

🖎 www.anacostia.si.edu

This museum of African-American social and cultural history focuses on Washington D.C., Maryland, Virginia, North Carolina, South Carolina, and Georgia. Established in 1967, the Anacostia was the first federally funded neighborhood museum. Exhibitions have highlighted the work of local Southern artists, as well as African-American culture and heritage in all walks of life, including music, religion, and more. Hours are daily, 10 A.M. to 5 P.M.

The Arts and Industries Building

✉ 900 Jefferson Drive SW

🚇 Metro: Smithsonian (Orange or Blue Line)

✆ 202-633-1000

🖎 www.si.edu/ai

This was the building where the Smithsonian collection was first shown, and it is a beautiful example of High Victorian architecture. The museum houses collections of American Victoriana, as well as crafts and special sociological exhibits of various peoples in America (Japanese-Americans in Hawaii, for instance). It is currently closed for renovation, so check before you make plans to visit.

The National Museum of the American Indian

✉ 4th St. and Independence Ave. SW

🚇 Metro: Federal Center SW (Orange or Blue Line)

✆ 202-633-1000

✒ *www.AmericanIndian.si.edu*

This museum, opened in the fall of 2004, houses the impressive George Gustave Heye collection, which features thousands of North American Indian masterpieces such as baskets, blankets, clothing, pottery, stone carvings, and masks. There are also artifacts from Mexico, the Caribbean, and Central and South American Indians. The museum is the result of a fifteen-year collaboration of various tribes and communities who designed the building, landscaping, and exhibits. It is located on the Mall, next to the National Air and Space Museum.

🧳 TRAVEL TIP

On July 1, 2006, after a six-year renovation project, the Smithsonian American Art Museum and the National Portrait Gallery reopened under one roof at the Donald W. Reynolds Center, a landmark building downtown, the former home of the Old Patent Office Building, the site of President Lincoln's second inaugural ball.

The National Portrait Gallery

✉ 8 & F Streets NW
🚇 Metro: Gallery Place–Chinatown (Red, Yellow, or Green Line)
✆ 202-633-1000
✒ *www.npg.si.edu*

Forget your preconceptions of a portrait gallery, this gallery's spankin' new quarters have made this incredible national treasure even more exciting than it was. Permanent exhibits feature Americans who have distinguished themselves in the performing arts, sports, and politics, using paintings, artifacts, memorabilia, and videos. The museum holds the only complete set of presidential portraits outside of the White House. Its impressive collection of daguerreotypes alone fills seventeen galleries and alcoves, and new galleries allow the show-ing of twentieth-century Americans.

The National Museum of American Art

✉ 8 & F Streets NW

🚇 Metro: Gallery Place–Chinatown (Red, Yellow, or Green Line)

✆ 202-633-1000

✍ www.americanart.si.edu

One of the few museums in the world dedicated solely to Ameri-can art, this permanent collection houses some great Colonial mas-terpieces, as well as the paintings that tell the story of our country. Visitors are introduced to the American experience on the first floor with some of Edward Hopper's iconographic paintings. Other galler-ies display folk art and American art through the 1940s.

The new building also houses a new way to experience art—the Luce Foundation Center for American Art, the first visible art storage and study center in Washington D.C. The kids (and you, too) will be fascinated visiting the Lunder Conservation Center, which allows the public a unique view of the preservation work that goes on behind the scenes of a museum.

The museum is open daily, 11:30 A.M. to 7 P.M.

CHAPTER 6

The Top Three Smithsonian Museums

VISITING ALL OR EVEN most of the Smithsonian museums and galleries might be too much for you, especially if you are in town for only a long weekend. In this case, you might wish to concentrate on the three must-see Smithsonian attractions—the National Air and Space Museum (the only one of its kind in the world), the National Museum of Natural History, and the National Museum of American History. Plan on dedicating at least three hours to fully explore each one of these museums.

The National Air and Space Museum

This is the most-visited museum in the Smithsonian complex, and some say the world, hosting more than 8 million museum-goers annually. It is a vast museum that chronicles the history of flight and aviation in twenty-three galleries, each devoted to a subject or theme, as well as 300 authentic spacecraft and rockets, space suits, a touchable moon rock, propellers, engines, and many interactive exhibits.

▐▌ TRAVEL TIP

Put aside at least three hours (or four, if you have children with you or if you are really interested in flight) to see the National Air and Space Museum. This time is necessary because there is no way you can rush through this incredible museum.

Milestones of Flight

This is the most popular exhibit in the museum; you can see it from the street through the glass wall of the museum. Here you will find:

- **The Wright Brothers' 1903** *Flyer*, the first human-propelled flying machine
- **The** *Spirit of St. Louis*, the aircraft in which twenty-five-year-old Charles Lindbergh made the first transatlantic flight, from New York to Paris, in thirty-three hours, thirty minutes, in 1927
- **The Bell X-1** *Glamorous Glennis*, in which Chuck Yaeger became the first pilot to fly faster than the speed of sound, in 1947
- *Gemini IV*, which carried astronauts Edward White and James A. McDivitt on the first manned space walk (exhibited with their space suits, too)
- **The** *Apollo 11* **command module**, which was the first spacecraft to land on the moon (with astronaut Michael Collins's space suit on display as well)

Other highlights include the world's only touchable moon rock, which was collected by *Apollo 17* astronauts; the *Viking Lander*, the test vehicle for the first spacecraft to explore the surface of Mars; Goddard rockets from 1926 and 1941; the Breitling Orbiter 3 gondola, the first balloon to successfully circle the earth, and the United States's Pershing II and USSR's SS-20 missiles, which are nuclear missiles banned by the INF treaty of 1987.

First-Floor Galleries

Galleries on the first floor include permanent exhibits on air transportation, how things fly, early flight, the golden age of flight, an interactive flight simulator, the space race, exploring the universe, and looking at earth. There is also an IMAX theater and a food court.

⟶ FAST FACT

As new as the headlines, the Milestones of Flight gallery now is permanent home to *SpaceShipOne*, the first privately built, piloted vehicle to reach space.

The first-floor exhibit on the history of early flight displays gliders that inspired the Wright Brothers, the first seaplanes, and a Bleroit IX, the most popular pre–World War I monoplane. In the How Things Fly exhibit, there are hands-on demonstrations of the scientific principles that enable airplanes to fly. You can also crawl into the cockpit of a Cessna 150 and manipulate the controls (a very popular experience for kids of all ages).

The first-floor gallery has you exploring the earth from above for mapping, weather, and spying purposes, and another gallery on the stars explains how satellites are used to map and examine radiant energy from the sun and the stars, with a host of solar instruments on display, as well as a film on the history of telescopes and our current knowledge of our galaxy and those beyond.

The Space Race gallery is one of the most popular exhibits on the first floor, with various models of American spacecraft, rocketry, missiles, space suits, and an overview of the space race. Here you will find a full-size test model of the Hubble space telescope, the *Apollo-Soyuz* spacecraft (the first manned international space mission), a model of the space shuttle *Columbia* on its launch pad, and the Skylab orbital workshop, which visitors can walk through (another very popular exhibit).

IMAX Theater

The Samuel P. Langley IMAX Theater features an IMAX screen that is five stories high and seven stories wide. Films on the history of flight and space exploration are shown daily. This is a unique experience, and children love films on this giant screen, especially the ever-popular *To Fly!* Tickets sell out quickly in the summer months, so purchase them early in the day even if you want to see a show in the afternoon (the 10 A.M. shows are usually not sold out). You can also purchase tickets at the box office up to two weeks in advance, so you might want to stop in the museum when you get to town and buy tickets for later in the week. Tickets are $8.50 for adults, $7.50 for seniors, and $7.00 for children. You can get a much better deal if you buy a combination planetarium/IMAX ticket. Call 202-633-IMAX(4629), 1-877-932-4629, or check out *www.si.edu/imax*.

Other Areas of Interest

You can enter the museum shop on the first floor, but it is a three-story, 12,000-square-foot emporium. It is also the largest of the Smithsonian museum stores, where almost every kid who ventures in walks out with the freeze-dried "astronaut" ice cream (at about two bucks, a bargain as far as purchasers of kids' souvenirs are concerned).

At the west end of the first floor is the very popular arcade with the fancy name "At the Controls," where children can pilot a flight simulator. There are dozens of aircraft to choose from, many of which are on display in the museum. The four-minute ride is $7.50 per person but worth every penny.

The Second Floor

Galleries on the second floor include exhibits on air and sea exploration from 1911 to the present and also display biplanes, World War I carriers, and navy fighters. There are two separate exhibit halls featuring aviation during World War I and World War II. The second is an extremely popular hall, displaying aircraft from five countries, including a Messerschmitt and a P-51D Mustang.

Another hall on this floor features an exhibit on exploring the planets, where you can see a full-scale replica of *Voyager*, the spacecraft that explored Jupiter, Saturn, Uranus, and Neptune, as well as a meteorite collected in Antarctica that scientists believe may be a piece of Mars.

≡ FAST FACT

It's hard to believe that only a little more than 100 years ago, on December 17, 1903, the first successful powered, controlled, sustained flight by humans took place in Kitty Hawk, North Carolina, using a plane designed and constructed by Orville and Wilber Wright. You'll see this same 1903 *Flyer* on the second floor at the Air and Space Museum.

The Pioneers of Flight exhibit houses many record-holding airplanes. The most popular is Amelia Earhart's Lockheed *Vega*. In this plane, Earhart became the first woman to make a transatlantic solo flight, in 1932 from Newfoundland to Northern Ireland in fourteen hours and fifty-two minutes.

Other galleries on the second floor include a look at space exploration in the future, including a realistic Martian landscape; an overview of the Apollo program, with examples of moon soil and space food and suits; and an exhibit of art about flight and space exploration. The final gallery looks at computers and space exploration and features the world's fastest computer, the brain of the Minuteman missile, and interactive displays for designing spacecraft.

The Albert Einstein Planetarium is located on the second floor, where there are various shows on the night sky, astronomy, and space projected onto a domed interior. Tickets for the planetarium shows can be purchased at the Langley Theater box office for $7.50 per person, but you can save by buying a combination planetarium/IMAX ticket.

If You Get Hungry

The Air and Space Museum has redesigned its Wright Place into a wonderful food court featuring a host of fast-food options, including Mezza Café, Boston Market, Donato's Pizza, and McDonald's (with a space-related trinket in the Happy Meal). It is perfect for this very busy museum.

The Steven F. Udvar-Hazy Center

If you have been inspired by the Air and Space Museum and/or you just can't get enough of aviation history, there is a spectacular sister museum near Dulles Airport that houses some of the larger aircraft that the museum just couldn't cram into its two stories (in fact, the original building can show only about a tenth of its collection).

The Udvar-Hazy Center opened to the public in 2003 on a 176.5-acre lot and features exhibit hangars, an observation tower where visitors can watch plane traffic, an IMAX theater, and restaurants. Noted exhibits include the fully restored *Enola Gay*, the space shuttle *Enterprise*, an F-40 Phantom Fighter, an SR-71 Blackbird, and one of the few surviving Concorde SST planes that flew between France and England. Another feature of the Center is the Wall of Honor, a permanent memorial to the tens of thousands of people who have contributed to air and space science. In total, the Udvar-Hazy Center displays more than 120 aircraft and 140 major space artifacts, plus thousands of smaller items, with the number growing monthly.

The National Museum of Natural History

The green-domed National Museum of Natural History is the second most visited museum in the Smithsonian complex, with more than 6 million annual visitors (with about a million during each of the summer months). To do this museum justice, you should expect to spend at least three or four hours there—its total area is more than 18 football fields!

☂ RAINY DAY FUN

The animal world comes alive at the Johnson IMAX 3-D Theater with the feature *Wild Safari*. You'll feel the walls disappear as you travel on a 3,000-mile journey through Africa and view the continent's most exciting creatures in their natural habitats. It's a popular show, so buy your tickets in advance and then plan your visit around showtime.

Highlights of the museum include the fabled Hope diamond, which always draws a huge crowd. The nearby Hall of Minerals is a favorite among children, with re-creations of a copper mine, many touchable geodes and rocks, and a good display of meteorites. Kids also love the insect zoo, where they can see inside termites' nests and a beehive and see a display of Madagascar hissing cockroaches.

The Hall of Bones is a great learning display on how mammal skeletons have evolved, and the replica of a giant blue whale and two preserved squid carcasses (two of only three *architeuthis*—giant squid—bodies in the country) are displayed and explained so even a parent can understand.

The Curse of the Hope Diamond

Many people say that the reason the Hope diamond lies behind glass in the Smithsonian is that the curse on the diamond can't harm anyone from there. According to legend, the diamond was once the eye of an Indian idol that was stolen, smuggled into Paris, and later turned up as the Blue diamond, part of the French royal jewels. Everyone who came in contact with the jewel was said to have met with tragedy, from Louis XIV's oldest son to his oldest grandson and his great-grandson. There's even a rumor that the stone was used as a bribe to get Louis XVI and Marie Antoinette out of France.

The diamond disappeared for a while—some think it appears around the neck of Queen Maria Louisa of Spain in a Goya painting—and resurfaced in Amsterdam, where it was recut. The jeweler died penniless because his son stole the gem, then the jeweler's son committed suicide after his father's death. It was purchased by Harry Hope in London in 1830 (from whom we get the name), whose son and daughter-in-law inherited the stone but also died penniless.

Later, an Eastern European prince bought the stone and gave it to a Follies Bergere actress, whom he later shot. After that, a Greek owner and his family were killed in a horrible car accident. The stone is said to have then turned up in Russia in the hands of Catherine the Great, who did not have a happy ending to her life.

A wealthy Turkish sultan bought the diamond and gave it to his favorite wife, who was later murdered after he was dethroned. Evelyn Walsh McLean, wife to the heir of *The Washington Post* fortune, had seen the blue stone while on her honeymoon in Turkey. She bought it, and, knowing about its history and the accompanying legend, supposedly had a priest bless it before she wore it. However, that precautionary measure did her no good because her only son was killed in a bizarre car accident right outside his home; her husband was committed to a mental institution after his involvement with the Teapot Dome scandal was revealed; and her daughter committed suicide.

New York jeweler Harry Winston bought the stone in the early 1950s and gave it to the Smithsonian on permanent loan, some say because his wife kept begging him to let her wear it. Winston sent the diamond to the museum by registered mail, and there's a story that after the mailman handled the package, his life was cursed: His leg was mangled in a car accident, his wife died of a heart attack, his dog died, and his house burned down.

Ground Floor

The ground-floor entrance on Constitution Avenue opens with highlights from the collection, including geodes and crystals, a 700,000-year-old hand ax, totem poles from the Pacific Northwest, a gigantic fossilized shark tooth, meteorites, and butterflies from South America. A collection of 300 local bird specimens is also on this floor.

The totally remodeled Atrium Cafeteria is here, too, offering many child-pleasing meals (hamburgers, pizza), as well as hot food and personally prepared sandwiches. The museum's gift shop is also on this level and has two wings—one exclusively for children. Museum artifacts, such as a lead coffin, are on display throughout the shop. The museum shop is extensive, and you could spend an hour in it as well. You can also buy a replica of the Hope diamond—with matching earrings!

First Floor

If you enter the museum from the Mall, you will walk into the museum's rotunda, where you will be greeted by a sight you won't soon forget—a giant African bush elephant trumpets your arrival with his extended trunk. This mighty creature has been a constant delight of childhood visits to Washington D.C. since before the baby boomers were kids.

There are eight exhibit halls on this floor, some of which have banners over their entrances from the rotunda.

📷 TRAVEL TIP

All the Smithsonian gift shops are worth exploring, but the shops in the National Museum of Natural History are among the best in the city. The ground-floor stores have a huge selection of toys, clothing, jewelry, and items for the home. On the second floor, the Gem Store has jewelry and geological samples, and the Mammals Museum Store is a miniature museum of "evolutionary treasures" for sale.

Early Life

This series of exhibits starts with a 4.6-billion-year-old meteorite containing amino acids, the building blocks of life. A relative newcomer is the oldest known fossil—of microorganisms—from 3.5 billion years ago, with a film explaining the law of evolution and various exhibits and fossils tracing the emergence of life from the ancient sea to the conquest of land. Some of the highlights of this exhibit include rare 530-year-old fossilized soft-bodied animals in shale, which were discovered by the fourth secretary of the Smithsonian in 1910, and the fossilized skeleton of an early whale.

The exhibit charts the evolution of ancient amphibians and plants and concludes with the dinosaur exhibit, where the skeletal remains of a diplodocus, an eighty-foot sauropod and the largest land-based dinosaur, is on display with a comptosaurus, stegosaurus, and an allosaurus. Informative, hands-on exhibits on dinosaur limbs, jaws, and teeth accompany this exhibit.

Ice Age Mammals

The next hall is dedicated to Ice Age mammals, where there are skeletons of saber-tooth tigers (one from the La Brea Tar Pits in California) and a woolly mammoth skeleton and tusk, as well as some preserved mammoth skin! Also on view is an Ice Age bison, freeze-dried by nature and recovered by Alaskan gold miners. This hall also features life-size tableaus of Neanderthal man and Ice Age mammals, and the FossiLab, where you may catch scientists working on fossils.

African Voices

The recently renovated exhibit hall makes African culture come alive as it explores the dynamism and diversity of African peoples from the Strait of Gibraltar to the Cape of Good Hope and the historical experience and influence of the African Diaspora. Highlights include a seventeenth-century Nigerian cast brass head, a carved door from Zanzibar, African headdresses from the nineteenth and twentieth centuries, and a contemporary portable Somali house called an *aqal*. Don't miss Discover Africa, an interactive experience for families.

The Behring Family of Mammals

The Mammal Hall has been completely renovated. It contains 274 specimens, such as a sloth hanging upside down in a South American rain forest; a giraffe drinking from an African watering hole; and a pair of African lions bringing down a water buffalo. The renovation reorganized the material so that visitors can see the evolution of the various mammal species and their traits. It includes an eight-minute video as well as fossils that can be touched, such as the skull of an extinct bear.

Second Floor

The second floor is home to the Janet Hooker Hall of Geology, Gems, and Minerals, which is always packed because the legendary blue Hope diamond is on display here.

JUST FOR PARENTS

In addition to the Hope diamond, the Janet Hooker Hall displays Marie Antoinette's diamond earrings and Empress Josephine's emerald necklace. Copies of these jewels are all available for purchase in the museum gift shop.

This exhibit hall also has a re-creation of a copper mine, a display of meteorites (including a fascinating story about meteorites that have dropped into people's homes), a moon rock, displays of ores and geodes to touch and examine, and many interactive displays on how minerals are formed.

The Hall of Western Culture

This is one of the most interesting exhibits in the museum. Its goal is to explain the history of Western civilization from the end of the Ice Age to 800 C.E., when the basic patterns of human existence were set.

The exhibit includes a diorama of the cave paintings of Lascaux, France, as well as excellent displays and informative short films about the ancient Egyptians and their burial and embalming processes. The Egyptian exhibits will hold even a child spellbound! Additional exhibits on Mesopotamian, ancient Greek, and Roman cultures are also on view here.

Osteology: The Hall of Bones

Floor-to-ceiling displays of hundreds of animal skeletons, grouped by order and species, dramatically show the law of evolution. Informative displays illustrate how bone structure adapted to the environment.

The Reptile Hall

This is an exhibit of alligators, frogs, turtles, and snakes in dioramas that duplicate their natural settings. Informative displays explain feeding habits, movement, and reptiles' influence on humans.

The Orkin Insect Zoo

This zoo is a relatively small but very entertaining exhibit on the world of insects. Here you can see a live beehive—put your hand on the glass and you can feel the bee's heat—along with an African termite mound and thrice-daily tarantula feedings (at 10:30 and 11:30 A.M. and 1:30 P.M. on weekdays). There are re-creations of rain forests and caves and swamps, all full of live bugs. The more docile members of the insect world can be held or touched by children (under supervision), including the ever-popular Madagascar hissing cockroach. There's also an insect lab where kids can see butterflies cocooning.

The Butterfly Garden

In the warmer months, there's an outdoor butterfly garden on the 9th Street side of the museum building where visitors can see the interaction between butterflies and plants. This is a nice follow-up to the insect zoo.

The Discovery Room

This is a hands-on, interactive room for children (and their parents) to touch and explore the many natural objects in the museum's collection. They have the opportunity to look into a crocodile's mouth; examine Discovery Boxes, which feature a variety of shells, fossils, plants, feathers, and bones; and touch an elephant tusk and a porcupine's spines. Look for a small room in the corner of the first floor near the museum store.

Restrooms

You may be tempted to think about finding restrooms in this immense museum as a safari, but not if you know where to look. Restrooms are located on the ground-floor Constitution Avenue lobby near the Information Desk; on the second floor next to the Discovery Room and the Ancient Seas exhibit; and on the second floor near the Hall of Western Culture.

The National Museum of American History

The National Museum of American History is closed to the public while it undergoes "a major architectural transformation." The planned work will upgrade the building's infrastructure and interior, and will construct a state-of-the-art gallery for the star-spangled banner. It is scheduled to reopen in the summer of 2008.

However, when open, this is another four-floor museum where you can expect to be fascinated for at least three hours (and perhaps an additional hour in the exhaustive gift shop). The exhibit about the first ladies is very popular, especially the section where you can see their inaugural gowns, and the huge Foucault's pendulum never fails to fascinate the visitors. There is so much that kids will enjoy that it is hard to know where to begin. The pop-culture touchstones on view include Archie Bunker's chair, Mr. Spock's phaser, and Dorothy's ruby slippers. There are a number of exhibits on the scientific innovations and technological advances that have made the United States a world leader, such as Thomas Edison's light bulb and Henry Ford's Model T. There are also halls on the historical events and sociological experiences that define our country.

First Floor

If you enter from Constitution Avenue, you will arrive on the first floor, which houses more than fifteen exhibit halls. These exhibits highlight the history and impact of science and technology on modern society.

≡FAST FACT

The legendary lunch counter from the F. W. Woolworth store in Greensboro, North Carolina, is on display on the main floor. Here, four African-American college students sat down, despite the "Whites Only" prohibition, and ordered lunch. Their nonviolent refusal to yield to the Jim Crow laws was a significant event in the movement to challenge segregation practices throughout the South.

The Country Store and Post Office

The first hall you will see displays an actual country store and post office that was transported in its entirety from Headsville, West Virginia. The post office continues to operate from within the museum— you can get your postcards stamped "Smithsonian Station."

The Material World

The purpose of this exhibit is to explain how things are made and how those elements have changed since the beginning of our country. There's a central section on new materials and reusing existing products (such as plywood and plastic) in new ways.

Technological Innovations

The next section of the first floor highlights technological innovations ranging from farm machines (harvesters and tractors) to ships (more than 100 models, including one of the *Mayflower*). On display is the engine room of a Coast Guard ship from the 1920s. There are also displays dealing with a sailor's life—kids find the re-creation of a 1940s tattoo parlor fascinating—including luxury liners, whaling, and disasters at sea (very popular since the movie *Titanic*).

A new permanent exhibit was added that highlights developments in transportation and how they influenced American society, from horses to trains to cars and public transportation. Especially fun and insightful pieces of this exhibit include the building of the famous Route 66 and the construction of the New York City subway system, complete with reproductions of the water pipes running beneath the city. There are cars and buses and trains for kids to entertain themselves in and with. For a child who loves cars and trucks, this is a dream come true.

Cars and Trains

The same exhibit wing also includes a hall on the development of the automobile, with more than forty antique cars on display (including the 1913 Model T), as well as the automobile's predecessors, the horse-drawn carriage, and alternate wheeled transportation such as bicycles and motorcycles. A hall on railroad innovations includes the Pacific-type steam locomotive 1401 used between 1926 and 1941, a stagecoach from 1836, and a Seattle cable car from 1888. There are additional exhibit rooms on bridge technology and engine design for power machinery.

Electric Power

The exhibit hall on electricity starts with the work of Benjamin Franklin and traces the development of electrical power through the nineteenth century, ending with the work of Thomas Edison and his light bulb. Other technological innovations highlighted on this floor include the development of the typewriter, the phonograph (with a display of one of Edison's first phonographs, from 1877), clocks, and locks.

The American Industrial Revolution

The exhibit on the American Industrial Revolution is vast, tying together industrial innovations and their effect on the population. It begins with a re-creation of the Crystal Palace, the site of the 1851 World's Fair in London, where American technological innovations were first heralded by Europe, and goes on to examine the impact of machinery and the factory system. On display are the world's oldest operable locomotive, the *John Bull*, as well as the Colt revolver and another 250 objects.

≡FAST FACT

When most people think of Thomas Edison, they think only of the light bulb, but Edison registered more than 1,000 patents for inventions in his lifetime. Other Edison inventions and improvements include the telegraph, phonograph, vote recorder, electric motor, talking doll, and storage battery.

Science in American Life

This exhibit chronicles scientific innovations over the past 125 years, such as nylon, the atomic bomb, and emerging technologies of bioscience. The hands-on science center is fascinating for children interested in science. Kids can put the four proteins of DNA together in varying patterns to create musical sounds or use a Geiger counter to test for radioactivity.

The Information Age

The final exhibit hall on the first floor is on the Information Age, which begins with the Morse telegraph and continues through the developments of the telephone, early computers, radio, and television. This exhibit is designed to be very interactive and offers visitors opportunities to have their fingerprints taken, decipher a German World War I code, and even produce an evening news program.

Second Floor

The emphasis on the second floor is the political and social history of our country, from the times of the Revolutionary War to the present. The second of two hands-on exhibits is also located on this floor, and visitors can operate machines featured on the floor, from sending a message by telegraph to turning the handle of a cotton gin.

The Star-Spangled Banner

One of the first exhibits you'll find on the second floor is the display of the flag, now restored, that Francis Scott Key saw by "the dawn's early light" was "still there," flying over Fort McKinley after a battle of the War of 1812. (After that sight, he wrote the poem "The Star-Spangled Banner," which became the national anthem.) The huge (9 × 10 feet) historic star-spangled banner is displayed under a protective cover.

🧳 TRAVEL TIP

On the second floor, be sure to visit Foucault's pendulum, an example of the nineteenth-century experiment that proved that Earth rotates. The pendulum dominates a second-floor gallery, where the hollow brass ball swings back and forth, periodically knocking down red markers set in a circle. It is somewhat mesmerizing and always surrounded by visitors.

After the Revolution

This exhibit looks at life in the United States in the 1780s and 1790s through the eyes of Native Americans, Europeans, and African-Americans, both slaves and freedmen, re-creating living spaces and the tools used during those times. It also re-creates the harrowing experience of coming to America on a slave ship.

Presidential Exhibits

As a hint that you are approaching the ever-popular exhibit featuring the first ladies, the next gallery displays a reproduction of the Ceremonial Court of the Cross Hall of the White House at the turn of the century, with original furnishings from Teddy Roosevelt's tenure in the White House. Adjoining galleries display presidential memorabilia, such as Thomas Jefferson's portable writing desk and the toys of the children who grew up in the White House.

The first ladies exhibit centers on the presidential wives of the twentieth century and gives a brief biographical and political background on each one. But it's the inaugural gowns that people really come to look at, especially those of Jackie Kennedy, Hillary Clinton, and Laura Bush.

The Suffragist Movement

A nearby exhibit focuses on the role of women in politics from 1890 to 1925, from the middle-class home to the tenement, and also includes some important memorabilia of the suffragist movement, such as Susan B. Anthony's desk.

Exhibits on Migration

This floor also has two exhibits examining the effect of migration on Americans. The first looks at African-American migration from the South to the North in the early part of this century, and the second hall, titled American Encounters, looks at the effect migration had on the western Native American populations.

Third Floor

The third floor features exhibits on the objects and innovations that have had an impact on the country, from coins to firearms. The section on the history of the armed forces features George Washington's field headquarters tent and a Revolutionary War vessel—the gunboat *Philadelphia*—from 1776, as well as many models of warships from the Revolution to World War I.

≡FAST FACT

The Hall of Armed Forces features the display of the stuffed and pre-served horse ridden by General Philip Sheridan in the closing months of the Civil War. Displayed intact beneath a glass case, the horse is decked in all its Union regalia. The horse was originally named Rienzi but was rechristened Winchester, in honor of the town where a potential defeat for the Union forces turned into a victory.

There is also a hall on the internment of Japanese-Americans during World War II that includes the executive order signed by Franklin Delano Roosevelt, a barracks room from the internment camp, and audio interviews with people who were kept in the camps.

Other galleries present collections of musical instruments, ceramics, textiles (magnificent quilts are on display), money, and medals. There's a permanent exhibit on the life and music of Ella Fitzgerald, with wonderful clips. The third floor also features a dollhouse from the turn of the century that has more than twenty rooms and is infinitely fascinating in both detail and content.

In addition to the previously mentioned pop-culture icons, cases filled to the brim with television memorabilia are on view around the escalators of both the second and third floor. These include Jim Henson's Muppets Elmo and Oscar the Grouch; Fonzie's jacket from *Happy Days*; and Howdy Doody, the talking, dancing puppet.

Ground Floor

The three restaurants and the gift shop are located on the ground floor. (There's a first-floor gift shop entrance as well.) The gift shop features a ton of fabulous knickknacks and Americana ranging from earrings made out of pennies to bags of old-fashioned candy and replicas of some of the White House china.

There is an old-fashioned ice cream parlor facing the Constitution Avenue entrance that offers a full lunch menu as well as wonderful ice cream desserts. The Palm Court Coffee Bar re-creates a turn-of-the-century restaurant, with wooden screens and ceiling fans, and features coffee and snacks such as brownies and scones. The Main Street Cafe is a large cafeteria with a full array of breakfast and lunch items. All the restaurants close by 4:30 P.M., even in the summer.

☂ RAINY DAY FUN

"The Hands On History Room" is an interactive exhibit that lets kids climb on a high-wheel bicycle and pedal, or explore the techniques and storytelling employed in buffalo hide painting.

Visitors' Information

Here are addresses, phone numbers, Web addresses, directions, and hours of operation for the National Air and Space Museum, the Steven F. Udvar-Hazy Center, the National Museum of Natural History, and the National Museum of American History.

National Air and Space Museum
✉ Independence Ave. at 6th Street SW
🚆 Metro: L'Enfant Plaza (Orange, Blue, Yellow, or Green Line)
✆ 202-633-1000
🖱 www.nasm.si.edu

The museum is located on the south side of the Mall, with entrances on Jefferson Drive and Independence Avenue. It is generally open from 10 A.M. to 5:30 P.M., but it may open earlier and close later in the summer, so call for hours. Free daily guided tours are offered at 10:30 A.M. and 1 P.M.; science demonstrations are conducted throughout the day.

Steven F. Udvar-Hazy Center
✉ 14390 Air and Space Museum Parkway
   Chantilly, VA
🚇 Metro: None
✆ 202-633-1000
🖎 *www.nasm.si.edu/museum/udvarhazy*

The Udvar-Hazy Center is located south of the main terminal at Dulles Airport in Chantilly, Virginia (near the intersection of Routes 28 and 50, about a half-hour drive from downtown D.C.). Parking is provided, but there is a parking fee. Hours of operation are 10 A.M. to 5:30 P.M.

National Museum of Natural History
✉ 10th St. and Constitution Ave. NW
🚇 Metro: Smithsonian or Federal Triangle (Orange or Blue Line)
✆ 202-633-1000
🖎 *www.mnh.si.edu*

The museum can be accessed from the Mall, with entrances on both Constitution Avenue and Madison Drive. General winter hours are from 10 A.M. to 5:30 P.M., and to 7:30 Friday and Saturday. Summer hours (beginning Memorial Day weekend) are 10 A.M. to 7:30 P.M. or later, so it's best to call and inquire. Guided tours are offered at 10:30 A.M. and 1:30 P.M. Tuesday through Thursday, and Friday at 10:30 A.M.

National Museum of American History
✉ 14th St. and Constitution Ave. NW
🚇 Metro: Smithsonian or Federal Triangle (Orange or Blue Line)
✆ 202-633-1000
🖎 *www.americanhistory.si.edu*

The National Museum of American History is closed for renovation until summer 2008.

The museum is located on the Mall, accessible from the Federal Triangle and Smithsonian Metro stations (Orange or Blue Line). When open, hours are from 10 A.M. to 6:30 P.M. (later during the summer). The museum also offers daily tours and demonstrations; times vary.

CHAPTER 7

Memorials and Monuments

WASHINGTON IS A SHOWPLACE of America's living history. The many statues, parks, and buildings erected in tribute to the people who have contributed to making the United States the proud country it is keep us close to our heritage. The most potent of these memorials commemorate four of our greatest presidents—Washington, Jefferson, Lincoln, and Roosevelt. Each of these presidential sites is awe-inspiring at any time, but the best way to see them is at night, when they are illuminated. It's also interesting to see them together so you can put their history into perspective.

The Washington Monument

✉ West end of Mall, between 15th and 17th Streets,
and Constitution and Independence Aves.
🚇 Metro: Smithsonian (Blue or Orange Line)
☎ 202-426-6841
🖱 *www.nps.gov/wamo*
🖱 *http://reservations.nps.gov (online reservations)*

The Washington Monument was the first memorial to be constructed in the nation's capital, and it's located at the center of the National Mall. Pierre Charles L'Enfant originally planned to erect a grand statue of George Washington on horseback. However, Congress failed to appropriate the necessary funds for the monument, and by the 1832 centennial of Washington's birth, a private society had been formed to raise funds for a national monument to the first president and Revolutionary War general.

The plans for an equestrian statue seemed too meager for this great man, and in 1845 a competition was sponsored to create something different. Robert Mills won the competition with his design for a Greco-Roman rotunda topped with an obelisk. It included a statuary group with Washington atop a chariot. Fortunately for posterity, they couldn't raise enough money for this grand scheme, and only the obelisk was constructed. The cornerstone was laid in 1848, but the Civil War interfered and the monument wasn't dedicated until 1885, with various descendants of Washington present.

The monument is 555 feet and 5⅛ inches high and is the tallest masonry structure in the world. A federal law prohibits any building in D.C. from being higher than this monument. Years ago, you could climb the 897 steps to the top, but now you have to take the elevator up. However, you can still walk down with a park ranger guide at 10:30 A.M. and noon when a ranger is available.

The view from the top is spectacular, and the whole upper tier and the observation tower were recently renovated. There is a visitors' center inside, which offers videos and displays on the life of the president. The monument receives close to a million visitors a year and underwent a major exterior restoration in 2000.

■ TRAVEL TIP

You can pay tribute to other fallen heroes by visiting the National Law Enforcement Officers Memorial commemorating federal, state, and local officers who have died in the line of duty. It is located between 4th and 5th Streets and E and F Streets; call 202-737-3400. The memorial is accessible from the Judiciary Square Red Line Metro station.

Location and Hours

The Washington Monument is located on the Mall, accessible from the Smithsonian Metro station (Orange or Blue Line). Open hours are from 8 A.M. until 4:45 P.M. The monument is closed on December 25.

You must have a ticket to get in to the monument, but tickets are free and you can get them at the ticket booth on 15th Street, at the bottom of the hill. Note that the booth opens at 8 A.M. and is often out of tickets by noon during the summer; also, there's a limit of six tickets per person. You can also purchase tickets in advance by calling 1-800-967-2283 or on the Internet at *http://reservations.nps.gov*. The tickets are free, but there is a fee of $1.50 per person, with a fifty-cent one-time processing fee.

The Lincoln Memorial

✉ 23rd Street between Constitution and Independence Avenues
🚇 Metro: Foggy Bottom-GWU (Blue or Orange Line)
✆ 202-426-6841
✐ *www.nps.gov/linc*

Lincoln's assassination in 1865 so affected the country that his memorial became the second presidential commemorative site to be built in the nation's capital. It is the second-most-visited of the presidential memorials, with 1.5 million viewers annually. The memorial's design, which we see every day on the back of the penny, is Henry Bacon's neoclassical interpretation of the Parthenon from ancient Greece. Thirty-six Doric columns represent the states of the Union at the time of Lincoln's assassination. Forty-eight decorative, wreathlike festoons above the columns symbolize the number of states at the time of the memorial's completion in 1922. Hawaii and Alaska are included on a terrace inscription.

The limestone walls of the memorial chamber feature the carved words of the Gettysburg Address and Lincoln's second inaugural address. There are also two murals by Jules Guerin depicting allegorical interpretations of Lincoln's achievements and beliefs on the north and south walls.

While the view of the Washington Monument across the Reflecting Pool from the front steps is serene, the power of the nineteen-foot-high seated white marble statue of Lincoln looking out onto the city makes you very aware of the magnitude of the Civil War. The statue, designed by Daniel Chester French from a death mask, took over four years to carve.

⬛ TRAVEL TIP

You can make your tour of the National Mall treasures more fun for the kids by requesting a Junior Ranger Program booklet from any park ranger on duty at the monuments. It will take you and the children on a self-guided tour of the Mall area.

Daniel Chester French

Many art historians consider Daniel Chester French to be one of America's greatest sculptors of the nineteenth century, but outside Washington D.C., his work is virtually unknown.

It was French's intention to depict Lincoln as "the war president" in the seated statue at the Lincoln Memorial. Lincoln sits in a curule chair like those used by Roman leaders, with his arms resting on the chair arms adorned with faces that are classical symbols of authority. The Union flag is draped over the back of the chair. Lincoln has one hand clenched in a fist and the other open. Some interpret this to suggest both his determination to preserve the Union and his compassion. Legend also has it that the position of Lincoln's hands spell out "A" and "L" in American Sign Language fingerspelling. While many think this is coincidental, French did later sculpt Thomas Gallaudet, founder of Gallaudet University for the deaf in D.C., in which French incorporated American Sign Language.

Other works by French in Washington D.C. include the statue of Samuel F. Dupont at Dupont Circle; the Butt-Millet Memorial (at 17th and E Streets), and the First Infantry Division Memorial (State Place near 17th Street).

An Inspiration to Many

The Lincoln Memorial has become a shrine to civil rights in the twentieth century. While many know that Martin Luther King Jr.'s famous "I Have a Dream" speech was delivered here in 1963, few are aware that as far back as 1939, the Lincoln Memorial was the site of a civil rights protest instigated by Eleanor Roosevelt. The first lady offered the memorial as the location for a recital by Marian Anderson when she was refused the stage at the Daughters of the American Revolution Constitution Hall because she was black. Roosevelt resigned her DAR membership over this snub.

Location and Hours

The Lincoln Memorial is located on 23rd Street between Constitution and Independence Avenues, at the western edge of the Reflecting Pool in Potomac Park. You can reach the memorial from the Foggy Bottom (Blue or Orange Line), but expect to do some walking.

You can enter the Lincoln Memorial from 8 A.M. until 11:30 P.M. any day but December 25. Park rangers offer lectures every thirty minutes. There is also a gift shop and a small bookstore (which closes at 10:30 P.M.). Wheelchairs are available.

The Thomas Jefferson Memorial

✉ South side of the Tidal Basin on Ohio Drive
🚇 Metro: Smithsonian (Blue or Orange Line)
📞 202-426-6841
🖋 *www.nps.gov/thje*

Although the concept of a memorial to the author of the Declaration of Independence and third president of the United States was planned in the L'Enfant city design, the actual location for the memorial was never laid out, so the cornerstone for this commemorative site was not broken until 1939, after land was purchased on what is now the Tidal Basin. The memorial was dedicated in 1943, the bicentennial anniversary of Jefferson's birth.

≡FAST FACT

The white marble memorial's colonnaded and domed design was created by John Russell Pope, who also designed the National Gallery of Art and the National Archives. The structure is neoclassic in tribute to Jefferson's influences.

The hollow bronze statue by Rudolph Evans, coated in wax to prevent ionization, depicts Jefferson (in a pose intended to represent the Age of Enlightenment) holding a document symbolic of his role as one of the authors of America's founding democratic principles. In this vein, the surrounding marble walls of the memorial are inscribed with the words of the Declaration of Independence, as well as of excerpts of various letters and bills Jefferson authored that articulate his belief in the American citizenry's ability to govern itself. The committee that drafted the Declaration of Independence is sculpted in bas relief above the entrance to the memorial.

The memorial also includes a gallery on Jefferson's life and works. He was also the founder of the University of Virginia, an amateur scientist, and an architect. The gallery is located on the lower level.

Location and Hours

The memorial is located on the south side of the Tidal Basin on Ohio Drive, accessible from the Smithsonian Metro station (Blue or Orange Line) and expect a long walk. Doors are open from 8 A.M. to midnight, but the memorial not open on December 25. Park rangers give talks every half hour. There is limited parking around the site. An alternative is to take the Tourmobile, which shuttles around the mall and its attractions.

🧳 TRAVEL TIP

During April and May, when the Japanese cherry blossoms are in bloom, the Jefferson Memorial is one of the most beautiful and inspirational sights in the city. It is said that President Roosevelt, who was the guiding force behind the construction of this memorial, had a number of trees removed so that his view of the Jefferson Memorial would be unobstructed.

The Franklin Delano Roosevelt Memorial

✉ West shore of the Tidal Basin in West Potomac Park
🚇 Metro: Smithsonian (Blue or Orange Line)
✆ 202-426-6841
🖱 www.nps.gov/fdrm

The newest of the presidential memorials, this four-room, open-air memorial to President Roosevelt sits on a 7½-acre site and is the most visited of the presidential memorial sites, with more than 3 million tourists a year. It is also the only presidential memorial that includes a tribute to a first lady, Eleanor Roosevelt, who was also the first U.S. representative at the United Nations.

The four "rooms" of the memorial represent Roosevelt's four terms in office, from 1933 to 1945, the years spanning the Great Depression through World War II. The first gallery represents his first term with a life-size statue of a poor Appalachian couple, the second room a bread line, the third a person listening to Roosevelt's fireside chats, and the fourth a statue of Eleanor Roosevelt.

There are also numerous fountains and green granite walls inscribed with Roosevelt's words, which are particularly moving when illuminated at night. A Social Programs mural depicts in images, writing, and Braille the fifty-four government programs implemented during Roosevelt's New Deal.

As with all commemorative works, there was some controversy associated with the Franklin Delano Roosevelt Memorial in that the images of Roosevelt do not portray him in a wheelchair, which he used from the age of thirty-nine until his death at age sixty-three as a result of polio. However, a statue of Roosevelt in a wheelchair was commissioned by President Clinton, and it is displayed at the entrance to the memorial. A replica of Roosevelt's wheelchair is also on view in the memorial's gift shop.

≡FAST FACT

While Roosevelt is best known for the statement "We have nothing to fear but fear itself," his thoughts on war should also be remembered: "I have seen war. I have seen blood running from the wounded. . . . I have seen the dead in the mud. I have seen cities destroyed. . . . I have seen children starving. I have seen the agony of mothers and wives. I hate war."

Although the memorial was in the works for more than fifty years, Roosevelt himself had said that he never wanted one. He told his close friend U.S. Supreme Court Justice Felix Frankfurter, that should posterity decide to erect a memorial to him, it should be no bigger than his White House desk. Until 1997, when the Franklin Delano Roosevelt Memorial was built, the only Roosevelt commemorative marker was a desktop-size granite stone outside the National Archives building.

Location and Hours

You'll find the Franklin Delano Roosevelt Memorial between the Lincoln and Jefferson Memorials, in West Potomac Park on the west shore of the Tidal Basin. The closest Metro stop is the Smithsonian on the Blue or Orange Line, but expect a fairly long walk from the metro station.

The memorial is open from 8 A.M. until 11:45 P.M., and the bookshop that's located on the premises operates 9 A.M. to 6 P.M. Audiotape guides are available.

The Vietnam Veterans Memorial

✉ Constitution Avenue and 23rd Street NW
🚇 Metro: Foggy Bottom (Blue or Orange Line)
✆ 202-426-6841
🖉 www.nps.gov/vive

Known as "the Wall," this is the most visited of the war memorials in Washington D.C. and certainly one of the most powerful war images ever created. It is impossible to walk by the sloped black granite 492-foot wall and not feel overwhelmed by the loss of lives. The wall is carved with the 58,249 names of those who were killed during the Vietnam War. The earliest recorded casualty dates from 1959, the last from 1975, and each is marked with either a diamond to denote a confirmed death or a cross to indicate that the remains were not found. There is a black bound book at the start of the memorial that lists the names of the dead.

This memorial is usually crowded, and viewers pass by the reflective wall in a single file. Relatives and friends of those whose names are inscribed on the wall often leave flowers, flags, and tokens or make a charcoal rubbing of their loved one's name. Park rangers collect the offerings at the end of each day, and a small sample is on display in the National Museum of American History. Park rangers will also provide a printout on the information for a specific name, as well as paper for rubbing.

The Vietnam Veterans Memorial Controversy

The design for the Wall was considered highly controversial in 1982, when it was erected. Yale architecture student Maya Ying Lin, then only twenty-two, won the competition sponsored by a private organization, and many were disturbed that the memorial did not follow more traditional war motifs.

Lin's stark design of a simple black granite wall bearing the names of the American soldiers who died in Vietnam was so different from all the war memorials in Washington that it immediately received criticism from just about every veterans' group, as well as special-interest groups and some politicians.

Critics cast aspersions on her vision, her ability, her talent, her age, and her gender. Some called it "dishonorable" and "a scar." But Maya Lin stayed firm to her vision for "the Wall" and refused to change her design. "I believed that this was going to help people," she said of her work.

Her entry described her vision for the Wall as follows:

> Walking through this park, the memorial appears as a rift in the earth. A long, polished, black stone, emerging from and receding into the earth. Approaching the memorial, the ground slopes gently downward and the low walls emerging on either side, growing out of the earth, extend and converge at a point below and ahead. Walking into this grassy site contained by the walls of the memorial, we can barely make out the carved names upon the memorial's walls. These names, seemingly infinite in number, convey the overwhelming numbers, while unifying these individuals into a whole. The memorial is composed not as an unchanging monument, but as a moving composition to be understood as we move into and out of it.

In the nearly twenty years since the memorial was erected, it has been accepted as a brilliant memorial to the sorrow and loss that most Americans feel when looking back on this war.

≡ FAST FACT

In the neighboring Constitution Gardens, there are two traditional sculptures dedicated to the soldiers of Vietnam and the female Vietnam veterans. Frederick Hart designed Three Servicemen, and Gloria Goodacre designed the Vietnam Women's Memorial.

Location and Hours

To reach the Vietnam Veterans Memorial, take the Metro to Foggy Bottom 9 Blue or Orange Line). The Memorial is located on Constitution Avenue and 23rd Street, NW, in Constitution Gardens, just northeast of the Lincoln Memorial. The memorial is open year-round from 8 A.M. to midnight. Closed December 25.

The Korean War Veterans Memorial

✉ Between 22nd and 23rd Street NW, in West Potomac Park
🚇 Metro: Foggy Bottom (Blue or Orange Line)
📞 202-426-6841
🖋 *www.nps.gov/kwvm*

This memorial is located within walking distance of the Vietnam Veterans Memorial and across from the Lincoln Memorial. This privately funded commemorative space in honor of the soldiers who fought in the Korean War of the 1950s is more traditional (as were the Cold War politics of that war), and it serves as a powerful counterpoint to the Wall. Like life-size chess pieces, nineteen statues of American servicemen, some wearing ponchos, are posed in various stages of advancement toward an imaginary hill where an American flag and a reflecting pool wait.

Like the Vietnam Veterans Memorial, the Korean War Veterans Memorial also has a black granite reflective wall, at the top of which are the words "Freedom Is Not Free." Etched on the surface of this wall are the faces of soldiers, chaplains, and war personnel, and around the perimeter of the memorial is a raised gray-granite curb that lists the twenty-two nations that sent men to this conflict. Though much shorter in duration (1950 to 1953), this war had almost as many casualties as the Vietnam War.

Location and Hours

The memorial is located between 22nd and 23rd Streets, directly across the street from the Lincoln Memorial. If you don't mind a fairly long walk, you can reach the memorial from the Foggy Bottom Metro station. The memorial is open from 8 A.M. until midnight. There are restrooms, a bookstore, and concessions.

The U.S. Navy Memorial and Naval Heritage Center

⊠ 701 Pennsylvania Ave. NW
🚉 Metro: Archives (Yellow or Green Line)
✆ 800-821-8892
✆ 202-737-2300
✎ www.lonesailor.org

The U.S. Navy Memorial, dedicated to the men and women who served in the U.S. Navy, is an outdoor circular plaza on an etched map of the world, with fountains and waterfalls flowing with the collected waters from the seven seas.

A bronze statue, *The Lone Sailor*, with a signature navy-blue coat, flared jeans, and a duffel bag, stands watching over the map on the plaza. The statue was cast from the remains of eight navy ships (and even a nuclear submarine) in service from the Revolutionary War through World War II.

Nearby is the Naval Heritage Center, which is a database, research center, and museum for the navy. There are informative displays on the history of the navy, its personnel, and its ships, as well as the President's Room, which profiles the six presidents who were navy officers. There is also a Navy Memorial Room, which houses the computerized record of navy personnel, both past and present (with more than 200,000 entries, including a young Tony Curtis in Hawaii in 1943 when he was still named Bernie Schwartz) and the showing of the film *At Sea*, which tells the story of today's navy. There is also a ship's store, which sells navy and nautical memorabilia and toys and games for the kids.

💼 TRAVEL TIP

Free concerts are held in the plaza in the summer months, and dramatic wreath-laying ceremonies are staged on Memorial Day and on Veterans Day. Call for more information.

Location and Hours

The memorial and center are located on Pennsylvania Avenue, near the National Archives Metro station (Yellow or Green Line). The U.S. Navy Memorial is open twenty-four hours. The heritage center is open Monday through Saturday, from 9:30 A.M. to 5 P.M. in the summer, closed Sunday and Monday in the winter. The center is closed Thanksgiving Day, Christmas Day, and New Year's Day. Admission is free.

Arlington National Cemetery and Arlington House

✉ Arlington, VA
🚆 Metro: Arlington National Cemetery (Blue Line)
✆ 703-697-2131
✆ 703-607-8052 (visitors' center)
🖰 www.arlingtoncemetery.org
🖰 www.nps.gov/arho (Arlington House)

Every year, 4.5 million people visit the 614 acres of the Arlington National Cemetery, a cemetery for the military. The many important sites on the grounds include the Kennedy gravesites, the former home of General Lee, the Tomb of the Unknown Soldier, the mast of the USS *Maine*, and the statue commemorating Iwo Jima. You should expect to spend at least two, if not three, hours here.

While probably not for young children, Arlington National Cemetery can be a somber but surprisingly educational experience, with its acres of symmetrically arranged white crosses on the green hills and the various gravesites and memorials on the property.

The Women in Military Service Memorial

When you enter the gates of the cemetery grounds, you will pass the newest war memorial in D.C.—the Women in Military Service Memorial—which honors the nearly 2 million women who have served in the armed forces. This memorial, which was designed by a husband-and-wife architect team and dedicated in October 1987, features a round reflecting pool within a semicircle of a curved granite wall. Arched entries in this granite wall lead to an upper terrace, which offers a sweeping view of the cemetery and the city of Washington.

TRAVEL TIP

Refer to Chapter 4 if you don't want to do a lot of walking and would prefer to take the Tourmobile. But if you do prefer to walk around the cemetery, make sure you wear comfortable shoes because there are a lot of hills.

Etched glass panels within the memorial include quotes about women's experiences in the military. Beneath the memorial is an education center, where the Hall of Honor traces the history of women in the military, as well as a computerized database of personnel and a shop.

The Visitors' Center

Here you can watch a video on the history of the Arlington cemetery and stop at the gift shop. Bathroom facilities are also available. If you plan to take the Tourmobile, tickets are available here, along with free maps of the grounds and information on specific graves.

The Curtis-Lee Mansion

Once out the door of the visitors' center, you should head to the grounds of the Curtis-Lee Mansion, where the history of the cemetery begins. The property was owned by the adopted grandson of George Washington (George Washington Parke Curtis, who is buried on the property). Curtis built the mansion to house his Washington memorabilia and left it to his daughter. She eventually married the man who would later lead the South against the North in the Civil War.

When the Lees left Virginia during the war, the Union took over the grounds and, some say out of spite, began burying the war dead on the property (1,800 casualties of the Battle of Bull Run are buried in front of the house). Their son did try to retain the property after the war, but the many graves on the grounds made it an unattractive home, and he eventually sold it back to the government.

Today, this property is known as the Arlington House. In front of the house is the sarcophagus of Pierre Charles L'Enfant, the man who designed Washington D.C. His marble tomb sits on a hill overlooking the city.

The The Kennedy Gravesites

The Kennedy gravesites are within walking distance of Arlington House. Many who remember the assassination of John F. Kennedy pass by the eternal flame, lit by Jacqueline Kennedy Onassis, who is now buried beside her first husband and the two babies they had who died in infancy. A short distance down the hill is the gravesite of Robert Kennedy, which is composed of a reflecting pool.

The Tomb of the Unknown Soldier

Located near the center of the cemetery, the Tomb of the Unknowns is one of the most visited sites on the grounds. The tomb honors the unknown soldiers of World War I, World War II, and the Korean War; the remains of the soldier who was interred in the Vietnam Tomb were identified in 1998 through DNA technology.

The tomb is guarded twenty-four hours a day by the Third Infantry Division (the Old Guard). The sentinels who guard the tomb perform a changing of the guard every half hour in the warm months and every hour during the winter. There are also many wreath-laying ceremonies at the Tomb of the Unknowns.

The Iwo Jima Memorial

Iwo Jima, the memorial to the United States Marine Corps, is a powerful tribute to the marines and World War II. If you can manage to drive around the monument, it will appear that the marines are raising the flag (an optical illusion). An Air Force Memorial and Museum are also being planned for the future on this site. Nearby is the Netherlands Carillon, a gift of chimes from the people of the Netherlands that has fifty bells.

Other Sites

At the Arlington National Cemetery, you'll also find the Confederate War Veterans' Memorial, which was erected in 1912 and designed by a Confederate war veteran who is buried beneath it, as well as the Civil War Memorial on the grounds of the Lee home. Also on the grounds of the Lee home is a former village for freed slaves, called the Freedman's Village, which thrived after the Civil War and even had its own hospital and a school with 900 students.

Other important commemorative sites include a memorial to the crew of the space shuttle *Challenger*, two of whom are buried at the memorial site; Lockerbee Memorial Cairn for the 259 people killed on Pan Am Flight 103; an Iran Rescue Mission Memorial for servicemen killed in the hostage rescue attempt; a monument to Teddy Roosevelt's Rough Riders of the Spanish-American War; a memorial to the Hmong, who helped the United States in the secret war in Laos; and the USS *Maine* Monument, which includes the actual mast and anchor of the ship.

💼 TRAVEL TIP

The District is home to other historic cemeteries you can visit, like the Congressional Cemetery that contains the remains of John Philip Sousa, J. Edgar Hoover, and Civil War photographer Matthew Brady. Rock Creek Cemetery, the oldest cemetery in Washington D.C., was established in the early eighteenth century on the grounds of St. Paul's Episcopal Church.

Arlington National Cemetery is also the final resting place of some of America's most famous military leaders, as well as people who made an impact on the nation. Arlington contains the gravesites of the following luminaries:

- **Thurgood Marshall**, U.S. Supreme Court justice
- **Audie Murphy**, most decorated World War II soldier and actor
- **Joe Louis (Barrow)**, World War II veteran and heavyweight boxing champion
- **Oliver Wendell Holmes Jr.**, Civil War veteran and U.S. Supreme Court justice
- **Daniel "Chappie" James Jr.**, the first African-American four-star general
- **Richard Byrd**, polar explorer and admiral

- **William Howard Taft**, president and chief justice of the U.S. Supreme Court
- **Virgil "Gus" Grissom**, astronaut
- **Medgar Evers**, World War II veteran and civil rights leader
- **Samuel Dashiell Hammett**, army sergeant and Sam Spade author
- **Lee Marvin**, U.S. Marine Corps private and movie actor
- **George Westinghouse**, Civil War veteran and inventor

There is an average of twenty funerals at Arlington National Cemetery a day, and approximately a quarter of a million gravesites. In 1980, a columbarium was erected to house cremated remains. Otherwise, it was estimated that at this present burial rate, the cemetery would have been full by 2002.

Location and Hours

The cemetery is located across from the Lincoln Memorial just over the Memorial Bridge in Arlington, Virginia. It's open 365 days a year to visitors from 8 A.M. to 5 P.M., and from April through September, the evening hours extend to 7 P.M.

There is public parking ($1.25 per hour for the first three hours, $2 per hour after that), but the Tourmobile is the best way to get there. (To make reservations, call 202-554-5100.) You can also go via the Metro to Arlington National Cemetery Metro station (Blue Line).

🯅 JUST FOR PARENTS

If your children have ever asked questions about the JFK assassination, this is a good place to start your own tale of where you were at the time and what it meant to you. You might also want to remind them that this is the president after whom the Kennedy Center is named and take them to see the giant bust of Kennedy later on in your trip.

The U.S. Holocaust Memorial Museum

✉ 100 Raoul Wallenberg Pl.
   (formerly 15th St. SW)
🚇 Metro: Smithsonian (Orange or Blue Line)
☎ 202-488-0400
🖰 www.ushmm.org

This museum and memorial is not for young children. A thoughtful permanent exhibit on the life of a young Jewish boy in Germany ("Daniel's Story: Remember the Children") is, however, suitable for slightly older children (8 to 12 years old). The museum has a sign posted recommending that children under twelve not view the material, but even teenagers need to be prepared for this museum.

Daniel's Story

This walk-through exhibit attempts to explain the events leading up to the Holocaust to children over eight years old. This exhibit is a Jewish child's personal account of life in Germany during the Holocaust. Daniel takes viewers through his town, his home, the streets of his town in the aftermath of Kristallnacht, the ghetto he was sent to, the cattle-car ride to a concentration camp, and what happened to his family after the war.

Each room of the exhibit has sample diary entries in Daniel's own words. Daniel's diary entries chronicle the confiscation of his parents' store, the burning of their synagogue, being able to buy food and other merchandise only from Jewish merchants, being taunted in school, and being forced to wear the yellow star of David. When his family is forced from their middle-class home and herded into a ghetto, both Daniel and his sister are forced to start working. His family is sent by cattle car to a concentration camp, and a film ends the exhibit explaining what happened to the family after the cattle-car journey, where Daniel was separated from his mother and sister, who were killed in the camps.

For the young and those who have never read *The Diary of Anne Frank*, this is as close to an interactive experience of what happened to those who were children during the Holocaust as one can come.

Other Exhibits

There are a handful of changing and permanent exhibits that you can view, including the Wall of Remembrance, tiles painted by schoolchildren to remember the 1.5 million children killed during the Holocaust, as well as a brief orientation film on the history of the Holocaust and the museum itself that is played every fifteen minutes.

When you get in line to enter the elevator to the fourth floor, where the chronological history of the persecution and elimination of European Jews under Hitler begins, you are given a reproduction of an identity card from one of the Holocaust's victims, two-thirds of whom were killed during this time. An estimated 12 million people were murdered by the Nazis during the Holocaust, a number that includes 6 million Jews as well as gypsies, homosexuals, Jehovah's Witnesses, Soviet prisoners of war, the disabled, and political dissidents.

The fourth floor tells the story of the Nazi rise to power, with examples of their propaganda against the Jews. The third floor continues the story of the increasing ghettoization of Europe's Jews and includes an authentic cattle car that was once used to transport victims to the camps. This will make the hair on your neck stand as you pass through it. There is also a replica of the wrought-iron sign that hung over the entrance to Auschwitz, *Arbeit Macht Frei* ("Work Will Make You Free"). Here you will also see a disturbing documentation of the Nazi scientific experiments on the camp prisoners.

On the second floor, the story of the liberation of the camps and the end of the war is told. There are relics and a graphic display of the cost of human lives as evidenced by a room full of the shoes of victims and pictures of piles and piles of removed wedding rings and human hair that was used to stuff upholstery. Here, too, are actual pieces of the crematoriums and camps.

The final exhibit is a thirty-minute film called *Testimony*, in which survivors tell their own stories. This leads to the solemn Hall of Remembrance, where an eternal flame burns to remember the victims of the Holocaust.

The museum is also a research center and Holocaust registry. There is a museum store that has a unique collection of books about the Holocaust and its survivors, as well as a museum café that serves both kosher and non-kosher meals.

Location and Hours

The museum is located off the Mall, and it is accessible from the Smithsonian Metro station (Blue or Orange Line). You can visit the museum from 10 A.M. to 5:20 P.M.; hours are extended to 7:50 P.M. April to June. Closed on the Jewish holiday of Yom Kippur and on Christmas Day.

You need tickets to see the permanent exhibitions—not because it costs money to view them but because there's a need to control the number of people walking through the exhibits at one time. (The memorial receives 2 million visitors a year, and the gallery spaces of the museum itself are small.) You can pick up the tickets at the museum's information desk, or you can order them ahead of time from Tickets.com or at 1-800-400-9373.

The National World War II Memorial

✉17th Street between Constitution and Independence Avenues
🚊 Metro: Smithsonian (Blue or Orange Line)
📞800-639-4WW2 (4992)
📞202-619-7222
🖊*www.wwiimemorial.com*

This memorial opened to the public in April 2004, made possible by private fundraising and ardent support from World War II veterans. Today, it is the only war memorial on the Mall's central axis.

The World War II Memorial is built on a 7.4-acre site between the Washington Monument and the Lincoln Memorial. The white-granite and bronze memorial has two forty-three-foot arches, symbolizing the Atlantic and Pacific theaters of the war, as well as fifty-six granite pillars that form an oval around a plaza with a pool. The pillars represent the states and territories that sent soldiers from the United States to war. Along the ceremonial entrance to the plaza, twenty-four bronze panels show various scenes from the war, both at home and overseas. Across from the pool is the Freedom Wall, where 4,000 gold stars symbolize the 400,000 Americans killed in combat.

TRAVEL TIP

The District is awash in security precautions, so be aware that there is a list of items that are not allowed in public buildings—weapons, of course, aerosol cans, strollers, animals, baggage, packages, food containers (except water in a clear container). No building has storage facilities for these items, so play safe.

As with all things in Washington, there was controversy over the construction of this memorial, from how the funds were raised (pitches from actor Tom Hanks and Senator Bob Dole) to its size and scale and even its location, claiming that it would obstruct the peaceful view of the Reflecting Pool.

Location and Hours

The memorial can be found at the Rainbow Pool site, at the east end of the Reflecting Pool between the Lincoln Memorial and the Washington Monument on the Mall. You can take the Blue or Orange Metro to the Smithsonian station, but it's a long walk to the site. Open twenty-four hours a day, seven days a week.

CHAPTER 8

Government Buildings

THE THREE BRANCHES OF federal government—executive, legislative, and judicial—are all headquartered in this showcase city. Being able to tour the facilities and actually see your government in action will bring you closer to those grade school social studies and civics lessons and give you real perspective on the nightly news. In addition to the three major branches, you can visit many other government agencies and service organizations to see how the principles worked out by our founding fathers have evolved over the last 200 years.

The White House

✉ 1600 Pennsylvania Ave. NW
🚇 Metro: McPherson Square (Blue or Orange Lines),
   Metro Center (Blue, Orange, or Red Lines)
   or Federal Triangle (Blue or Orange Lines)
✆ 202-456-2121
🖰 www.whitehouse.gov/history/tours

The White House is the oldest public building in D.C. and has been the home of all presidents except George Washington. It was designed by Irishman James Hoban, who won a competition in 1790, beating out fifty-one designers including Thomas Jefferson, who used a pseudonym when submitting his entry. Originally called the "presidential palace," it acquired the nickname "the White House" after continuous applications of whitewash were painted on the exterior to fix it up after it was set on fire during the War of 1812.

📷 TRAVEL TIP

Since the terrorist attacks of September 11, you must get White House tour tickets in advance through your local representative's or senator's office, and there are no tours on Sunday or Monday. Also, the Bureau of Engraving and Printing and U.S. Supreme Court are closed on the weekends, so head there first on a Friday or save them for Monday.

James Hoban guided the subsequent restoration of the White House, adding space for the presidential staff. In 1902, a West Wing, with the Oval Office, and the Rose Garden were added under Teddy Roosevelt's administration. The third floor was added in 1927 to provide more living space for the first family. The entire White House was rehabbed in 1948 after the leg of a piano Margaret Truman was playing crashed through the dining room ceiling. The Trumans lived at Blair House, the presidential guest house, for four years, during which time the East Wing, an air-raid shelter, an interior movie theater, and a balcony on the south portico were added.

White House Ghosts

A walk-through of the Executive Mansion will take on some new excitement for the kids when you tell them that many people believe it is haunted by a few ghosts. (A good way to get some "living" history in there, too!) By far the most famous ghost is that of President Lincoln, but ghost hunters and former White House personnel claim he's not the only one. According to various tales and legends, the presidential mansion is haunted by the ghosts of Abigail Adams, Dolley Madison, Lincoln's son Willie (who died at age twelve in the White House), Presidents Jackson and Harrison, and a British soldier who was killed during the burning of the White House in 1814.

The ghost of Abigail Adams is forever attempting to hang her laundry in the grand East Room, and her ghost has been seen approaching the room with her arms out as if carrying a laundry basket. Some have said that they can smell a whiff of soap and damp cotton when her ghost is near.

💼 TRAVEL TIP

When you tour the White House, remember that this is not just any museum. Videotaping and photography are not allowed. The bathrooms inside the White House are not open to the public, so it's a good idea to make a pit stop before you start the tour. The nearest restrooms and public telephones are in the White House Visitor Center.

Dolley Madison cared a great deal about the White House and planted her own garden where the Rose Garden is today. It is reported that when Edith Wilson attempted to tear up this plot of land, the ghost of Dolley Madison terrified the gardeners. Instead, the roses were planted to appease her, and she has not reappeared since then.

The ghost of Lincoln's son is said to appear in the room where he died, and his mother reported that she felt him with her in the White House. A great believer in the spirit world, she also said she could hear Thomas Jefferson playing the violin. The presence of Abraham Lincoln has been recorded throughout the White House ever since his assassination. He is said to walk through the halls and knock on the door of the Lincoln Bedroom when guests are staying there.

Even before Lincoln's ghost was said to roam the halls, White House servants had said that they could hear laughter coming from the bed where Andrew Jackson slept in the Rose Room, and Mrs. Lincoln reported that she often heard his ghost stomping and swearing. President Harrison is said to haunt the White House attic.

The White House Tour

When you tour the White House, you won't be able to have access to all of it. Generally, only seven rooms and various hallways and corridors of the White House are open to the public. The second and third floors of the White House are the private domains of the first family. The Oval Office and the Lincoln Bedroom are not open to the public.

The Library

First stop on the tour is the Library, where you'll see 2,700 books on display and a chandelier that once belonged to James Fenimore Cooper (author of *The Last of the Mohicans*). The Library is where the president holds private interviews.

The China Room

The next room on the tour is where examples of the table settings from each presidential administration are on display. It is interesting to note that Nancy Reagan wasn't the only first lady to cause an uproar over her china pattern choice. Mary Todd Lincoln's pattern uses a bright purple, which many thought was too royal, and caused quite a stir at the time.

The East Room

The gold-and-white East Room on the second floor has been the site of many of the mansion's biggest events, including the wedding receptions of Nellie Grant, Alice Roosevelt, and Lynda Bird Johnson. It has also been the viewing room for seven presidents' funerals, the site of Susan Ford's senior prom, and the site of President Nixon's resignation speech. During the Civil War, Union troops were housed in this room.

The famous life-size painting of George Washington by Gilbert Stuart that was saved by Dolley Madison as the White House burned in 1814 is also on display here. The four walls of the East Room are the oldest parts of the White House left after the fire.

≡FAST FACT

The East Room is the largest room in the White House and, according to the secret service tour guide, in the nineteenth century it was the room where Abigail Adams hung the presidential laundry to dry because she didn't want people to see it hanging on the lawn (and this is now the room supposedly haunted by her ghost).

The Green Room

This room once served as Jefferson's dining room; today it serves as a parlor. The room gets its name from the green silk that has adorned its walls since the Monroe administration.

The Green Room is furnished in the federal style of the early 1800s. There's a marvelous painting of Bear Lake, New Mexico, by Georgia O'Keeffe as well as a street scene of Philadelphia that was purchased by an antiques dealer for $10 and turned out to be one of the original White House paintings.

The Blue Room

The most formal room in the White House, this is where presidents often receive guests and where the largest Christmas tree in the mansion is on display. This was also the site of President Cleveland's marriage to Frances Folsom. Cleveland, incidentally, was the only president to get married while in office.

The Red Room

In this room, the first lady traditionally does her entertaining. The Red Room features red walls and red satin chairs, as well as a painting of the Rocky Mountains by Albert Bierstadt. This was also the room in which Abraham Lincoln rescinded Confederate President Davis's citizenship during the Civil War.

≡FAST FACT

The White House Web site is a wealth of information about the building and its inhabitants. You can virtually tour many of the rooms that are not open to the public, view a movie, call up its history, and read the latest news. There is also a separate kid's site, *www.white housekids.gov*. Parents might first want to tour both sites themselves, because some might find them too heavily politicized.

The State Dining Room

The dining room, which seats 140 people, is also the site of the G.P.A. Healy portrait of Lincoln, which was given to the White House by Lincoln's heirs. Carved above the fireplace mantel are the words of President John Adams from his second evening in the White House: "I Pray Heaven to Bestow the Best of Blessings on THIS HOUSE and All that shall hereafter inhabit it."

The Vermeil Room

Also known as the Gold Room, this room was refurbished in 1991. It serves as a display room and has also been the room where first ladies have received visitors. Portraits of seven first ladies are on display here, as well as furniture from the nineteenth century.

The White House Visitor Center

You and the kids will have a more fruitful experience if you visit the White House Visitor Center. It has a number of interesting exhibits on the history of the mansion, its architecture, furnishings, and first families; there is also a thirty-minute video. Other facilities include a small gift shop and bathrooms. (The public is not allowed to use the bathrooms in the White House.) When you go through the visitor entrance, there are displays along a hallway looking out onto the Jacqueline Kennedy Gardens that explain the architectural and interior changes within the mansion over the past 150 years.

≡FAST FACT

In 1961, First Lady Jacqueline Kennedy decided to make the White House the showplace it once was. She sent out a worldwide request for original furnishings from the house, and restored many of the rooms to their earlier splendor. To preserve the historical decor, Congress passed an act declaring all furnishings and decorations used by the first family during their stay to be the property of the White House.

Location and Hours

The White House is not far from the McPherson Square (Blue or Orange lines), Metro Center (Blue, Orange, or Red lines) or Federal Triangle (Blue or Orange lines) Metro stations; the visitor center is accessible from the Federal Triangle station. The White House Visitor Center is located at the southeast corner of 15th and E Streets. The White House is a little further up, at 1600 Pennsylvania Avenue NW.

The visitor center is open from 7:30 A.M. until 4 P.M., seven days a week. White House self-guided tours of up to ten people at a time are available between 7:30 and 11:30 A.M. Tuesday through Saturday (excluding federal holidays). Don't forget that you'll need to obtain tickets in advance through your congressional representative's office. They are accepted up to six months in advance, and are scheduled on a first come, first served basis approximately one month in advance of the requested date. The White House is occasionally closed for official functions, so call ahead for scheduling on the twenty-four-hour line at 202-456-7041.

👥 JUST FOR PARENTS

If your tour is early, you might consider having a leisurely breakfast at Old Ebbitt Grill (see Chapter 14), which is almost across the street, or an exquisite breakfast in the Willard Room of the Willard InterContinental Hotel. Nothing else nearby is open that early.

Before the tour, you'll need to go through a security check that includes walking through a metal detector and having your belongings X-rayed. The list of prohibited items is long and can be found on the White House Web site. Note that there are no storage facilities on or around the complex. Visitors who arrive with prohibited items will not be permitted to enter the White House.

For the Physically Challenged

Visitors with special needs can be easily accommodated. Those scheduled for tours who require the loan of a wheelchair should notify the officer at the visitors entrance upon arrival. Note that they don't take reservations. Tours for visually- or hearing-impaired groups of ten or more may be requested through one's member of Congress. The Visitor Center TDD (telephone device for the deaf) is 202-456-2121. Guide animals are permitted in the White House.

The United States Capitol

✉ E and 1st Streets SW
🚇 Metro: Capitol South (Orange or Blue Lines)
    or Union Station (Red Line)
☎ 202-225-6827
🖥 *www.aoc.gov*

The Capitol is home to the U.S. House of Representatives and the U.S. Senate, which together make up the legislative branch of the federal government. House and Senate galleries are open to all visitors, but you must obtain passes when Congress is in session (call 202-224-3121). *The Washington Post* also lists the schedule in its "Today in Congress" section.

Because of increased security and construction of the Capitol Visitor Center, contact the U.S. Capitol Guide Service if you have any questions before your visit. Recorded information is available at 202-225-6827. Visitors are not permitted to bring certain items into the Capitol. Visit the Web site at *www.aoc.gov* for the list.

If you want to observe the workings of Congress from the galleries, contact your representative or senator for tickets several months ahead of time. You can also try to get them (they are very limited) by presenting acceptable ID at your senator's office on the Constitution Avenue side of the building or your representative's office on the Independence Avenue side of the building. When either the House or the Senate is in session, a flag flies over the respective side of the building.

The Capitol's east front is where most of the recent presidents have taken their oath of office. Aside from being the seat of our government, where the daily business of legislation is enacted, the Capitol building is itself a work of art, and there's much to see there. The building was designed by William Thornton and amended by Benjamin Latrobe; the cornerstone was laid by Washington in 1793. The Capitol was ready for Congress to open its first session in 1800. The Capitol was burned down by the British in 1814, and the famous dome wasn't actually added until the Lincoln administration.

As this is being written, the finishing touches are being put on the new Capitol Visitor Center that will house a variety of amenities, including an exhibition gallery, orientation theaters, a 600-seat cafeteria, gift shops, and restrooms. Scheduled completion is July 2007. It will be a welcome, secure oasis for families.

The Rotunda

The Capitol's round structure, the rotunda, is covered by a dome that's 180 feet high and 96 feet wide, and it is jam-packed with more than 800 works of art and artifacts.

≡ FAST FACT

The rotunda also has a number of statues, including the controversial group sculpture of the three leaders of the women's suffrage movement—Elizabeth Cady Stanton, Susan B. Anthony, and Lucretia Mott—that had been kept in the crypt until women's groups campaigned successfully to have it moved to a more prominent position in the building.

The rotunda's bronze doors are a bas relief that depict the life of Christopher Columbus. On the walls are eight giant oil paintings by John Trumbull depicting events in American history, such as the signing of the Declaration of Independence and the presentation of Pocahontas to British royalty. On the dome's ceiling is a fresco by Constantino Brumidi, who has been called the "Michelangelo of the Capitol" for this painting, *Apotheosis of Washington*. It's an allegorical portrait of the first president surrounded by Roman deities who are watching the development of the nation.

The Rest of the Capitol

Beyond the rotunda is the National Statuary Hall, which was the original chamber for the House of Representatives. Each state was invited to send two statues of important regional leaders, and the hall is now so full that statues spill out into adjoining halls and corridors and even show up haphazardly throughout the building.

Some of the more prominent figures whose statues are on display include Ethan Allen, Daniel Webster, and Henry Clay; some of the more unusual works of art and personages that can be found elsewhere are Utah's sculpture of Philo Farnsworth, the father of television, and Colorado's painted bronze statue of Jack Swigert Jr., an *Apollo 13* astronaut.

The vaulted ceilings of the first floor of the Senate wing have paintings and panels celebrating American democracy, progress, and technology painted by Brumidi. Known as the Brumidi Corridors, they are based on the loggia of the Vatican. This tradition continues throughout the halls and galleries in the House wing by other artists (after Brumidi's death) and depicts such events in American history as the Boston Tea Party, the Women's Suffrage Movement, the signing of the Declaration of Independence, and the burning of the Capitol in 1814. These scenes continue to the present and include a panel on the space shuttle *Challenger* disaster.

The south and north wings of the Capitol are the House and Senate chambers. The House of Representatives chamber is the largest legislative body in the world and the site of the president's annual state of the union address.

Location and Hours

The Capitol is located at the east end of the Mall, where E and First Street intersect. The closest Metro stations are Capitol South (Orange or Blue Lines) or Union Station (Red Line).

You can visit the Capitol from 9 A.M. until 4:30 P.M. Monday through Saturday. It is open on all federal holidays except Thanksgiving Day and Christmas Day. Guided tours of up to forty people are given throughout the day. To take the tour, you'll need timed tickets, which you can pick up at the Capitol Guide Service kiosk located along the curving sidewalk southwest of the Capitol (near the intersection of First Street S.W., and Independence Avenue). Tickets are available after 9 A.M. on a first-come, first-served basis. The Congressional Special Services Office provides information about tours for the disabled by telephone at 202-224-4048 (voice) or 202-224-4049 (TDD).

☂ RAINY DAY FUN

If you've got time, you can visit the two museums on site: the original U.S. Supreme Court chambers, which have been restored to their original appearance with red velvet upholstery (the Supreme Court moved out of the Capitol to its own building in 1935), and the old Senate chamber, also restored to its original nineteenth-century appearance.

The Supreme Court

✉ 1st St. NE
🚇 Metro: Capitol South (Orange or Blue Line)
   or Union Station (Red Line)
☎ 202-479-3000
✎ www.supremecourtus.gov

Keeping watch over the Congress, literally and figuratively, the building that now houses the U.S. Supreme Court building was built across from the Capitol in 1935. Previously, the Court met in the Merchants Exchange building in New York City and moved a number of times; it was (ironically) housed in the Capitol prior to 1935. The building is classic Corinthian, with sixteen marble columns topped by a sculpted pediment. (The building was once nicknamed the Marble Palace.) Check out the statues *Contemplation of Justice* and *Authority of Law* flanking the entrance. The five-story marble and bronze spiral staircases are considered masterpieces.

The U.S. Supreme Court is the highest court of the judicial branch of our government. It is besieged by close to 7,000 requests a year for retrial of controversial cases that bear on issues affecting the nation, but it hears only about 100 cases annually.

Educational programs, a theater, and changing exhibits are located on the ground floor. The Court's Great Hall features a twenty-minute film on how the Supreme Court works, as well as its history and some of its more famous cases. There's a gift shop on the premises, as well as two restaurants.

≡FAST FACT

The first bill introduced in the U.S. Senate was the Judiciary Act of 1789, which established the U.S. Supreme Court, originally composed of five associate justices and a chief justice. Today there are eight associate justices and one chief justice. Members of the U.S. Supreme Court are appointed by the president and subject to approval by the Senate.

Location and Hours

The U.S. Supreme Court building is located behind the Capitol, on First Street SE, between East Capitol Street and Maryland Avenue. Take the Orange or Blue Line Metro to Capitol South or the Red Line to Union Station. Visitor hours are Monday through Friday from 9 A.M. to 4:30 P.M. (The Court is closed on weekends and all federal holidays.) Lectures in the courtroom are given every half hour. The Court is in session Monday through Wednesday from 10 A.M. until noon, beginning the first Monday in October and ending in late April; brief sessions are held in May and June. *The Washington Post* regularly publishes the Supreme Court's calendar. The business of the Court or unforeseen factors such as inclement weather may affect public access to the building, requiring changes in the Courtroom lecture schedule and/or the building's hours of operation. To obtain case information or updated information on visiting the Court, including any schedule changes, call 202-479-3211. There are only 150 public seats, so arrive early if you want to get in. No cameras or videotaping are allowed. Check the excellent Web site before you go for a wealth of information on the Court, as well as items prohibited in the building.

The Library of Congress

✉ lst St. SE
🚊 Metro: Capitol South (Orange or Blue Line)
✆ 202-707-8000
📧 *www.loc.gov*
📧 *www.americaslibrary.gov*

This is the world's largest library, with more than 29 million books and other printed materials, 2.7 million recordings, 12 million photographs, 4.8 million maps, and 58 million manuscripts, as well as letters, prints, movies, personal papers from scholars and celebrities (from Jefferson to Groucho Marx), and musical instruments. The total collection has more than 131 million items. Of course, only a fraction of this material is on display at any given time, so the exhibits change constantly.

History of the Library

The Library of Congress was created by John Adams in 1800, "for the purchase of such books as may be necessary for the use of Congress." It was originally housed in a boarding house and later moved to the Capitol, where the entire collection was torched by the British in 1814. Thomas Jefferson sold his personal collection of close to 7,000 books to the government to restart the library.

The first permanent home of the library—the Thomas Jefferson Building—was erected in 1897 and was expected to house the growing collection for decades, but it filled up in a mere thirteen years. Two additions have been built: the John Adams Building in 1939 and the James Madison Memorial Building in 1980. The Jefferson building underwent a major twelve-year renovation and reopened to the public in 1997.

There is a twelve-minute orientation film shown in the visitors' center in the Jefferson building, which gives you an overview and history of the library.

Halls and Galleries

The exterior of the Jefferson building was designed to look like the Paris Opera House and has a very European fountain with a bronze statue of Neptune outside its front doors. The Great Hall of the Jefferson building features a domed interior and a stained-glass ceiling plus paintings, sculptures, and mosaics by fifty artists.

JUST FOR PARENTS

Anyone over eighteen may use the Library of Congress, but its holdings do not leave the premises. You have to obtain a user card, which is available by showing a valid driver's license or passport or by filling out an information sheet. The library's Web site has an interesting Kids and Families section.

The American Treasures exhibition showcases some 300 items that represent the breadth and depth of the Library's American historical items. The Bob Hope Gallery of American Entertainment, on the ground floor, includes items from the newly acquired Bob Hope Collection, materials from the rich and varied collections of the Library, and objects borrowed from the Bob Hope Archives. The comedian was a friend of every president of the United States since Franklin D. Roosevelt. On view are engaging photographs of Bob Hope making the presidents laugh and scores of political jokes from Hope's 89,000-plus-page personal Joke File, displayed in its entirety at the Library. Other items that have been on temporary display in the Library include Jefferson's handwritten draft of the Declaration of Independence, with notations from other signatories; Jelly Roll Morton's early compositions; Maya Lin's original drawing for the Vietnam Veterans Memorial; Alexander Graham Bell's notebooks; and George Gershwin's orchestral score for *Porgy and Bess*. The gift shop is also located in this building.

The John Adams Building has murals illustrating scenes from *The Canterbury Tales* painted on its interior walls, and the Madison building is the home of the library's restaurants and a theater that shows rare films.

The library has a wealth of services for the physically challenged, including those with sight problems.

Location and Hours

The Library of Congress faces the front of the Capitol (between East Capitol Street and Independence Avenue). If you plan to take the Metro, hop the Orange or Blue Line and get off at the Capitol South Metro station. The Visitors' Center is located inside the west front entrance of the Thomas Jefferson Building, Ground Level, and is open 10 A.M. to 5 P.M., Monday to Saturday. Here you'll find information and brochures about the Library of Congress and a twelve-minute (open captioned) film about the Library. The Jefferson building is open Monday through Saturday, 10 A.M. to 5 P.M. The Madison building is open from 8:30 A.M. to 9:30 P.M. on weekdays and until 6:30 P.M. on Saturdays. All buildings are closed on Sunday and on federal holidays. One-hour guided tours are available every hour on the half hour by reservation, but these are not recommended for children under ten. There is a security check when you enter.

🧳 TRAVEL TIP

Hours for the various buildings and facilities of the Library of Congress fluctuate, and even the newest of guidebooks has them wrong at times. Check with the Web site for the latest visitors' information.

Eats

The Madison Cafeteria is open weekdays from 9 A.M. to 10:30 A.M. and 12:30 to 3 P.M., Saturday from 12:30 to 3 P.M. The Madison Coffee

Shop is open weekdays from 9 to 10:30 A.M. and 12:30 to 3 P.M.; the Cappuccino Bar stays open to 5 P.M. The Shop is open Saturday from 8:30 A.M. to 2 P.M. The Montpelier Room (LM 619) is open weekdays from 9 A.M. to 2 P.M. Vending machines in room LM G49 are available weekdays 8:30 A.M. to 9:30 P.M. and Saturday 8:30 A.M. to 5 P.M. All times may change, so check beforehand. The LOC Web site lists other nearby eateries.

The National Archives

✉ 700 Pennsylvania Ave. NW
🚇 Metro: National Archives–Navy Memorial (Yellow or Green Line)
✆ 1-86-NARA-NARA
✆ 202-50l-5000
🖰 www.archives.gov

The National Archives and Records Administration is home to the Rotunda for the Charters of Freedom, which permanently exhibits our nation's most precious documents: the Constitution, Bill of Rights, and Declaration of Independence, all in glass cases in which the air has been replaced by helium.

Surrounding these cases are documents, photos, and artifacts that tell the story of our nation's history from the colonies to the present, from the Emancipation Proclamation to the Japanese surrender in World War II. In the interactive Public Vaults exhibit, you actually feel you are going beyond the walls of the Rotunda into the stacks and vaults of the National Archives to "touch" and explore history's most fascinating original records (including Abraham Lincoln's telegrams to his generals and an audio recording from the Oval Office).

Although it was constructed relatively recently, in 1932, the building matches the Greek revival style of many other federal buildings with its colonnade facade topped by a pediment and a dome. The design was created by John Russell Pope, who also worked on the National Gallery of Art and the Jefferson Memorial.

Location and Hours

The National Archives is located off the Mall. The entrance is on Constitution Avenue, between 7th and 9th Streets. You can reach the archives from the National Archives-Navy Memorial Metro station (Yellow or Green Line). During the spring, the archives are open from 10 A.M. until 7 P.M., and in the summer until 9 P.M. After Labor Day, it closes earlier, at 5:30 P.M., and it is closed on Christmas Day. Public tours of the National Archives are available, but you must call to make a reservation at least a month in advance. There is a security check at the door.

Eats

The building has a small snack bar, and food may be purchased at nearby attractions: the National Gallery of Art, National Museum of Natural History, National Museum of the American Indian, National Air and Space Museum, Old Post Office Pavilion, and the Hirshhorn Museum and Sculpture Garden.

The Mint and the Bureau of Engraving and Printing

✉14th and C St. SW
🚇 Metro: Smithsonian (Orange or Blue Line)
✆ 1-866-874-2330
www.moneyfactory.com

The Bureau of Engraving and Printing, an arm of the U.S. Department of the Treasury (and also known as the U.S. Mint), is a real kid-pleaser and makes for a fun family tour. Timed tickets are required during the busy season and can be obtained at the visitors' center in front of the building or by writing to your representative or senator ahead of time. Once you have a ticket, you may have to wait awhile for your thirty-minute tour, but it is fascinating to see the bills, stamps, and White House invitations being printed. (Coins are minted in Texas and Philadelphia.)

To enter, you must pass through a security checkpoint. While you wait in line for your tour to begin, you will see a brick of $20 bills that totals a million dollars and television displays of interesting facts about our currency. Did you know, for instance, that dollar bills aren't made out of paper? They're actually 75 percent cotton and 25 percent linen. And did you know that the average lifespan for a dollar bill is a year and a half?

The tour begins with a brief film about the history of the Bureau of Engraving and Printing. (In 1862, it consisted of six employees who separated $1 and $2 bills printed by a private company; the staff is currently about 3,000 people.) The presentation also includes an introduction to the printing of money, with a description of how the U.S. currency was recently redesigned to include a watermark portrait that you can see by holding the bill up to the light. These changes were implemented to make counterfeiting more difficult.

≡FAST FACT

Everyone knows that a dollar bill travels extensively in its lifetime, but now there's a Web site that tracks its journey. If you log onto *www.wheresgeorge.com* you will be able to enter the serial number of a bill currently in your possession, and someone will e-mail you back its travel history. One sample dollar bill was tracked at traveling 193 miles in six months.

The "money factory" prints 35 million notes a day, totaling approximately $635 million. The tour leads you through the actual printing process. You witness the giant presses in action behind a Plexiglas wall and smell the paint-like odor of the green and black inks. The production process of U.S. currency involves sixty-five steps, including examining the bill sheets, overprinting, slicing the sheets, and shrink-wrapping the bills.

After the tour, you are let out into the gift shop, which sells such novelties as bags of shredded money and imperfect sheets of currency. It has a number of interactive displays for kids, as well as a photo booth where kids can have their picture imprinted on a $20 bill.

Location and Hours

The Bureau is located on 14th and C Streets, not far from the Smithsonian Metro station (Orange or Blue Line). During the winter, tours are given from 9 A.M. to 2 P.M., Monday through Friday. In the summer, afternoon hours are added from 4 to 7:30 P.M. The Bureau is closed on weekends, federal holidays, and the week between Christmas Day and New Year's Day. The Bureau is open on the Friday after Thanksgiving, but this is one of its busiest tour days of the year, so plan ahead.

TRAVEL TIP

Because of heightened security, all tour policies are subject to change without notice. If the Department of Homeland Security level is elevated to Code Orange, the Bureau of Engraving and Printing will be closed to the public unless otherwise noted.

Tickets are required for all tours during the peak season from March through August. They are free on a same-day, first-come, first-served basis from the ticket booth located on Raoul Wallenberg Place (formerly 15th Street). The ticket booth opens at 8 A.M. Monday through Friday and closes when all tickets have been distributed. Lines form early and tickets go quickly; most days' tickets are gone by 9 A.M. No tickets are required during nonpeak season, from September through February. Just line up at the Visitors' Entrance on 14th Street.

Eats

Street vendors along 14th Street and Independence Avenue offer quick refreshment. The U.S. Department of Agriculture Cafeteria is open to the public from 6:30 A.M. to 2 P.M. Present a valid picture ID at the Wing 3 entrance, 12th and C Streets SW, in the South Building. The Museum Cafe, located on Raoul Wallenberg Place adjacent to the Holocaust Museum, is open from 9:30 A.M. to 3 P.M. Delicatessens can be found in the buildings at 12th Street and Maryland Avenue SW.

The U.S. Department of Treasury

✉ 15th St. and Pennsylvania Ave. NW
🚇 Metro: Metro Center (Blue, Orange, or Red lines) or Federal Triangle (Blue or Orange lines)
✆ 202-662-0896
✍ www.ustreas.gov

Once money is printed and bundled, it is sent off to the U.S. Treasury, and from there it is dispersed to banks. The white granite building of the U.S. Treasury Department should be familiar to all Americans, because it appears on the back of the $10 bill. It is the third-oldest federal building in the city, after the White House and the Capitol. The building itself is a prime example of the Greek revival architectural style that swept the nation in 1800s, with a facade full of Ionic columns and topped by a pediment. After decades of neglect and misplaced "modernization," the building underwent restoration beginning in 1985 and has since been returned to its former glory.

≡FAST FACT

The best reason for visiting the Treasury Department and going through the annoying tour-request bureaucracy is the Cash Room. A U.S. Treasury–operated bank until the mid-1970s, this small marble room (32 by 72 feet) with chandeliers was the site of President Grant's inaugural reception. Six thousand invitations were sold, and the crowd was so tight that people passed out.

At the U.S. Department of the Treasury, you can take a tour that will take you through the restored interior of both the east and west wings, featuring vaulted ceilings, chandeliers, and period furniture that includes some chairs with dollar signs on their backs.

Location and Hours

You can reach the Treasury from Metro Center (Blue, Orange, or Red lines) or Federal Triangle (Blue or Orange lines) Metro stations. Guided tours of the Main Treasury Building are conducted on Saturday mornings at 9:00, 9:45, 10:30, and 11:15 A.M. The approximate length is sixty minutes. Advance reservations are required and must be made through your senator or representative. Tours are available only for citizens and legal residents of the United States. The name, date of birth, and social security number for each visitor must be provided when making a reservation. In addition, everyone must show a photo ID to gain admittance to the building on the date of their scheduled tour.

The Federal Bureau of Investigation (FBI)

✉ J. Edgar Hoover Building, 935 Pennsylvania Ave. NW

🚇 Metro: Metro Center (Blue, Orange, or Red lines)
   or Federal Triangle (Blue or Orange lines)

📞 202-324-3447

💻 www.fbi.gov

The Bureau of Investigation was established in 1908 during the Teddy Roosevelt administration by U.S. Attorney General Charles Bonaparte as a force of special agents to investigate a corrupt public land scheme in Idaho. There were nine newly hired detectives, thirteen civil rights investigators, and twelve accountants. The first public enemies list was released in April 1930 and was composed mainly of Chicago gangsters. (Surprisingly, the notorious Al Capone was only number four.)

In 1933, the Bureau of Investigation merged with the Prohibition Bureau and the Bureau of Identification, establishing the FBI as we know it today. At the head of the FBI was J. Edgar Hoover, who had 266 agents and 66 accountants under his direction. As of March 31, 2006, the FBI had a total of 30,430 employees, 12,515 special agents, and 17,915 support staff, such as intelligence analysts, language specialists, scientists, information technology specialists, and other professionals. In fiscal year 2005, the total budget was approximately $5.9 billion, including $425 million in net program increases to enhance counterterrorism, counterintelligence, cyber crime, information technology, security, forensics, training, and criminal programs. Along with headquarters in Washington D.C., there are 56 field offices in major cities throughout the United States, more than 400 resident agencies in smaller cities and towns across the nation, and over 50 international offices, called Legal Attaches in U.S. embassies worldwide. The Bureau's motto is "Fidelity, Bravery, and Integrity."

On October 7, 1964, the National Capital Planning Commission, as part of a grand scheme to upgrade Pennsylvania Avenue, approved the major design concept for a new FBI headquarters. It consisted of 2,800,876 square feet of space for 7,090 employees. For reasons of economy, the approving agencies insisted on poured concrete as the major outside building material.

Construction started December 6, 1967, using a unique composition containing an aggregate of crushed dolomite limestone. While contrasting with the traditional marble, granite, or limestone government buildings, it echoed a major architectural style of the 1960s. The concrete was poured into reusable steel forms separated by metal ties. The ties remained in the concrete when the molds were removed. This technique produced an architectural feature of evenly spaced holes throughout the exterior. Thirty-eight years after the first proposal for a separate FBI building and fifteen years after Congress approved construction on the Pennsylvania Avenue site, the last employees moved into the building in June 1977. When completed, the building cost $126,108,000—$106,000,000 more than when it was first proposed in 1939. But, at last, FBI employees housed in nine separate locations finally had a home.

The Bureau offers open captioned tours (monitors are placed on the tour gallery) in seven languages: English, Chinese, French, German, Hebrew, Japanese, and Spanish. Tour guides with sign language skills are also available if requested in advance. An audiotape is available for visitors who are sight impaired. Visitors in wheelchairs and their party (limit 10), may report to the 14th Street entrance even during the peak season. Wheelchairs are available upon request.

Location and Hours

The FBI building is located on E Street between 9th and 10th Streets in the J. Edgar Hoover Building. Take the Metro to the Metro Center (Blue, Orange, or Red lines) or Federal Triangle (Blue or Orange lines) Metro station. The FBI building has been undergoing renovations and is closed to tours, but it should reopen soon, so check with the tour office at 202-324-3447. Once it does reopen, you should be able to obtain tickets from your representative's or senator's office.

CHAPTER 9

Other Museums

WASHINGTON D.C. HAS THE largest number of museums per capita of any city in the world. In addition to the national monuments and the Smithsonian museums and galleries, the capital also has a number of fabulous private museums. The fact that they are private establishments means that you do have to pay for entrance, but it's well worth it. The one exception to this rule is the National Gallery of Art, which is free even though it's not part of the Smithsonian Institution. Also, the International Spy Museum, which opened in 2003, has caused quite a stir in the city as one of the more offbeat educational experiences in the city.

The National Gallery of Art and Sculpture Garden

> ✉ 6th Street & Constitution Ave. NW
> 🚇 Metro: Archives (Yellow or Green Line), Judiciary Square (Red Line), or Smithsonian (Blue or Orange Line)
> ✆ 202-737-4215
> 🖱 www.nga.gov

This monumental museum of art takes up two city blocks and continues across the street with a new outdoor sculpture garden. Half a day is hardly long enough to see everything. The Web site will guide you to the must-sees if you have only limited time (even less than an hour).

The original neoclassical West Building was designed by John Russell Pope (who also designed the Jefferson Memorial and the nearby National Archives building). The newer East Building is connected via an underground passageway that includes a gift shop and restaurant. Its H-shaped façade and signature skylights were designed by Chinese-American architect I. M. Pei, who also designed the controversial glass pyramid addition at the Louvre museum in Paris.

The West Building

The gallery was created by Congress after financier Andrew Mellon donated his world-renowned art collection to the nation; the collection included two of the Raphaels on display. Today, the National Gallery has one of the finest collections of Renaissance art outside Italy. It may house the only bona fide painting by Leonardo da Vinci in the United States—*Ginevra de Benci*, a noblewoman's portrait, is a double-sided wooden panel, and believed to be a Da Vinci. The museum also displays *Madonna and Child with a Pomegranate*, a painting that some believe was also completed by Da Vinci while apprenticing in Verrocchio's studio. Other highlights of the Renaissance collection, which takes up fifteen rooms of the West Building, include five Botticellis, Raphael's *St. George and the Dragon*, a number of Fra Angelicos and Filippo Lippis, and a room of Italian frescoes that are the only representatives of their kind in the United States.

🧳 TRAVEL TIP

Because of so many recent destructive acts aimed at artworks, to say nothing of plain thoughtlessness, none of the city's art museums will allow backpacks or large, unwieldy bags inside. You must check them in the coat-check areas.

The Flemish and Dutch collections are equally stupendous, with some of the finest Rembrandts, Vermeers, Halses, Rubenses, and Van

Eycks in America. The eighteenth- and nineteenth-century galleries displaying French works include some marvelous rococo Watteaus and Bouchers, as well as David's *Napoleon*, Georges de La Tour's *Repentant Magdalen*, fourteen paintings by El Greco, and Jean Baptiste Siméon Chardin's *(Boy with) Soap Bubbles*, a classic work.

In the galleries that display nineteenth-century English paintings, there are marvelous landscape paintings by Turner and Constable, as well as portraits by Thomas Gainsborough.

≡ FAST FACT

One of the most popular Colonial American paintings on display in the American collection—John Singleton Copley's Watson and the Shark—tells the story of fourteen-year-old Watson's fall into Havana Harbor, where a shark ate his right foot. Watson survived to become a successful British merchant and politician. This is sure to be a shocker (and pleaser) for bored boys who are tired of all the portraits and landscapes.

You can also view American classics, including a terrific selection of early American paintings by unknown artists, such as *Strawberry Girl*; Augustus Saint-Gaudens's life-size sculpture of the Shaw Memorial; a tribute to the Buffalo Soldiers of the Civil War; and Thomas Coles's four paintings of the stages of man's life. The nineteenth-century American collection also includes a number of Homers, Sargents, Eakinses, Bellowses, and Hassams.

The indoor sculpture collection downstairs spans the fifteenth to nineteenth centuries and includes a fabulous Rodin collection, including studies for *The Kiss* and *The Thinker*, as well as some ballerinas by Degas. This floor also features furniture, tapestries, and ceramics.

Break for lunch after you've seen the West Building, and eat in the full-service Terrace Cafe, which offers a good selection of sandwiches, pastas, and hot meals. You can even enjoy a glass of wine and use your credit card to pay. Then head through the ground-floor gift shop, which features mainly prints, scarves, and posters, and look at the twentieth-century art housed in the East Building.

The East Building

The East Building features an impressive number of large-canvas moderns from the abstract expressionist movement, including Robert Motherwell's gigantic black-and-white painting *Reconciliation Elegy*, Pollock's *Number 1*, and Mark Rothko's *Orange and Tan*. Alexander Calder's orange-and-black finned mobile hangs above you. Barnett Newman's *Stations of the Cross*, as well as works by pop artists Roy Lichtenstein, Claes Oldenburg, and Andy Warhol are also on display. Early twentieth-century works include thirteen Picassos and paintings by Braque, Kandinsky, Mondrian, Rene Magritte, and Edward Hopper.

The Sculpture Garden

The outdoor sculpture garden on 8th Street features about thirty works from the late twentieth century and is a wonderful marriage of large-scale art and public space. A large circular fountain shoots jets of water in the center of the garden—during the winter it's an ice-skating rink—and there is an outdoor cafe. People flock to the giant typewriter eraser by Claes Oldenburg and Lichtenstein's *House I*, a two-dimensional primary-color sculpture that plays with the spatial illusion of the house, as well as the metaphorical. Other artists represented include David Smith, Alexander Calder, Sol Lewitt, and Lucas Samaras.

Location and Hours

The museum is located on Constitution Avenue, between 3rd and 7th Streets on the north side of the Mall. Take the Metro to Archives (Yellow or Green Line), Judiciary Square (Red Line), or Smithsonian (Blue or Orange Line) Metro station.

You can visit Monday through Saturday from 10 A.M. to 5 P.M. and on Sunday between 11 A.M. and 6 P.M. Closed on December 25 and January 1. Inquire about free tours, special exhibits, concerts, and films.

Wheelchairs and strollers are available on a first-come, first-served basis at all entrances. The exhibition spaces and public facilities are accessible by elevator. You can get a free copy of the *Brief Guide and Plan*, which lists all accommodations, including accessible restrooms, at any Art Information Desk in the West or East Buildings. Sign-language interpreters for the hearing-impaired and guides for visitors who are blind or visually impaired may be made available on request from Visitor Services. Print materials and audio devices can be provided to those who are hearing impaired.

Visitors must present carried items for inspection. Luggage and oversize bags must be presented at the Fourth Street entrance of the East or West Building to be X-rayed and checked. Checkrooms, located at each entrance, are free to use. Backpacks are not allowed inside.

≡FAST FACT

Augustus Saint-Gaudens created the *Shaw Memorial*, a bronze relief in tribute to Robert Gould Shaw and the Buffalo Soldiers of the Massachusetts Fifty-Fourth Regiment. The original is on display at the top of Boston Common, but a full-scale plaster cast can be seen at the National Gallery of Art. The memorial is considered one of the most powerful pieces of art dealing with the American Civil War.

Eats

There are five places to eat at the National Gallery. In the East Building, the Terrace Café offers a nice theme buffet lunch, or you can watch a waterfall as you munch on the goodies at the Cascade Café. For java and sweets, there's The Espresso & Gelato Café. The Garden Café in the West building also offers a theme menu. For a view of the Sculpture Garden, there's the Pavilion Café. All are child-friendly.

The Corcoran Gallery of Art

✉ 500 17th St. NW

🚇 Metro: Farragut West (Orange or Blue Line, 17th St. exit)
   or Farragut North (Red Line, K St. exit)

📞 202-639-1700

✍ www.corcoran.org

A renowned private collection in a beautiful Beaux Arts museum building, the Corcoran was D.C.'s first art museum and is still the city's only college of art and design. Originally housed in what is now the Renwick Gallery, the collection outgrew its space and moved to its current location in 1897. It is currently undergoing another expansion, having once again outgrown its space with thousands of new objects added in recent years, with a new wing designed by Frank Gehry. Work is scheduled to be completed by 2009.

Collection Highlights

The collection was amassed by William Corcoran (1798–1888), a Washington banker and philanthropist who realized how important it was to begin collecting American art, not just the European masters that everyone else with money was buying. Highlights of his personal collection include Bierstadt's *Last of the Buffalo* and Frederick Church's *Niagara*, as well as Healy's portrait of Abraham Lincoln (a second one is in the White House) and the controversial sculpture of the naked female *Greek Slave* by Hiram Powers.

There are a number of important works by European artists here as well, such as Rubens, Delacroix, Renoir, Monet, Corot, Degas, and Turner. You can also see a working clock that once belonged to Marie Antoinette.

Contemporary Works

Newer works by American artists include canvases by almost all the members of the Hudson River school, as well as paintings by Mary Cassatt, Thomas Eakins, Mark Rothko, and Helen Frankenthaler. In the lower level of the gallery, near the cafe, is a changing exhibit of works by African-American artists—the Corcoran has the largest collection of works by African-American artists in any American art museum and includes 350 works dating back to 1806. The museum has an especially energetic program of exhibitions and activities that has featured such diverse shows as "Picturing the Banjo," "Dutch Royal Silver," "Italian Renaissance Ceramics," "Joan of Arc," the history of photography, and a huge retrospective of American contemporary art.

The Corcoran is accessible to those with disabilities. Wheelchairs are available on a first-come, first-served basis.

Restaurant and Gift Shop

The museum restaurant, Café des Artistes, offers wonderfully creative meals often tied to the show. You can fantasize that you are eating in ancient Greece, surrounded by stately columns with a copy of a frieze from the Parthenon on the walls above. There's also a Sunday gospel brunch accompanied by local gospel musicians. Price, which includes museum admission, is $24.95 for adults, and $11.95 for children. Seating begins at 10:30 A.M.

The museum shop offers an eclectic mix of unusual art-related gifts, apparel, kid stuff, books and one-of-a-kind items. You can also order from the Web site. Because the Corcoran has an art school, it often supports the work of local artists.

Location and Hours

The Corcoran Gallery is located on 17th Street NW, between E Street and New York Avenue. Take the Metro to Farragut North (Red Line, K St. exit), or Farragut West (Orange or Blue Line, 17th St. exit).

The Corcoran is open Wednesday through Sunday between 10 A.M. and 5 P.M. and Thursday to 9 P.M. The gallery is closed on Monday, except holidays, and Tuesday, as well as on Thanksgiving, Christmas, and New Year's Day.

Admission for adults is $8, $6 for seniors and military, and $4 for students with valid ID. Children under twelve get in free. There are fees for special exhibits. Visitors may pay as they wish on Thursdays after 5 P.M. Every Sunday afternoon there is an art-making workshop for kids ages five to ten. Reservations are required, and there are free family days four times a year with performances and art demonstrations.

≡FAST FACT

One of the most influential architects of Washington in the nineteenth century was James Renwick, who brought an American sensibility to the neoclassic style that was prevalent at the time. He designed the Smithsonian Castle, the original Corcoran Gallery (now the Renwick Gallery), the gatehouse at Georgetown's Oak Hill Cemetery, St. Patrick's Cathedral and Grace Church in New York City, and Vassar College.

The Phillips Collection

✉ 1600 21st St. NW
🚇 Metro: Dupont Circle (Red Line)
✆ 202-387-2151
✎ *www.phillipscollection.org*

The Phillips Collection is a private collection of steel-fortune heir Duncan Phillips (1886–1966) and his wife, Marjorie Phillips. The collection spans the twentieth century, rivaling any modern art museum in the world. In fact, it is considered to be the first modern art museum in the country. Today, the collection is still housed where it was originally shown to the public—in the Phillipses' Georgian mansion. In 2006, the Phillips Collection's most recent addition opened to the public following a three-year, $27-million building project. The Sant Building was built mostly underground to preserve the mansion's intimate scale and residential quality.

Collection Highlights

Highlights of this incredible personal collection include Renoir's *Luncheon of the Boating Party* and the Rothko room, which features four works in a small room. Marjorie was an artist herself, and her American impressionist work is also on display here. Sometimes when a museum benefactor is also an artist, the work is included to appease the family, but Marjorie Phillips's *Night Baseball* is an American classic. Using post-Impressionistic techniques for its very middle-American subject, it deserves the treatment it receives as one of the icons of this museum.

The collection has grown immensely from the time it was started by the Phillips family. Today, it includes 2,500 works and is known throughout the world for its breadth of European impressionist and postimpressionist works, which the Phillipses felt started with El Greco, because he was "the first impassioned expressionist," and Chardin because he was "the first modern painter." There are also works by Van Gogh, Monet, Degas, Gauguin, and Cezanne, as well as Pisarro, Bonnard, Vuillard, and Braques (thirteen of these). American painters in the collection include O'Keeffe, Marin, Dove, Hartley, many of the Ashcan School artists, and four striking works by Jacob Lawrence from his *Migration of the Negro* series.

Gift Shop and Café

The museum gift shop is small, eclectic, and clever, featuring many reproductions from the collection as well as unusual modern art items such as a Man Ray teapot. There's a good selection of children's items as well. The newly renovated cafe, operated by the locally famous Firehook Bakery (recently named one of the five best bakers in the world) is located on the lower level.

Location and Hours

The Phillips is located on 21st Street NW at Q Street. If you take the Metro Red Line to Dupont Circle (and the Q Street exit), it's a short walk to the museum.

Permanent collection admission is free on weekdays; on weekends and for special exhibits, the admission price varies, but is usually $12 for adults and $10 for seniors and students. This includes admission to the permanent collection. Children under eighteen can enter free.

The museum is closed Monday. It is open Tuesday through Saturday from 10 A.M. to 5 P.M. (on Thursday, open until 8:30 P.M.), and on Sunday from noon to 7 P.M. but only until 5 P.M. June through September. The Phillips is closed for some national holidays, such as Fourth of July, Thanksgiving Day, December 25, and New Year's Day, so call ahead. For advance tickets only, outside D.C. call 800-551-SEAT.

JUST FOR PARENTS

The famous Phillips Sunday Concerts are held October through May and are included in the price of admission. Seating is nonticketed and unreserved, so get there early. Concerts start promptly at 5 P.M.

Parents must stay with their children at all times. Strollers and front-facing baby carriers are allowed, but backpacks and back baby-carriers are not. The entire museum is wheelchair accessible, and a limited number of wheelchairs are available at the coat check.

The Kreeger Museum

✉ 2401 Foxhall Rd., NW
🚇 Metro: Tenleytown (Red Line)
✆ 202-337-3050
🖰 *www.kreegermuseum.org*

The Kreeger Museum is one of those incredible places that you can't believe everyone in the world doesn't know about—it is one of the best-kept secrets in Washington. Off the beaten track in the city's exclusive suburbs, the Kreeger houses a breathtaking collection of nineteenth- and twentieth-century modern art.

The Kreeger is located in a private mansion built by noted architect Philip Johnson in the late 1960s when he was at the beginning of his postmodern style. The architecture and the art complement each other so well that it's hard to decide which is the more impressive.

Museum Layout

The Kreeger Museum, a private home until 1994, was a design challenge. The architects were told to design a building that would serve as a residence, a museum, and a recital hall. It was to be a modern building yet reflect historic influences. The result was a building of stunning innovation built according to a module system. Every room and public space (including the stupendous pool) is constructed on some variation of a box measuring twenty-two feet on all sides. Areas sometimes consist of two modules, sometimes just half of one, and they are often topped by a dome reminiscent of Byzantine architecture. There are hints of Egyptian and Roman influences as well. The structure is composed of beige limestone with marble, glass, aluminum, steel, teak, and brick. The museum's acoustics (both indoors and outside in the sculpture garden) are wonderful.

Although there are more than 180 works in this collection, the most memorable are in the dining room, where nine paintings by Monet catch the sunlight through glass door panels that overlook the sculpture terrace.

Collection Highlights

David Kreeger, founder of Geico insurance, and his wife, Carmen, were responsible for amassing the collection, and it is said that they agreed on every piece they purchased, although Carmen was more partial to nineteenth-century works and David liked those of the twentieth century. The collection begins with French masters of the nineteenth century, such as Corot, Courbet, and Renoir and continues through every modern art movement from the Cubists to the Symbolists to Pop. The Kreegers also collected African art, from masks to sculpture, and the presence of it here certainly helps to reveal the connections among the influences this art had on the art of the twentieth century.

Artists in the collection read like a Who's Who in modern art, from thirteen Picassos that span his entire career to Braque, Cezanne, Man Ray, Kandinsky, Degas, Bonnard, Van Gogh, Léger, Mondrian, Munch, Stella, Rodin, and Chagall, to name only a few. It is truly amazing that all these wonderful works once hung on the walls of a private home, which itself is a work of art, and that the owners had the generosity and vision to leave it all to the public.

Location and Hours

The Kreeger is located in a residential neighborhood and isn't conveniently accessible by public transportation. But you can get off at the Tenleytown station of the Red Line and walk. The Web site tells you how. If you have a car, parking is available. A taxicab ride from downtown will run about $10.

There are two ways to see the museum. You may choose to take a docent-led tour, available at 10:30 A.M. and 1:30 P.M. Tuesday through Saturday. The tour takes about an hour and a half and is limited to fifteen people. Call to make a reservation at 202-338-3552, or send an e-mail to *visitorservices@kreegermuseum.com*. The museum is also open for visitors to browse the collection on Saturday from 9 A.M. to 4 P.M. Admission is $8 for adults and $5 for seniors and students. Children under twelve are discouraged, except during Saturday Open Hours, when all ages are welcome. If your children are used to touring museums and they are well-behaved, this is a not-to-be-missed experience. Also note that the museum is closed the entire month of August and several days during the year-end holidays.

The museum is child-friendlier than it sounds. There are several programs for children. "Storytime at the Kreeger" is aimed at little ones from three to five, every second Thursday at 10:30 A.M. and every third Tuesday at 1:30 P.M. There are Saturday workshops for kids ages eight to twelve. The museum is mostly wheelchair accessible.

The National Museum of Women in the Arts

✉ 1250 New York Ave. NW

🚃 Metro: Metro Center (Red, Orange, or Blue Line)

📞 1-800-222-7270

📞 202-783-5000

🖰 *www.nmwa.org*

Do you have a daughter or granddaughter who is interested in art? This is a must-see museum that is sure to inspire her. Another gem in D.C.'s museum crown, the National Museum of Women in the Arts features more than 250 works by female artists housed in a restored Masonic temple.

Collection Highlights

In this museum, you will find the work of two of the Peale sisters, who were as talented as their father and his brother (nineteenth-century portrait painters James and Charles Peale) but whose work is virtually unknown. The permanent collection also features early Italian Renaissance and Flemish works by female artists, as well as seventeenth-century female silversmiths. Rosa Bonheur, considered the best painter of animals in the nineteenth century, had to dress as a man to paint in public.

Also on display are works by Elizabeth Lebrun, who was the court painter to Marie Antoinette and one of the few known female portrait painters of her time. Mary Cassatt's Japanese-inspired prints are all on view here, as are two Frida Kahlos, including her *Self-Portrait Dedicated to Leon Trotsky*, which some art historians believe was a visual love letter between the painter and the Communist philosopher.

≡FAST FACT

The niece of one of the first successful artists in America, Sarah Miriam Peale is considered one of the first American women to have a successful career as an artist. Her uncle was Charles Wilson Peale, whose portraits of pals George Washington and Thomas Jefferson are famous. Her sister's work can also be found at the National Museum of Women in the Arts.

Other Highlights

Other works on display include those by Georgia O'Keeffe, Lee Krasner, and Helen Frankenthaler, as well as Alice Neel's powerful *T. B. Harlem*. There's a quirky sculpture on the landing outside the second-floor elevator near the restaurant: Petah Coyne's dripped pink-and-white wax ballerina costume suspended from the ceiling.

The museum's small but relaxing restaurant has a surprisingly good selection of soups, salads, gourmet sandwiches, a daily entrée, and desserts given clever names. The gift shop features a terrific collection of books and posters about female artists, as well as a creative jewelry display, a large children's selection, and sale items. It is open weekdays, 11:30 A.M. to 2:30 P.M.

Location and Hours

The National Museum of Women in the Arts is located on New York Avenue and is accessible from Metro Center (Red, Orange, or Blue Line). Hours are Monday through Saturday, 10 A.M. to 5 P.M., and Sunday noon to 5 P.M. Admission is $8 for adults, $6 for seniors and students, children eighteen and under get in free. Additionally, admission on the first Sunday of the month is free. The museum is closed on Thanksgiving Day, December 25, and New Year's Day. All public areas are wheelchair accessible. Wheelchairs and strollers are available. You can get a large-print edition of the permanent collection's wall labels at the information desk.

The National Museum of Health and Medicine

✉ 6825 16th St. NW, Bldg. 54

🚇 Metro: Silver Spring (Red Line), then taxi, or Tacoma (Red Line), then taxi or bus

📞 202-782-2200

🖥 *www.nmhm.washingtondc.museum*

Does your child want to be a doctor? Okay, does he or she love horror movies? This is the museum for kids interested in biology and slightly gross stuff (which means it's not for kids under five). If this sounds like something your kids (or you) may enjoy, you should go; they'll be talking about what they saw here for the next year!

A Heady Collection

A little off the beaten track, but certainly one of the most interesting and unusual museums in existence, the National Museum of Health and Medicine is one of the nation's oldest medical museums, with 12,000 medical and anatomical items in its collection. Where else could you find the bullet that killed Lincoln or see Civil War–era surgical tools? You can also see centuries-old Inca skulls that show the results of head surgery, and Paul Revere's dental tools.

The National Museum of Health and Medicine, which was founded after the Civil War, was primarily focused on military medicine and pathology until World War II. It has a wonderful collection of old medical instruments and machines, as well as an extensive collection of skeletons and body parts, the first heart-lung machine, and prosthetic limbs.

It will take about two hours to fully explore this unusual museum. Its four permanent exhibits include "To Bind Up the Nation's Wounds," which focuses on medicine during and after the Civil War; "Living in a World with AIDS"; "Human Body, Human Being," which offers a look at a smoker's lung and the opportunity to touch a human brain; and the Billings Microscope Collection, which features the world's most comprehensive collection of microscopes from the earliest in the 1600s to the first electron microscopes of the 1930s.

The museum also has a changing panorama of special exhibits, so call or check the Web site for more information.

Location and Hours

The museum is housed in the Walter Reed Army Medical Center, accessible via the Elder Street NW gate off of Georgia Avenue NW. To get there, you'll have get off at Silver Springs or Tacoma on the Red Line and take a short bus ride. Hours of operation are from 10 A.M. until 5:30 P.M. Guided tours are available at 1 P.M. on the second and fourth Saturday of each month. The museum is closed on Christmas Day. You'll need a photo ID to get on the grounds.

There are plenty of places to eat both on- and off-campus, from fast food to great ethnic restaurants, including the hospital's cheap meals.

The U.S. Navy Museum

✉ 805 Kidder Breese Street, SE, Building 76, Washingon Navy Yard

🚇 Metro: Navy Yard (Green Line)

✆ 202-433-4882

✐ *www.history.navy.mil/branches/nhcorg8.htm*

Lovers of the sea and its battles will be in rapture over this museum. Among the treasure trove of America's Naval history are a rigged foremast fighting top from the frigate *Constitution*, period uniforms, ship models, a Gulf War Tomahawk missile, and an atomic bomb ("Little Boy" version). Outside, a decommissioned Navy destroyer allows visitors a peek into life at sea.

Location and Hours

Located near the Navy Yard Metro station on the Green Line. The museum is open Monday through Friday from 9 A.M. to 5 P.M. and on weekends and holidays, 10 A.M. to 5 P.M. Visitors without Defense Dept. or military identification must call the museum twenty-four hours in advance for weekday visits and by noon Friday for weekend visits: 202-433-6897.

The International Spy Museum

✉ 800 F. St. NW
🚆 Metro: Gallery Place–Chinatown (Red and Green Line)
✆ 1-866-Spy Museum
✆ 202-393-7798 (EYE-SPY-U)
🖰 *www.spymuseum.org*

A really fun and quirky museum—a must-see with something for everyone in the family, which is why there are lines for the International Spy Museum on most weekends. This is a private (for-profit) museum dedicated to the history and craft of spying, the only one in the country.

An Intriguing Collection

Although there are some exhibits from ancient and European history, the bulk of the museum covers twentieth-century espionage involving Americans, and the exhibits are fascinating and fun.

Kids can crawl though an air-duct tunnel, place a bug, spot a bug, listen to conversations with the KGB, and learn how to disguise themselves. James Bond's famous Aston Martin is on display, with all its wonderful gadgets, and there's a media room of pop culture spying, with I Spy games and *Get Smart* gadgets that never fail to entertain.

What's Covered in the Exhibits

It will take about two hours to see the museum from start to finish. You can pick an alias when you enter, which you are quizzed on when you leave to see if you have successfully completed your mission. The next section is the School for Spies, where the tricks of the trade (use of cameras, bugs, disguises) are explained. Then it's on to the Secret History of History, with displays on spying in the Soviet Union, female spies throughout history, and use of birds and balloons in early spying. There's even a section on spying during the American Revolution.

Then you'll meet celebrity spies of World War II, where you are reminded that Josephine Baker and Marlene Dietrich did some espionage work for the Allies, with an overview of spying during World

War II. Then it's on to the Cold War and spying in Berlin during the 1950s and 1960s, and Eastern Europe until the present. When you exit, you are asked a number of questions about your cover to see if you have been successful at your own spying missions.

The International Spy Museum store is a kick, and there's something for everyone, from Spy Museum T-shirts for teens to espionage kits to a pen shaped like a lipstick holder modeled after a KGB pistol. The Spy City Café is large and offers a good selection of "Killer Sandwiches," salads, and soup.

Location and Hours

The museum is located on F Street, accessible from the Gallery Place/Chinatown Metro station (Red and Green Lines) in the heart of the city. It is open at varying times, generally from 9 A.M. April to August, 10 A.M. the rest of the year. Last admittance is 7 P.M. April to October and 5 P.M. November to March. But you should call or check the Web site, which is a riot. Expect lines during the season and school holidays. Admission is $16 for adults; $15 for seniors, active military and the Intel community; and $13 for children. Children under four are free (but the permanent exhibits are not appropriate for kids under twelve). Advance tickets can be purchased at the museum or through TicketMaster at 1-800-551-7328 or at ticketmaster.com.

≡FAST FACT

The Martin Luther King Jr. Memorial Library is the main city library of Washington D.C. and an architectural landmark. It is the only building in this city designed by the founder of the international style of architecture, Ludwig Mies van der Rohe. It is a stark black and glass-paneled rectangle on the street facing the Museum of American Art and the National Portrait Gallery.

The Newseum

✉ Pennsylvania Avenue and 6th Street NW

🚇 Metro: Archives–Navy Memorial (Yellow or Green Line)
   or Judiciary Square (Red Line)

📞 1-800-NEWSEUM (639-7386)

📞 703-284-3544

🖱 www.newseum.org

Scheduled to open in the fall of 2007, the new Newseum promises to be a bright star in the galaxy of iconic Washington D.C. buildings and a favorite of visitors. The original Newseum, located in Arlington, Virginia, was a museum of news and journalism, a role it will continue to play, but with a dramatically larger physical plant. The new building, to cost $435 million was designed from the first to be a landmark by architects Ralph Appelbaum, who designed the original Newseum, and James Stewart Polshek, creator of the Rose Center for Earth and Space at the American Museum of Natural History in New York City. It will have 600,000 square feet, containing the museum, six levels of displays, including more than a dozen galleries, an interactive newsroom, a broadcast studio, a 535-seat theater, a conference center, and office space for the museum staff and the staff of the governing Freedom Foundation. The building's facade will feature a "Window in the World" looking out over Pennsylvania Avenue and the Mall, which will allow passersby to see inside. The forty-five words of the First Amendment will be etched onto a stone panel facing the street.

Location and Hours

The museum is located on Pennsylvania Avenue and 6th Street next door to the Canadian Embassy. It is near the Archives-Navy Memorial Metro stop on the Orange or Green Line, or the Judiciary Square stop on the Red Line. Hours, tour information, and fees were not yet determined at press time.

More Museums

Washington D.C. has no shortage of museums. Most tourists gravitate toward the National Gallery or the Corcoran, but there is a multitude of smaller museums that have something for everyone. Here are your many options.

The Art Museum of the Americas

✉ 201 18th St. NW
🚇 Metro: Farragut West (Blue or Orange Line)
📞 202-458-6016
✍ *www.museum.oas.org*

Free admission is just one reason to check out this museum, which you'll find located a stone's throw from the White House and just behind the House of the Americas in a Spanish Colonial structure that was once the home of the Organization of American States. In keeping with the international theme set down by that history, the museum is dedicated to Latin American and Caribbean art. See contemporary works on all kinds of themes by artists and sculptors from Mexico, Venezuela, the Galapagos Islands, and more. The permanent collection includes works by Botero, Roberto Matta, and others, and there is a sculpture garden.

☂ RAINY DAY FUN

Step out of the rain and into the National Building Museum (*www. nbm.org*), which is dedicated to the architecture and technology of American building. It offers tours, a gift shop, and a café.

Location and Hours

The Art Museum of the Americas is located on 18th Street and is accessible from the Farragut West Metro station on the Blue or

Orange Line. Visitors are welcome on Tuesday through Sunday from 10 A.M. to 5 P.M. Closed on federal holidays and Good Friday.

The Black Fashion Museum

✉ 2007 Vermont Ave. NW
🚇 U Street–Cardozo (Green Line)
✆ 202-667-0744
🖱 www.bfmdc.org

This is a private museum started by Lois K. Alexander-Lane, founder of the Harlem Institute of Fashion, and author of *Blacks in the History of Fashion*. The museum is housed in the former Sojourner Truth Home for Women located in the historic U Street/ Shaw neighborhood, home of Duke Ellington. It is a research center and museum displaying garments and memorabilia from the Black fashion experience, from slave dresses to garments of distinguished African-Americans, past and present. You can visit the museum by appointment only, and a small donation ($2 for adults, $1 for children) is requested.

The College Park Aviation Museum

✉ 1985 Corporal Frank Scott Dr.
   College Park, MD
🚇 Metro: College Park–U. of Maryland (Green Line)
✆ 301-864-6029
🖱 www.collegeparkaviationmuseum.com

This is a great place to take the kids. The world's oldest operating airport was established here in 1909, when two guys by the names of Orville and Wilbur brought their "aeroplane" to a field in Maryland. It led to the creation of the first Army Aviation School, one of many firsts to occur at this site. The airport continues to operate today, and your brood will love to watch the planes take off and land right outside the large window. Visitors step into an open exhibition space 1½ stories high filled with displays and artifacts that dramatically recount the history of flight from the Wright brothers to today. (Because of security, the museum has had to cancel the popular annual Air Fair that featured stunt shows and historical aircraft.)

Location and Hours

College Park Aviation Museum is located in College Park, Maryland, near the University of Maryland, between Route 1 and Kenilworth Avenue (Route 201). You can reach it via the Metro—it's accessible from College Park/University of Maryland Metro station (Green Line). Hours of operation are from 11 A.M. to 3 P.M. Wednesday through Friday, and the museum is open until 5 P.M. on weekends. Hours of operation are daily from 11 A.M. to 5 P.M., except major holidays. Admission is $4 for adults, $3 for seniors, and $2 for children and students. Children under two get in free.

The Daughters of the American Revolution Museum

✉ 1776 D St., NW

🚇 Metro: Farragut West (Blue or Orange Line)
   or Farragut North (Red Line)

📞 202-628-1776

🖳 www.dar.org/museum

This is the museum of the National Society of the Daughters of the American Revolution. It houses a collection of American decorative arts from the seventeenth to the nineteenth century in thirty-one period rooms organized around thirty-one states. There is also an extensive genealogy library. Members donated all objects in the museum's extensive collection.

Location and Hours

The museum is located on D Street and is a ten- to fifteen-minute walk from either of the nearest two Metro stations Farragut West (Blue or Orange Line) or Farragut North (Red Line). Museum and shop are open 9:30 A.M. to 4 P.M. on weekdays and from 9:00 A.M. to 5 P.M. on Saturday. The museum is closed on Sunday, federal holidays, and for special events. Check the Web site for tour and special-collection hours.

The Textile Museum

✉ 2330 S St. NW

🚇 Metro: Dupont Circle (Red Line)

📞 202-667-0441

🖱 *www.textilemuseum.org*

This museum features samples of textiles and fabrics from all over the world. Exhibits also display looms and hand tools. The Textile Activity Center has hands-on activities for adults and kids. On the fourth floor, there is an interactive exhibit on textile-making for children.

≡ FAST FACT

In what may be a sign of the times, the museum at American Red Cross Headquarters has been discontinued and replaced by a virtual museum. Go to *www.redcross.org/museum/history* and you will see a museum complete with exhibitions, children's activities, even a store. It's very well done, with wonderful old graphics and lots of goodies, like downloadable coloring books.

Location and Hours

Located near the Woodrow Wilson House on S Street, the museum can be reached from the Dupont Circle Metro station on the Red Line. Hours of operation are Monday through Saturday, 10 A.M. to 5 P.M., and on Sunday from 1 to 5 P.M. Free; a donation of $5 per visitor is suggested.

CHAPTER 10

Sites of Historical and Special Interest

WASHINGTON D.C. IS ONE of the oldest cities in the nation, and because the city was planned from the first as the nation's capital, it is full of historic places that tell its exciting story. What makes D.C. different is that many of these historic moments were preplanned. Their importance was known from the onset, and preservation was in mind at the time of their occurrence. Washington is also a city that has expanded outward, around the Potomac, so that the older, original parts of the city never had to be torn down and rebuilt for the next generation.

Ford's Theatre

> ✉ 517 10th St. NW
> 🚊 Metro: Metro Center (Red, Orange, or Blue Line)
>   or Gallery Place–Chinatown (Red, Yellow, or Green Line)
> 📞 202-426-6924
> 🖥 *www.nps.gov/foth*

In 1865, less than a week after General Lee had surrendered, actor and Confederate sympathizer John Wilkes Booth shot President Lincoln at close range in the back of the head while the president was watching the play *Our American Cousin*. Ford's Theatre has remained occupied in one way or another to this day, and the second-story balcony booth where Lincoln was shot is now draped in presidential bunting.

From the time of Lincoln's death until the 1930s, Ford's Theatre was used as an office building and storage space, but when the Lincoln Museum was opened there in 1932, funds were raised for its restoration, and it has been managed by the National Park Service since then. The theater was beautifully restored and now hosts a full season of theatrical performances, including an annual production of Dickens's *A Christmas Carol*.

 **RAINY DAY FUN**

Although the Lincoln Museum at Ford's Theatre has a wealth of items from Lincoln's assassination, other artifacts from that night can be seen at different locations throughout the city. The National Museum of Health and Medicine has the bullet that killed Lincoln, the Library of Congress has the contents of Lincoln's pockets from the night he was killed, and a blood-soaked pillow can be seen at the Petersen House (see page 178).

Downstairs you will find the extensive Lincoln Museum, which exhibits artifacts from the night Lincoln was shot, such as the gun Booth used, the clothes Lincoln was wearing when he was shot, bloodstained pillowcases and towels, mourning memorabilia collected from throughout the nation, a cast of Lincoln's face and hand, and photos of the other conspirators in the assassination. Across the street you can visit the Petersen House, where Lincoln was taken and eventually died (see page 178).

There is also an extensive bookstore that includes videos, biographies, and even puzzles featuring Abraham Lincoln.

Location and Hours

Ford's Theatre is located on 10th Street, NW, and is accessible from Metro Center Metro station (Red, Orange, or Blue Line) or Gallery Place-Chinatown (Red, Yellow, or Green Line). You can tour the theater each day of the week from 9 A.M. to 5 P.M., and historical talks are presented in the theater at fifteen minutes past the hour, except during rehearsals and performances. The theater is closed on December 25. Note that this attraction gets extremely busy during the spring and summer seasons—70 percent of the annual visitors come from March through July.

The Martin Luther King Jr. Memorial Library

✉ 901 G St. NW

🚍 Metro: Gallery Place–Chinatown (Yellow, Green, or Red Line, Museum exit) or Metro Center (Red, Orange, or Blue Line, Woodies exit)

✆ 202-727-1126

🖱 www.dclibrary.org

The great architect of the International style, Ludwig Mies van der Rohe, designed the main branch of the Washington D.C. library and an architectural landmark, the Martin Luther King Jr. Memorial Library. The library has served as a memorial to the slain civil rights leader and contains a large mural by Don Miller on the life of Martin Luther King Jr. that rivals any of the WPA murals of the 1930s. The library often hosts events related to the life of Martin Luther King Jr. as well as special events during Black History Month.

Location and Hours

The library is located on G Street, diagonally across from the National Museum of American Art. It is accessible from Metro stations Gallery Place/Chinatown (Yellow, Green, or Red Line) "Museum" exit and Metro Center (Red, Orange, or Blue Line) "Woodies" exit. Visit on Monday through Thursday, 9:30 A.M. to 9 P.M., Friday and Saturday from 9:30 A.M. to 5:30 P.M., and Sunday from 1 P.M. to 5 P.M.

The Charles Sumner School

✉ 1201 17th St. NW
🚇 Metro: Farragut North (Red Line)
☎ 202-442-6060
🖥 www.cr.nps.gov/nr/travel/wash/dc58.htm

Local legend has it that U.S. Senator Charles Sumner petitioned for this school for freed slaves to be taxed so that it could be accredited. It opened in 1872 and became the city's first public school for African-Americans. Today it is also the archive center for the D.C. public-school system, and contains extensive memorabilia on display. It is also a fine museum illustrating the history of Martin Luther King Jr., Frederick Douglass, and Washington D.C. The building was meticulously reconstructed to its "modernized Norman style" in 1984–86.

Location and Hours

The Charles Sumner School, where the museum and archive are housed, is located on 17th Street NW. It is accessible from Farragut North (Red Line) Metro station. You can visit the museum on Monday through Saturday from 10 A.M. to 5 P.M.; the archives are open by appointment only, Monday through Friday, from 8 A.M. to 4 P.M. Closed school holidays.

The African-American Civil War Memorial

✉ 10th and U Sts. NW
☎ 202-667-2667
🚇 Metro: U Street–Cardozo (Green Line)
🖥 www.afroamcivilwar.org

This interesting site contains a monumental sculpture and museum. The memorial is a stone-and-bronze commemorative statue grouping created by sculptor Ed Hamilton in honor of more than 200,000 African-American Union soldiers and their white officers who fought during the Civil War. The relatively new memorial, the first and only in the nation, stands on the former grounds of Union barracks for black soldiers. There is a visitors' center and museum with a large selection of contemporary Civil War artifacts—from uniforms and weaponry to newspaper and magazine articles, photographs, and unique items such as an 1834 bill of sale for a young Alabama girl. You can use the database to look up the history of those honored by the memorial.

Location and Hours

The memorial is located between 10th and U Streets NW, near the U Street-Cardozo Metro station (Green Line). It is across the street from the famed Ben's Chili Bowl. The visitors' center is open Monday through Friday from 10 A.M. to 5 P.M., and Saturday from 2 to 5 P.M.

💼 TRAVEL TIP

L'Enfant Plaza, near Maine and Water Streets, SW, is a commemorative to the African-American mathematician and astronomer Benjamin Banneker, who worked with Pierre L'Enfant to create the original design for the city of Washington D.C. in 1791.

Howard University

✉ 2400 6th St. NW
🚇 Metro: Shaw–Howard U (Green Line)
✆ 202-806-7070
🖱 www.howard.edu/library/art@howard/goa

Howard University was founded in 1866 as a liberal arts college and university to educate the nearly 4 million emancipated African-Americans of the time. Famous alumnae include U.S. Supreme Court Justice Thurgood Marshall and novelist Toni Morrison.

The University was named after white Civil War General Oliver O. Howard, who was Commissioner of the Freedman's Bureau, one of the university's founders, and its third president. His home on Georgia Avenue is a historic landmark.

The Gallery of Art in the College of Fine Arts features the permanent Alain Locke African collection, the Kress Foundation Collection of Renaissance and Baroque paintings, and the Gumbel Collection of European prints. It hosts an ever-changing program of traveling exhibitions. The Moorland-Springarn Research Center houses the country's largest collection of information on the history and culture of African-Americans.

Location and Hours

Howard University is accessible from the Shaw/Howard U Metro station on the Green Line. Gallery hours are weekdays, 9:30 A.M. to 4:30 P.M.; weekends, 12:30 P.M. to 6 P.M. Tours are available, but call ahead for scheduling.

Georgetown University

Georgetown, founded in 1751, is the oldest part of Washington D.C. It was a town before there was even a nation for which to build a capital city. It was named after King George II and featured cobblestone streets, some of which still exist around Georgetown University, where Bill Clinton went to school. (Clinton is the only president to have gone to college in D.C.) Many of the houses are very narrow—a pink one-bedroom on M Street is only 9.5 feet wide—because houses in the colonies were taxed by width.

A Tour of Georgetown

Start your walking tour at the Old Stone House (3051 N Street), believed to be the oldest building in the city. It was built in 1765 by carpenter Christopher Layman, who had his workshop on the first floor. This four-room museum is now furnished in eighteenth-century décor, and it is open free to the public Wednesday through Sunday from 9 A.M. to 5 P.M.

Walk down Jefferson Street to the Chesapeake & Ohio Canal Lock (between M and K Streets), where you can see this important link to the shipping history of Georgetown. The C&O Canal was supposed to connect with the Ohio River so that products could be shipped a total of 185 miles, but the quick development of the railroad made this method of transportation obsolete. Visitors can still travel on barges (mule-drawn ones, at that) and canoes along the canal.

≡ FAST FACT

According to Georgetown University records from 1967, William Jefferson Clinton ran for president of the East Campus Student Council. However, he lost to a classmate. G.U. legend has it that Clinton lost to a much less widely known candidate on the basis of Clinton's desire to unite all five of G.U.'s undergraduate schools. Many felt he had collaborated with the university's administration, which wanted the unification.

Walk down K Street until it intersects with Wisconsin Avenue, and you should find a fence, inside of which is a worn plaque identifying this site as Suter's Tavern, where George Washington and Pierre L'Enfant are said to have planned the city of Washington in 1790. No one knows for sure exactly where the tavern was situated.

Up Wisconsin Avenue and on the corner of Grace Street, you will find the C&O Canal Commemorative Marker. This granite stone is the only record of the canal in existence today, and it commemorates the completion of the canal in 1850. It lies right outside The Shops at Georgetown, a four-story mall that features a food court, Benihana, and Clyde's restaurants, and everything from bead stores to barber shops.

At 1066 Wisconsin Avenue is the Vigilant Firehouse, the oldest volunteer firefighter brigade in Washington, which was founded in 1817. The firehouse was built in 1844 and is now a restaurant that still bears the large "V" for Vigilant near its roof.

Further along M Street is the City Tavern (3206 M Street). Built in 1796, this tavern was the main terminal for the stagecoach line in Georgetown. It once hosted President John Adams for dinner on his inspection of the new city.

≡ FAST FACT

Georgetown has always been home to the city's influential and well-known persons. Houses here have belonged to Alexander Graham Bell, Louisa May Alcott, Sylvester Stallone, Arnold Schwarzenegger, and countless politicians such as John F. Kennedy and Henry Kissinger. A number of movies have been filmed in Georgetown as well. The most famous are *The Exorcist*, *St. Elmo's Fire*, *The Pelican Brief*, and *No Way Out*.

It's hard to believe that a city that has preserved so much of its history allowed Francis Scott Key's house to be torn down to make way for a freeway exit ramp. All that is left is the Francis Scott Key Memorial Site (3518 M St.), which is a public park and a marker for the former home of the author of "The Star-Spangled Banner."

Further along M Street, turn at 35th Street and you will reach Prospect Street. Here you will find the site of *The Exorcist* stairs, which were built on the site of Southworth Cottage (3600 Prospect St.), the former home of a Victorian novelist. There are now two townhouses and the long stairs to Canal Street, where the movie was shot. This is a favorite haunt of the university crowd around Halloween.

Walk up 35th Street to N Street, and on the corner of 33rd Street you will find The Marbury House (3307 N St.), where U.S. Senator and Mrs. John F. Kennedy lived before they moved into the White House in 1961. It had been built for William Marbury in 1812.

Walk up 33rd Street and turn right at Q Street, and you will come to Tudor Place (1644 31st Street, 202-965-0400). William Thornton, who designed the Octagon and had a hand in the design of the U.S. Capitol, designed this home for Martha Washington's granddaughter, who married the mayor of Georgetown. The house is now a museum of Washington memorabilia. Tudor Place is open Tuesday through Sunday for guided tours only with admission.

Walk along Q Street until you get to 29th Street, and then head to R Street, where you will come to the large, fenced Victorian Oak Hill Cemetery. The cemetery was established by William Corcoran, who is also buried here, in 1850.

Just around the corner from the Oak Hill Cemetery is Evermay (1623 28th Street NW), a huge, quirky, red-brick mansion that looks like something out of an Edgar Allan Poe story. You can't enter, but you can walk along its brick wall and peer in at this home of Scottish bachelor Samuel Davidson, who once took out an ad about his property that warned his neighbors to avoid "Evermay as they would a den of evils, or rattlesnakes, and thereby save themselves and me much vexation and trouble." When he died, his will forced his nephew to change his name to Davidson in exchange for the estate.

💼 TRAVEL TIP

The chapel of Oak Hill Cemetery was designed by James Renwick, and even the gatehouse (3001 R Street) is quite beautiful. If you stroll the grounds, you will see Southern-style Victorian mourning sculptures, like winged angels. You can get a map of the gravesites at the gatehouse, and the cemetery is open from 10 A.M. to 4 P.M. on weekdays.

On Q and 28th Streets is the Gun Barrel Fence, which stretches about a half a block and looks wholly unspectacular—until you realize that it was made from the guns and metal that were recovered from the Old Navy Yard after it was burned by the British in 1814.

Walk back down 28th Street to N Street until you get to 30th Street, and you will be standing in front of The French House (3017 N Street), which is where Jacqueline Kennedy lived for a year after her husband's assassination in 1963.

Historic Houses

Washington D.C. is a terrific city for visiting historic homes that have been wonderfully preserved. Because so many of them were the sites of historic events, such as the Petersen House, they have been left almost unchanged since the event that made them a piece of living history.

The Petersen House
✉ 516 10th St. NW
🚇 Metro: Metro Center (Blue or Orange Line) or Gallery Place-
   Chinatown (Red, Yellow, or Green Line).
📞 202-426-6924
💻 www.nps.gov/foth/hwld.htm

Lincoln died in a first-floor back bedroom of the home of William Petersen, a tailor. Doctors knew immediately after he was shot that the head wound was mortal, and they did not dare move him to the Civil War hospital less than two blocks away.

The bed Lincoln was laid in was too short for him, and he lay sideways for part of the night until the end piece was sawed off so his feet could hang out. Blood from his head injury is said to have soaked through seven pillows. It's said that a psychic who visited the room claimed she could see a mist rising from one of the blood-soaked pillows.

You can pay a visit to the Petersen House, which is now maintained by the National Park Service. It's accessible from the Metro Center station (Blue or Orange Line) or Gallery Place-Chinatown (Red, Yellow, or Green Line). And say hello to Miller the guard if he's on duty; you'll never forget him.

≡FAST FACT

According to John Alexander's *Ghosts: Washington Revisited*, one evening Lincoln dreamed that he heard crying throughout the White House. In the dream, he left his bedroom to see what was going on and discovered a crowd of people around a coffin. When he asked who had died, he was told, "The assassinated president." It was reported that when he looked in the open casket, he saw himself.

The Dumbarton Oaks Estate and Gardens

✉ 1703 32nd St. NW
🚋 Metro: No Metro nearby; take bus 30, 32, 34, 36, D2, D4, or M12
✆ 202-339-6401
🖳 *www.doaks.org*

Dumbarton Oaks was the site of an international conference that led to the creation of the United Nations in 1944. Today, the original Georgian mansion is the site of a museum of Byzantine art, and a newer addition designed by Philip Johnson houses a pre-Columbian art collection.

This Georgetown mansion sits on a sixteen-acre plot that features some of the most beautiful gardens in Washington D.C., which are open to the public in warm weather as part of the house tour. The historic music room, where the Dumbarton Oaks conversations took place, has a sixteenth-century stone fireplace as its focal point. It also features French tapestries on the walls and El Greco's Visitation.

Location and Hours

The mansion is located on 32nd Street NW, and is accessible by car, taxi, or bus (routes 30, 32, 34, 36, D2, D4, or M12). At this writing, the mansion and shop were closed for renovation and due to reopen in 2007. Check the Web site or call for updates. The garden remains open daily, except Monday, federal holidays, and Christmas

Eve. Hours are March 15 through October, 2 P.M. to 6 P.M.; November 1 to March 14, 2 P.M. to 5 P.M. Garden admission in the summer is $7 for adults, $5 for seniors and children. Admission is free in the winter.

The Hillwood Museum
✉ 4155 Linnean Ave. NW
🚊 Metro: Van Ness (Red Line)
✆ 1-877-HILLWOOD (445-5966)
✆ 202-686-5807
✑ *www.hillwoodmuseum.org*

This is the restored mansion of Post cereal heiress Marjorie Merriweather Post, who, with her ambassador-to-Russia husband, managed to buy up many of the Russian aristocracy's confiscated trinkets and jewels when the Communists were selling them for cash in the 1930s. She had a splendid collection of Faberge eggs and rare Russian books, as well as icons. There is also a lovely Japanese-style garden on the grounds. You will find a museum shop and a café on the premises.

Location and Hours
Located on Linnean Avenue NW, between Upton and Tilden Streets, the Hillwood Museum is accessible from the Van Ness Metro station (Red Line). Parking on the premises is also available.

🧳 TRAVEL TIP

If you're interested in feminist history, visit the Sewall-Belmont House, 144 Constitution Ave. NE, 202-546-1210. This feminist museum, library, and store—in the home of suffrage leader Alice Paul, founder of the National Woman's Party and drafter of the Equal Rights Amendment—is the oldest house on Capitol Hill, with some parts dating back to 1680.

The museum is open Tuesday through Saturday from 10 A.M. to 5 P.M. Reservations are required for house tours and are obtainable on the same-day at the mansion, by telephone, or via the Web site. Admission is $12 for adults, $10 for seniors, $7 for full-time college students, and $5 for children six to eighteen. Children under six are not permitted in the mansion but may visit the gardens. Closed January and most federal holidays.

The Woodrow Wilson House

✉ 2340 S St. NW
🚇 Metro: Dupont Circle (Red Line)
📞 202-387-4062
🖥 www.woodrowwilsonhouse.org

The Wilson House is the only museum in Washington D.C. of a former president. After Wilson left the presidency, private groups of friends and benefactors bought him this Georgian Revival townhouse and a car to make sure that he lived the remainder of his years in comfort.

Wilson and his second wife, Edith, lived here from 1921 until his death in 1924. The house offers a wonderfully preserved glimpse into the 1920s, with an antique phone, Victrola, radio consoles, and even an early GE refrigerator. The parlor still holds wedding presents the couple received, such as a tapestry from the ambassador to France. Long after Wilson left the presidency, rules were passed to prevent presidents from taking official gifts and memorabilia from the White House, but the Wilson House is peppered with bits and pieces from his days in the White House, such as his White House desk chair and even presidential china.

≡FAST FACT

Rumor has it that Wilson's ghost haunts the house, shuffling up and down stairs with the aid of his cane (which he used after a stroke), still disgruntled that his plans for the League of Nations did not come to fruition in his lifetime.

Special events at the Wilson House include a preservation garden party in May and a spot on the annual Kalorama House and Embassy Tour in September. There is a small gift shop on the premises that sells Wilson memorabilia, including replicas of the Wilson china pattern.

Location and Hours

The Woodrow Wilson House is located on S Street NW and is accessible from Dupont Circle (Red Line) Metro station. Hours of operation are Tuesday through Sunday from 10 A.M. to 4 P.M. You cannot wander through the house on your own, but docents offer tours beginning every half hour. You can sign up for a general tour when you arrive, or reserve in advance over the Internet if you have special needs or requirements. Admission is $7.50 for adults, $6.50 for seniors, and $3.00 for students. Children under age seven get in free. The house is closed on major holidays.

The Decatur House

✉ 748 Jackson Place NW
🚇 Metro: Farragut West (Orange or Blue Line)
    or Farragut North (Red Line)
✆ 202-842-0920
🖎 www.decaturhouse.org

This red-brick Federal-style home was considered one of the first "decent" homes in the city when it was built in 1817. A War of 1812 naval hero and commodore, Stephen Decatur hired Benjamin

Latrobe, who also contributed to the design of the U.S. Capitol, to design his home. It quickly became a gathering place for the city's upper crust until Commodore Decatur was killed in a duel only fourteen months after moving in.

His widow moved to Georgetown and quickly sold the house. Visitors are treated to a fascinating history of the building and its inhabitants; over the years it has been home to several foreign ministers, three secretaries of state (Henry Clay and Martin Van Buren were two), and many politicians.

≡FAST FACT

Although only one Civil War battle took place in Washington D.C., it is amazing how much of the city's history, from the Arlington House and Arlington National Cemetery to Ford's Theatre and the Petersen House, was shaped by the Civil War years.

There is a large gift shop with an excellent selection of Americana and Victorian gifts. You may visit in time for one of the many scheduled special events, which include a showing of quilts with architectural themes in January and February; Mother's Day Open House in May; participation in the Federal City walking tour and Lafayette Square Open House in September, and a three-week-long nineteenth-century Christmas display in December.

Location and Hours

Located on the corner of Jackson Place and H Street in Lafayette Square, the Decatur House is accessible from Farragut West (Orange or Blue Line) or Farragut North (Red Line) Metro stations. Hours of operation are Tuesday through Saturday from 10 A.M. to 5 P.M. and Sunday from noon to 4 P.M. Docents lead tours every 15 minutes past the hour that last about forty minutes. Admission is by donation.

The Octagon Museum

✉ 1799 New York Ave. NW
🚇 Metro: Farragut West (Orange or Blue Line)
✆ 202-638-3221
✒ *www.archfoundation.org*

One of the oldest houses in the city (finished in 1801), and the oldest museum in the United States devoted to architecture and design, the Octagon house was the temporary home of Dolley Madison and President Madison. They lived here while the White House was rebuilt after it burned down. The Madisons could watch the White House being constructed from the windows of this house; the children of its first occupants gave it its current name. Madison signed the Treaty of Ghent that ended the War of 1812 in the circular room at the circular desk on the second floor.

🧳 TRAVEL TIP

The Freedom Plaza is a national park that lies between the Ronald Reagan Building, the National Theatre, the Warner Theatre, and the J. W. Marriott Hotel near the Federal Triangle Metro station. The park is named after the freedom rally in which Martin Luther King Jr. delivered his "I Have a Dream" speech. In the summer, there are concerts and performances here.

The townhouse was designed by Dr. William Thornton, one of the many architects of the U.S. Capitol building. It was built for the wealthy Tayloe family, which included fifteen children, and their slaves. The house has a number of unique design features, such as a three-story oval staircase and hidden doors. The English basement features a working kitchen and the servants' quarters, which offer a glimpse of what life was like for servants during this time.

After the Tayloes moved out, the house became a girls' school and eventually became a boarding house, then a tenement. The museum is now run by the American Architectural Foundation, which houses its amazing collection and mounts changing exhibits about American architecture.

Location and Hours

The Octagon Museum is located on New York Avenue NW and is accessible from Farragut West Metro station (Orange or Blue Line). Hours of operation are Tuesday through Sunday from 10 A.M. to 4 P.M.; the museum is closed Monday. Guided tours are offered every half hour at a fee of $5 for adults and $3 for students and seniors. The museum has temporarily been restricted only to prearranged group tours and has announced it will again be open to walk-in visitors in 2007. Contact the museum before you show up.

The Heurich House

✉ 1307 New Hampshire Ave. NW
🚈 Metro: Dupont Circle (Red Line)
✆ 202-429-1894
🖎 *www.brewmasterscastle.com*

Even if you do not like meandering around old houses, the Heurich House is a one-of-a-kind experience and should not be missed. Eccentric beer magnate Christian Heurich (pronounced HI-rich), whose grandson has revived the family business and now offers a Foggy Bottom Ale on sale throughout the city, built it at the turn of the century.

The house, the most intact late-Victorian structure in the country, is a unique combination of German beer garden and ornate Victorian flourishes. From the outside it looks like a castle, with a tower and arched portico doorway and a handful of gargoyles and carved human heads and animals thrown in as design elements.

Inside, the Heurich House is crammed full of the carved wooden panels, wainscoting, and matching furniture that was popular with the nouveau riche of the time but that rarely survives today. The front parlor's ceiling is a painting of blue sky with angels of the seasons. The dining room is wall-to-ceiling carved oak and mahogany with matching fireplaces; carved wooden tables and chairs feature berries, fruit, and animals. The hallway is mauve with a stenciled gold fleur-de-lis-pattern. On the lower level, where the kitchen is, there is a tavern room where Heurich had eight German drinking mottoes painted as frescos on the walls, offering such wisdom as "There is room in the smallest chamber for the biggest hangover."

Heurich had suffered two fires in his beer factories, so he ordered that his home be fireproof. As a result, this house on Dupont Circle is one of the first private residences in the country that used poured concrete as a foundation and is the first fireproof building in the city. Heurich was ahead of his time in many building innovations. His was one of the first homes to use electricity throughout the house (because of his fear of fire) as well as a "speaking tube" to communicate from one floor to the other and an electric bell system. He also used a coal-burning steam boiler to heat the house.

There's a small shop on the premises that sells old postcards of Washington D.C. and Victorian tea items and that features a section for children. You will also find a Victorian garden that is open to the public. During the holiday season, the house is done up with Victorian Christmas decorations.

Location and Hours

The Heurich House is located on the corner of 20th Street and New Hampshire Avenue NW. You can get there from the Dupont Circle Metro station (Red Line). The museum is raising money to save it from developers. It offers tours Wednesday through Sunday for $5 a person. This is a worthy cause.

Cedar Hill

✉ 1411 W St. SE

🚇 Metro: Anacostia (Green Line), then transfer to the B2 bus

📞 202-426-5961

✎ www.nps.gov/frdo

This last home of Frederick Douglass—freed slave, author, civil and women's rights orator, and U.S. Marshall of the District of Columbia in 1877—is far off the beaten track, but the tour is well worth it.

👥 JUST FOR PARENTS

If you want to take a break from museums, take a stroll around Lincoln Park. Although the park honors Abraham Lincoln, the real draw here is the Emancipation Statue. This statue, which was built from funds raised by freed slaves, depicts Archer Alexander, the last slave captured under the Fugitive Slave Law, breaking the chains of slavery while President Lincoln reads the Emancipation Proclamation.

Frederick Douglass was the first African-American who was nationally renowned as a civil rights leader. After he escaped from slavery and purchased his freedom, he wrote and published his autobiography, *Narrative of the Life of Frederick Douglass*, which became an international bestseller. He traveled extensively throughout the north and the world, telling firsthand of the injustices and horrors of slavery in the South.

When he returned to the United States, he printed an abolitionist newspaper out of Rochester, New York, and oversaw the Rochester activities of the Underground Railroad. When he attended the first women's rights convention in 1848, he also became an ardent supporter of rights for women.

Douglass became a confidant to Presidents Abraham Lincoln and Andrew Johnson regarding black suffrage, but he turned down Johnson's offer to be the head of the Freedman's Bureau. Instead, he became the first president of the Freedman's Bank, where he thought he could do more good.

He served the country as U.S. Marshall, recorder of deeds in Washington D.C., and the American consul-general to Haiti. When he died in 1895, thousands attended his funeral.

≡FAST FACT

Starting with its role as a mecca for freed slaves during and after the Civil War, and continuing through this century as the site of many major civil rights demonstrations, Washington D.C. has one of the nation's most extensive groupings of sites of historic significance to African-Americans. However, most of them are scattered around the city.

Douglass bought Cedar Hill, a twenty-one-room mansion on a hill overlooking the Capitol, for $6,700 as a bankruptcy foreclosure and broke the neighborhood's "whites only" barrier. He moved into the house at the age of sixty, and walked the two miles to the Capitol every morning. He lived here with his first wife and five children for years. When she died, he married his white secretary, an act that many considered scandalous; in response, he said that his first wife had been the color of his mother and his second was the color of his father.

The house is furnished with the memories of a long career in public service. He was a close friend of Harriet Beecher Stowe and Abraham Lincoln, and Mrs. Lincoln had given him one of the president's canes. He had served as the U.S. Ambassador to Haiti, and a prized possession in the house is a leather rocking chair bestowed on him from the people of Haiti. He also had an extensive library and built himself a small brick house in the back of the property where he liked to work alone. Family members dubbed it "the Growlery" because he growled at anyone who bothered him there.

There is a short movie of Douglass's life, which is extremely well done, that plays in the visitors' center. There is also a gift shop that sells copies of his famous autobiography.

Location and Hours
You can reach Cedar Hill by taking the Metro to Anacostia (Green Line) and transferring to the B2 bus, which stops in front of the house.

The house is open daily from 9 A.M. to 4 P.M.; to 5 P.M. April 15 to October 15. It is closed Thanksgiving Day, December 25, and New Year's Day. Admission is free, but there is a $2 fee for tour reservations. The Douglass House is undergoing renovation and will be closed until early 2007. The visitors' center will remain open. Contact it for the latest developments.

The Mary McLeod Bethune House

✉ 1318 Vermont Ave. NW
🚇 Metro: McPherson Square (Blue or Orange Line)
📞 202-673-2402
💻 www.nps.gov/mamc

Every July 10, there is a birthday celebration at the Victorian residence of Mary McLeod Bethune. Bethune, one of seventeen children of freed slaves, advised Franklin Delano Roosevelt and three other presidents and created the National Council of Negro Women. She was also the founder of Bethune-Cookman College in Daytona, Florida. The visitors' center shows a twenty-five-minute film on Bethune's life. This is also the site of the National Archives for Black Women's History, which is open by appointment. There is a treasure hunt through the Council house for children.

Location and Hours

You can reach the Mary McLeod Bethune House from McPherson Square Metro station (Blue or Orange Line). Tours are available Monday through Saturday from 10 A.M. to 4 P.M.

Houses of Worship

Washington D.C. has several historic churches, synagogues, and cathedrals that are open to visitors. You don't have to be religious to appreciate their art and architecture.

The Franciscan Monastery
✉ 1400 Quincy St. NE
🚇 Metro: Brookland-CUA (Red Line)
📞 202-526-6800
💻 www.myfranciscan.org

Located on forty-four acres of land, Mount St. Sepulchre, a Franciscan monastery, is dotted with replicas of Holy Land shrines surrounding a turn-of-the-twentieth-century Byzantine-style church. Tours of the monastary, shrines, and Roman-style catacombs are given on the hour from 10 A.M. to 3 P.M. and Sunday from 1 P.M. to 3 P.M. The grounds are open daily, 10 A.M. to 5 P.M. The monastery is about three-quarters of a mile away from Brookland/CUA Metro station (Red Line). It's about a 15-minute walk, or you can take the H6 Metro bus.

The Sixth & I Historic Synagogue
✉ 600 I Street NW
🚇 Metro: Gallery Place–Chinatown (Yellow, Green, or Red Line)
📞 202-408-3100
💻 www.sixthandi.org

This half-century-old building has recently been reborn into a vibrant force for the Jewish community in Washington. The building is an outstanding example of American synagogue architecture in the early twentieth century. With Moorish, Romanesque, and Byzantine elements, the structure was constructed of vitrified brick with beautiful terra-cotta accents and an impressive dome. Built in 1908, it served as a synagogue for half a century, then it was sold and converted to a church and used for another fifty years. In 2002, it was purchased and restored to its classic beauty using old photographs and architectural elements still preserved in the building. Original lighting fixtures held in the collection of the Jewish Historical Society were given their rightful place, and a magnificent ceiling painting was added using eighty-two square feet of gold leaf. The building now serves as a venue for music, theater, festivals, exhibits, lectures, and religious services.

St. John's Episcopal Church

✉ 16th & H Sts. NW

🚇 Metro: McPherson Square (Orange or Blue Line)

✆ 202-347-8766

✑ www.stjohns-dc.org

Called the Church of Presidents, this nineteenth-century Episcopalian church has seen every president from James Madison to Bill Clinton worship here. The church is located in Lafayette Square.

St. Matthew's Cathedral

✉ 1725 Rhode Island Ave. NW

🚇 Metro: Farragut North or Dupont Circle (both on the Red Line)

✆ 202-347-3215

✑ www.stmatthewscathedral.org

Most Washingtonians pass this red-brick church without realizing that it was the site of John F. Kennedy's funeral in 1963. Recently undergoing a three-year renovation, it has been cited as having "one of the most beautiful church interiors of modern times." St. Matthew's is open Sunday through Friday from 6:30 A.M. to 6:30 P.M. (7:30 A.M. in the summer) and on Saturday from 7:30 A.M. to 6:30 P.M. Federal holiday hours are 7:30 A.M. to 1 P.M. You can take a guided tour on Sunday at 2:30 P.M. You can reach St. Matthew's Cathedral from Farragut North or Dupont Circle Metro stations (both on the Red Line).

Calvary Baptist Church

✉ 777 8th St. NW

🚇 Metro: Gallery Place–Chinatown (Red, Yellow, or Green Line)

✆ 202-347-8355

✑ www.calvarydc.com

One of the oldest black churches in D.C. and one of the stops on the Underground Railroad, this church was attended by General Oliver Howard, one of the founders of Howard University. It is undergoing extensive renovation and rebuilding to the point where only the historic façade of one building is left standing, and a modern office building is built behind it. The church is accessible from Gallery Place/Chinatown Metro station (Red, Yellow, or Green Line).

Ebenezer Methodist Church

✉ 420 D St. SE

🚇 Metro: Capitol South (Blue or Orange Line)

☎ 202-544-1415

🖱 www.gbgm-umc.org/ebzumc

This church was the site of the first public school for African-Americans. In 1975, the Ebenezer Methodist Church was designated as a landmark by the D.C. government. The church is open to visitors Monday through Friday from 8:30 A.M. to 3 P.M. You can get there by taking the Metro to Capitol South station (Blue or Orange Line).

CHAPTER 11

Other Attractions

NOT ONLY IS WASHINGTON D.C. a great city for museums and historical and government sites, but it has some truly fabulous buildings and arts centers that compete with those of other major cities. Much of D.C. was built in the 1950s and 1960s. It is an American city that features significant architectural accomplishments of the international architectural style of glass and steel, such as the Martin Luther King Jr. Memorial Library and the Kennedy Center.

The John F. Kennedy Center for the Performing Arts

✉ 2700 F St. NW
🚇 Metro: Foggy Bottom (Blue or Orange Line),
   transfer to a free shuttle
📞 1-800-444-1324
📞 202-467-4600
🖥 *www.kennedy-center.org*

The John F. Kennedy Center for the Performing Arts (known as the Kennedy Center) is a living memorial tribute to President Kennedy and is our nation's premier performing arts center. It houses four theaters and is home to the National Symphony Orchestra, the Washington Opera, and the American Film Institute.

The Kennedy Center is built on seventeen acres of land overlooking the Potomac. It was designed by Edward Stone (who designed the General Motors building in New York) in the international architectural style of the '70s, with lots of marble and glass.

The John F. Kennedy Center Tour

The free fifty-minute guided tour starts at the Hall of Nations, where the flags of the countries that the United States has diplomatic relations with are on display, in alphabetical order. Throughout the Kennedy Center are gifts sent by various nations, such as the Swedish modern chandeliers and the Belgian mirrors. Even the marble was a gift, contributed by Italy.

■ TRAVEL TIP

The Millennium Stage at the John F. Kennedy Center for the Performing Arts features free concerts for 400 people every evening at 6 P.M. The series was started in 1997 as part of the Performing Arts for Everyone Initiative, and it has been so successful that a mirror project was started in 1998 on the grounds of the U.S. Capitol during the summer months. No tickets are needed.

The next stop on the tour is the Grand Foyer, where free concerts are given and the signature giant bronze bust of President Kennedy (sculpted by Robert Berks) is on view. It is also the reception area for all three theaters on the main floor.

The tour will take you through the Israeli Room, where panels depicting scenes from the Hebrew Bible adorn the walls, and the African Room, which displays beautiful tapestries donated by various African nations. You'll then continue through the Concert Hall, which is the largest auditorium in the building with 2,700 seats, where the National Symphony Orchestra performs.

Next, you'll tour the Opera House, which has 2,200 seats and an interior décor of red and gold. There is also a smaller Eisenhower Theatre, which seats 1,100 and is wood paneled, and the newer Terrace Theatre, which was donated by Japan as a bicentennial gift. The Terrace Theater is used for chamber concerts.

There are also two smaller theaters: the Theatre Lab, which seats 380 people, and the American Film Institute's theater, which seats 200. You will end your tour in the Hall of States, where the flags of the fifty states and four territories are displayed in the order they joined the nation.

The view from the Roof Terrace Restaurant is stupendous. If there are no performances, you will be allowed to visit. If a performance is in progress in the restaurant, the staff doesn't want to disturb the diners who are watching. You can just go up to the Roof Terrace and take a look as part of the tour or on your own, if it's not closed. In addition to the Roof Terrace Restaurant, the center boasts the KC Café, and there's also a gift shop.

Location and Hours

The Kennedy Center is located on F Street, near New Hampshire Ave. and 25th Street NW (at Rock Creek Parkway at the tip of F Street). Take the Metro to Foggy Bottom station (Blue or Orange Line) and transfer to a free shuttle. Parking is also available on site.

The Kennedy Center is open daily for visitors from 10 A.M. until the last show closes, which can vary. Free guided tours are given Monday through Friday from 10 A.M. to 5 P.M. On Saturday and Sunday the hours are 10 A.M. to 1 P.M. For more information, call 202-416-8340.

Tickets to performances can run from the cheap to the pricey, but depending on the event, half-price discounts for seniors and students may be available. The box office is open Monday through Friday from 10 A.M. to 5:30 P.M.

The Folger Shakespeare Library

✉ 201 E. Capitol St. SE
🚇 Metro: Capitol South (Blue or Orange Line)
📞 202-544-4600
🖥 *www.folger.edu*

A national treasure, this incredible collection of Shakespearean plays, memorabilia, and artifacts was amassed by an Amherst student after hearing Ralph Waldo Emerson lecture on his love of the Bard. Henry Clay Folger began the collection by buying a cheap set of Shakespeare's plays and from there went on to put together the world's largest collection of Shakespeare's printed works, now housed in the Folger Shakespeare Library.

🌂 RAINY DAY FUN

The Folger Library has a great interactive Web site for kids, featuring games and fun facts from the collection. In addition, on Saturdays, groups can book performance workshops for families on such things as Elizabethan swordplay. There's usually a matinee performance at the theater, so it might be fun to perform in a Shakespeare play in the morning and then see one that afternoon!

On the exterior of the marble building are nine raised art deco reliefs depicting scenes from Shakespeare's plays. A statue of Puck, from *A Midsummer's Night Dream*, stands in the west garden, and there are quotes from Shakespeare and his contemporaries etched onto the façade.

On the east side of the building is an Elizabethan garden, with flowers and herbs from Shakespeare's time. In warm weather the garden is included in the library tour.

The Library

The Folger Library is an active research center for both Shakespearean scholars and those who wish to research English and Renaissance history and literature. There are more than a quarter of a million books on hand, many of which are very rare, such as early editions of Shakespeare's plays. The collection also features a number of rare Renaissance manuscripts, musical instruments, costumes, and paintings. The Reading Room, which is open to the public in April only, during the library's annual celebration of Shakespeare's birth, houses a replica of the bust of Shakespeare on view at Stratford's Trinity Church. At the other end is a stained-glass window showing the seven ages of man from *As You Like It*.

TRAVEL TIP

Washington D.C. has one of the best Shakespearean theater companies in the country, dedicated to classical theater. The Shakespeare Theatre in the nation's capital performs five plays a year (not all Shakespeare) at its home—downtown at 450 7th Street—and two weeks of free Shakespeare every summer at the "Shakespeare Free for All" in Rock Creek Park. Call 877-487-8849 or 202-547-1122 for information.

The interior Great Hall is chock-full of Shakespeare-related decor, from the wood-paneled walls with a carved relief of the Bard to the painted plaster ceiling depicting Shakespeare's coat of arms to the tiled floor inlaid with the masks of Comedy and Tragedy.

Other Facilities

Special exhibits on the works of Shakespeare, as well as other Renaissance interests, are on view throughout the year. The Library also hosts PEN-Faulkner readings, poetry readings, and a concert series. There is a performance space designed to resemble an Elizabethan theater with a three-tiered gallery, carved oak columns, and a sky balcony at the end of the Great Hall. Performances are given here throughout the year.

There is also an extensive gift shop on the premises.

Location and Hours

The Folger Shakespeare Library is located on Capitol Street, near the Capitol South Metro station on the Blue or Orange Line. Visitor hours are Monday through Saturday from 10 A.M. to 4 P.M.; the library is closed on federal holidays. Free guided tours are offered Monday to Friday at 11 A.M. and Saturday 11 A.M. and 1 P.M. Matinee performances are held every Saturday.

Union Station

✉ 50 Massachusetts Ave., NE
🚆 Metro: Union Station (Red Line)
✆ 202-289-1908
✑ www.unionstationdc.com

Built at the turn of the century during the great railroad age, Union Station was once the largest railway station in the world. It was an important center of Washington D.C. life for many years. (Roosevelt's funeral train left here amid thousands of mourners.) The station later fell into disrepair and became a place that people avoided. In 1981 it was renovated to the tune of $160 million and has once again become an important part of Washington's bustling life. It is now the site of a number of charity events and gala evenings, hosted in the station's Main Hall beneath its ninety-six-foot-high gilded vaulted ceiling. The Main Hall is visited by 25 million people annually, making it the most visited site in the capital.

Daniel Burnham incorporated a number of neoclassical design elements and American motifs in his designs of the station. The design was based on the ancient Baths of Diocletian and the Arch of Constantine in Rome, featuring arches, Ionic columns, and 100 eagles on the white-granite façade. In front of the building is a replica of the Liberty Bell, and a huge statue of Columbus greets visitors as they disembark and grab a cab. Above the arched entryway are six carved figures representing Fire, Electricity, Freedom, Imagination, Agriculture, and Mechanics.

Inside the Main Hall are a total of forty-eight statues of Roman soldiers designed by Augustus Saint-Gaudens (one each for the states that were in existence at the time of the station's construction). The East Hall, with its marble walls, a hand-stenciled skylight, and bright murals, is now a shopping arcade that features more than 135 stores from Ann Taylor to Alamo Flags.

═FAST FACT

The larger-than-life bronze statue that welcomes visitors to Union Station when they arrive by train at Gate C depicts Philip Randolph, the founder of the Sleeping Car Porters Union and the civil rights activist who organized the famous 1963 March on Washington.

A number of very good restaurants are featured in the Main Hall of the Station (America, B. Smith, Thunder Grill), as well as a food court on the lower level that supplies more than forty varieties of faster food, from burgers to sushi. The lower level also features a nine-theater movie complex, where films are shown in the carved-out underground passageways of the former train station.

Location and Hours

Amtrak trains, Greyhound buses, and the Metro Red Line come and go from the station, as well as the D.C. Ducks and Old Town Trolley tours. The station is open twenty-four hours a day, but most restaurants and the movie theaters close by 11 P.M. Store hours are Monday to Saturday 10 A.M. to 9 P.M., and Sunday from noon to 6 P.M.

If you go to the Union Station Web site, *www.unionstationdc.com*, you can print out a coupon for 15 percent off at many of the 135 shops and eateries in the station.

The Washington National Cathedral

✉ Massachusetts and Wisconsin Avenues, NW
🚇 Metro: Tenleytown-AU (Red Line)
✆ 202-537-6200
🖰 *www.cathedral.org*

Designed to be "Your Church in the Nation's Capital" (it is an Episcopal church with a nondenominational congregation), the Washington National Cathedral stands higher than the Washington Monument and crowns a fifty-seven-acre plot of land at the capital's highest point. It is the sixth largest cathedral in the world and took a total of eighty-three years to complete (in 1990).

This church is designed in the fourteenth-century English Gothic style, complete with flying buttresses. It has many beautiful stained-glass windows, but the one that draws the most attention is the "space" window commemorating *Apollo 11*, which contains a chunk of moon rock. Its exterior and interior feature an incredible collection of gargoyles from the traditional to one that looks like Darth Vader, which was designed by a twelve-year-old boy in an annual competition. New gargoyles are added every year.

In the crypts on the lower level lie the sarcophagi of President and Mrs. Wilson, as well as Helen Keller and her teacher, Anne Sullivan.

There is an observation gallery that you get to by elevator where you can see a panoramic view of Washington D.C. from a very different perspective. There is also a lovely garden and an extensive gift shop that offers many gargoyle-related items, tea services, and cookbooks. The selection of jewelry for sale is quite comprehensive.

There are wonderful programs for children offered throughout the week, and an occasional medieval arts-and-craft workshop for children on some Saturdays from noon to 4 P.M. You can find afternoon tea being served on Tuesday and Wednesday afternoons. (See Chapter 15 for more information.)

≡ FAST FACT

The Darth Vader gargoyle at the National Cathedral is one of the most famous offbeat sights in the capital. It was designed by twelve-year-old Christopher Rader, who read of the national competition for children in *National Geographic* magazine. The Darth Vader gargoyle is located on the northwest corner of the nave, and you really need binoculars to see it well.

Location and Hours

The cathedral is located at the intersection of Massachusetts and Wisconsin Avenues NW and is accessible from Tenleytown Metro station (Red Line), though you should expect a fairly long walk along Wisconsin Avenue or to catch the bus.

Visiting hours and tour times vary with the season, as do the hours when the nave level is open. Services are held throughout the day. Call 202-364-6616 for the latest information.

Guided tours are given all day and highlight many of the different and offbeat aspects of the cathedral, from a gargoyle tour to a behind-the-scenes tour that takes you up slender staircases. There's a suggested donation for tours of $3 per adult, $2 for seniors and military, and $1 per child.

The Pentagon

✉ Arlington, VA
🚇 Metro: Pentagon (Blue or Yellow Line)
☎ 703-697-1776
🖱 *www.pentagon.afis.osd.mil/tours.cfm*

Since the Pentagon was attacked on September 11, 2001, public touring has been greatly curtailed, but tours are available for certain groups, and you may be able to schedule a tour or join an existing tour by calling at least two weeks ahead. The side of the building that was hit by the airplane has been completely restored, and the Pentagon has been operating at full capacity.

The World's Largest Office Building

The five-sided headquarters of the U.S. military is the world's largest office building and houses more than 24,000 employees. It is huge in every sense of the word, from the 583 acres of land it occupies on to the 17.5 miles of interior corridors, about a mile of which you will have to walk through on the hour-and-a-half tour, so wear very comfortable shoes. Here are some other facts about the Pentagon:

- It is twice the size of the Mercantile Mart in Chicago and has three times the office space as the Empire State Building in New York.
- The 24,000 people who work in the Pentagon park approximately 8,770 cars in sixteen parking lots. There are 4,200 clocks, 691 water fountains, and 284 bathrooms. About 200,000 telephone calls are made daily through 100,000 miles of telephone cables.
- The building was designed in such a way that even though there are 17.5 miles of corridors, it takes only seven minutes to walk between any two points in the building!

The Tour

You have to pass through airport-quality security before you begin the tour, which starts at the Concourse area of the Metro station. There is a short film about the development of the Pentagon, which was built just after World War II in sixteen months on former swampland. The new structure consolidated seventeen buildings of the War Department. Tours were offered to the public in 1976 and were expected to be discontinued after the Fourth of July, but they turned out to be very popular, so the Pentagon has continued the service.

Part of the tour is a visit to the Air Force Art Collection, which includes some of Walt Disney's early cartoons, which he did while he was an ambulance driver in World War I, as well as more traditional art depicting historic events in air force history. You then pass the executive offices of the U.S. Air Force and the POW Alcove, where paintings of prisoner-of-war camps are displayed. Next you will pass the Marine Corps Corridor and then the Navy Corridor, where models of ships and submarines are on display in glass cases. Then you'll tour the Army Corridor, which displays the army command and divisional flags and 172 army campaign streamers from just after the Revolutionary War to the present.

Next up is the Time-Life Corridor, where civilian artists' paintings of war commissioned by the Time-Life Company during World War I hang. The MacArthur Corridor honors General MacArthur's fifty-two-year military career. The hall of heroes commemorates the 3,409 Medal of Honor recipients. The Military Women's Corridor tells the story of women in the military. The Navajo Code Talkers Corridor honors the 400 Navajo marines who created an indecipherable-to-enemies communication code based on the Navajo language to use during World War II. The two newest additions to the Pentagon tour are the African-Americans Corridor and the Hispanic Heroes Corridor. The Flag Corridor displays state and territorial flags throughout the nation's history.

The Pentagon cafeterias are not open to the public, but there is a mall inside the Pentagon with two banks, an Amtrak station, and a post office.

Location and Hours

The Pentagon is located off I-309; you can get there on the Metro Pentagon station (Blue or Yellow Line); if you choose to drive, be aware that limited parking is available. The Tour Office will accept only requests from educational and religious institutions, government agencies, or military organizations. Tours are conducted Monday through Friday, 9 A.M. to 3 P.M. No tours are held on weekends or federal holidays. Groups interested in touring the Pentagon should contact the Pentagon Tour Office at 703-697-1776.

The National Geographic Society's Explorers Hall

✉ 17th & M St. NW
🚇 Metro: Farragut North (Red Line)
    or Farragut West (Blue or Orange Line)
📞 202-857-7588
🖱 *www.nationalgeographic.com/museum*

Kids love this place almost as much as the huge National Museum of Natural History, and because it's much smaller, it's also easier to visit in a short period of time. There are many interactive exhibits, such as giant slides in a microscope and a display in which kids can touch a tornado. Everyone comes here to see the *Aepyornis maximus* egg from the extinct elephant bird. Other objects on display include a replica of a giant Olmec stone from 32 B.C.E., the dogsled from Admiral Perry's trek to the North Pole, and a full-scale model of Jacques Cousteau's diving craft.

There's a geology exhibit where you can see inside the Earth and another where you can explore Martian terrain. A theater-in-the-round exhibit explains Earth's weather and ecology.

The Explorer's Hall also has exhibits that change monthly. The museum store has an extensive display of books, science-related toys, and ecological items for kids.

Location and Hours

Located at the intersection of 17th and M Streets NW, the museum is accessible from Farragut North (Red Line) and Farragut West (Blue or Orange Line) Metro stations. Visiting hours are Monday through Saturday and holidays, 9 A.M. to 5 P.M. and Sunday from 10 A.M. to 5 P.M. The museum is closed on December 25. Admission is free.

The National Aquarium

✉ 14th and Constitution Ave. NW
🚇 Metro: Federal Triangle (Orange or Blue Line)
☎ 202-482-2825
🖱 www.nationalaquarium.com

This is a 125-year-old aquarium, and certainly one of the quirki-est—where else would you find piranhas in a government building? It's small by big-city standards, but that's one of its charms. It's also old and much less high-tech than many other aquariums around the country, which makes it very child-friendly. There's a tidal pool where kids can touch horseshoe crabs and rather large snails, and there's a fairly large and ominous-looking electric eel.

≡FAST FACT

According to the guides at the Aquarium, piranhas have been given a bad rap. When President Roosevelt saw a school of piranhas furi-ously eat a cow that had been lowered into the water, the fish hadn't been fed in a month. To prove that piranhas are usually not that vicious, a fillet of flounder is lowered into the piranha tank, and it takes a good ten minutes for the fish to eat it.

The big kid-pleasers are the shark and piranha feedings, which take place on alternate days at 2 P.M. You can visit the aquarium in the morning (on your way to the Mall) and have your hand stamped to return for the feeding in the afternoon. The alligator exhibit has recently been expanded, and new touch-tanks have been added.

Location and Hours

The aquarium is located on the corner of 14th Street and Constitution Avenue, in the basement of the Department of Commerce

Building. It is accessible from Federal Triangle Metro station (Orange or Blue Line).

Hours of operation are from 9 A.M. to 5 P.M. every day of the week; the last admission is at 4:30 P.M. There are daily animal feedings: sharks on Monday, Wednesday, and Saturday, piranhas on Tuesday, Thursday, and Sunday, and alligators on Friday. Admission is $5 for adults, $4 for seniors and military, and $1 for children ages two to ten. The aquarium is closed on Thanksgiving and December 25.

The National Academy of Sciences

✉ 2100 C St. NW
🚆 Metro: Farragut West (Blue or Orange Line)
✆ 202-334-2436
✍ www.nasonline.org

Do you have a young scientist in the family? The National Academy of Science manages exhibits at three locations that he or she would love to see. At the headquarters building, you can pose in front of the twenty-one-foot statue of Albert Einstein (by Robert Berks, the same sculptor who did the bust of Kennedy at the Kennedy Center) that adorns the front of the building, and have a picture taken. Inside are two gallery spaces; one relates the history of science up to 1926, so you can see how far we've come.

🧳 TRAVEL TIP

The relatively new Marian Koshland Science Museum (6th and E Streets NW, 202-334-1201) offers visitors an interactive look at cutting-edge science and how it affects the world. DNA analysis and criminal investigations, global warming, and medical research are illustrated and explained. And you can do it in less than an hour.

The other two locations are the Marian Koshland Science Museum (see Travel Tip), and the Keck Center at 500 5th Street, NW, where there are permanent installations in the lobby.

Location and Hours

The National Academy of Sciences is located on the corner of C Street and 22nd Street. The hours of operation are Monday through Friday, 9 A.M. to 5 P.M.

The Pope John Paul II Cultural Center

✉ 3900 Harewood Rd. NE
🚇 Metro: Brookland-CUA (Red Line)
✆ 202-635-5400
🖥 www.jp2cc.org

The cultural center is a relatively new museum, opened in 2001 in a postmodernist building. The center is devoted to faith and culture and offers a variety of exhibits, programs, performances, family festivals, and lectures throughout the year. One room features Pope John Paul II's personal memorabilia, another is devoted to the heritage of his homeland, Poland. The Center of Imagination offers appropriate interactive activities for kids up to eight years old, such as bell ringing. There is a chapel, a museum store, and an inexpensive café where you can also bring your own food.

Location and Hours

The Pope John Paul II Cultural Center is located on Harewood Road, NE. If you don't mind a walk of about a mile, you can get there from the Brookland/CUA Metro station on the Red Line. The center is open Tuesday and Thursday to Saturday, 10 A.M. to 5 P.M., and Sunday, noon to 5 P.M. It is closed Monday and Wednesday. Admission is free, but a donation is suggested of $5 for individuals, $4 for seniors and students, and $15 for families.

Freedom Park

✉ 1101 Wilson Blvd., Arlington, VA
🚇 Metro: Rosslyn (Blue or Orange Line)
✆ 703-284-3710
🖰 *www.newseum.org/newseum/abouttheewseum/freedompark
.htm*

Until recently, Freedom Park was the site of the Newseum, a popular interactive museum dedicated to journalism, its history, and its changing technology. The Newseum has moved to a new site near the Mall in downtown D.C. (see page 163). However, Freedom Park is still worth visiting.

The park is dedicated to the spirit of freedom throughout the world. On display in the park are articles that represent freedom all over the world, including the following:

- A chunk of the Berlin Wall
- A former watchtower
- A toppled, headless statue of Lenin
- A bronze casting of Martin Luther King Jr.'s Birmingham, Alabama, jail-cell door
- Stones from the Warsaw ghetto
- A cast of a South African ballot box

At the center of Freedom Park is the glass and steel Freedom Forum Journalists Memorial, which honors journalists who have died while trying to report the news. The monument bears 1,000 names of journalists, whose deaths date back to 1812.

Location and Hours

Freedom Park is located on Wilson Boulevard in Arlington, Virginia. It is accessible from Rosslyn Metro station (Blue or Orange Line). The park is open from dawn until dusk. Guided tours are available by reservation on a first-come, first-served basis. Call for information.

The Reagan Trade Building

✉ 1300 Pennsylvania Ave. NW

🚊 Metro: Federal Triangle (Orange or Blue Line)

✆ 202-312-1300

🖃 *www.itcdc.com*

One of the newest federal buildings in the city, the Ronald Reagan Building and International Trade Center was designed by James Ingo Freed, the architect for the U.S. Holocaust Museum and Memorial. You'll see a giant slab of the Berlin Wall covered with graffiti when you enter from the Federal Triangle side, and an underground food court that caters to office workers. The walls are lined with contemporary artworks, and there is a gift shop selling Reagan memorabilia. With its Federal Triangle entrance, the Trade Center is also a great air-conditioned shortcut to the Mall on an extremely hot day (or a heated one on a cold day).

Location and Hours

The Reagan building is open during business hours and closed Sunday. The food court is open from 7 A.M. to 7 P.M., Saturday from 1 P.M. to 6 P.M., and Sunday from noon to 5 P.M. It is open all holidays except New Year's Day, Easter, Thanksgiving, and Christmas. Guided tours are available on Monday, Wednesday, and Friday at 11 A.M. Self-guided tours are also available.

≡FAST FACT

Inside the Reagan Trade Building are two valuable assets for the visitor. The beautiful office of the Washington D.C. Visitor Information Center has loads of help and material to make your trip even more memorable. It also houses a Ticketmaster outlet where you can get half-price tickets to the Kennedy Center and other local theaters.

The Old Post Office Pavilion

✉ 1100 Pennsylvania Ave. NW
🚇 Metro: Federal Triangle (Orange or Blue Line)
✆ 202-606-8691
🖰 *www.oldpostofficedc.com*

Built in 1899, the Old Post Office Pavilion was once the largest government building in Washington D.C. It was the first public building with a clock tower and electric power. Only eighteen years after it was built, people began referring to it as "old" because a new post office had been constructed at Union Station.

The old post office was slated for demolition in the 1920s, but the Depression saved the building, which many now appreciate for its design. The building houses a number of shops, a food court, and the office of TICKETplace (202-TICKETS) where you can buy half-price tickets for concert and theater events the day of the show. The Clock Tower is open for tours and offers a splendid view of the city from a vantage point that is the second highest in the city (after the Washington Monument). A statue of Benjamin Franklin stands outside the building to remind us that he was our first postmaster general.

Location and Hours

The pavilion is located on Pennsylvania Avenue NW and is accessible from the Federal Triangle Metro station (Orange or Blue Line). Free self-guided tours are available Monday to Saturday between 8 A.M. and 8 P.M., and Sunday from 10 A.M. to 6 P.M.

The Washington Post Newsroom

✉ 1150 15th St. NW
🚇 Metro: Farragut North (Red Line)
   or McPherson Square (Orange or Blue Line)
✆ 202-334-7969
🖰 *http://washpost.com/community/you/tours.shtml*

This is a great group tour for a budding journalist or anyone interested in Watergate lore. The tour is led by a specially trained *Post* guide who will take you through the newsroom, where you can see reporters gathering information and writing their stories. Stops include prepress production and a visit to the presses, which print the day's papers. You will also be taken to the circulation department and the hot type museum, where you'll see how newspapers were once produced.

Location and Hours

The Washington Post building is located on 15th Street NW, near the Farragut North Metro station on the Red Line or McPherson Square stop on the Blue or Orange Line). Group tours with a minimum of ten people are offered Monday from 11 A.M. until 3 P.M. and take about an hour. To tour the newsroom, you must make reservations up to four weeks in advance. Children under ten years old are not admitted.

CHAPTER 12

Gardens, Parks, and Recreation

WASHINGTON D.C. IS A great outdoor city, with a terrific array of outdoor public spaces—parks, playgrounds, recreational facilities, and gardens, as well as circles and squares where you can sit and relax. In fact, from spring until late fall, the National Mall is alive with energy, where you will often see people running, walking dogs, playing Frisbee, or flying a kite. Because of its moderate weather, Washington D.C. is a gardener's dream. There are many places to have family picnics and enjoy outdoor sporting activities from ice skating in the winter to sailing, bicycling, and fishing in the warmer months.

The National Mall

The long lawn that runs between the Jefferson Memorial on the south to the Lincoln Memorial on the west and to the Capitol on the east is really a giant park, which is why the National Park Service oversees it. More than just grass, the Mall is lined by 2,000 American elms and the famous 3,000 cherry trees.

🧳 TRAVEL TIP

If you visit Washington D.C. in the spring or early summer, don't miss the Twilight Tattoo on the Jefferson Memorial Grounds every Wednesday at 7 P.M. The kids will love the pageantry as a fife and drum corps, drill team, jazz ensemble, and a chorus and chorale put on a show they will never forget. Call first at 202-685-2888, or visit *www.mdw.army.mil/tlt.*

At the turn of the last century, the area was a railway yard, but construction of the Smithsonian museums turned it into the public space it is today. Sometimes called the nation's backyard, the Mall is a wonderful public space for national expressions of remembrance, observance, and protest. In the summer months, free "Screen on the Green" screenings of classic movies are shown Monday nights at sunset, but people start staking out their territory at 5 P.M. Bring a blanket and bug spray.

≡ FAST FACT

The Smithsonian Carousel is a nineteenth-century merry-go-round that features beautiful horses for kids to ride when the weather is nice. It may remind you of the many merry-go-rounds in Paris. The carousel is located across the street from the Arts and Industries Building on the Mall. Kids can take a ride for $2 daily from 10 A.M. to 5:30 P.M.

The Mall is accessible from Smithsonian or L'Enfant Plaza Metro stations on the Orange or Blue Line, or the Archives–Navy Memorial Metro station on the Yellow or Green Line.

The U.S. Botanic Garden

✉ 100 Maryland Ave. SW
🚇 Metro: Federal Center SW or Capitol South (Orange or Blue Line)
📞 202-225-8333
🖊 *www.usbg.gov*

The U.S. Botanic Garden is a really fun place for kids and parents alike. The concept for the creation of a national garden was conceived by our founding fathers, and many of the plants on view here have their roots (literally) in our nation's past.

America's living plant museum, the newly renovated facility reopened in December 2001 (and continues to be improved upon), with a new conservatory and lots of exhibits for kids, such as a Jurassic plant re-creation, a tropical rain forest, and many exhibits on endangered plant species, as well as a children's garden. Among its many highlights is the orchid collection, which features 10,000 varieties.

Visitors to the reopened botanical gardens will find new exhibits, upgraded interiors, an enlarged gift shop, and an entrance on Independence Avenue. Themes within the Conservatory (the glass house) focus on plant conservation and endangered species, plant discoveries, orchids, and tropical medicinal plants. Case exhibits explore how plants have influenced the development of civilization, their therapeutic value, and how plants are represented in the arts.

Exhibits in the east half of the Conservatory focus on the ecology and evolution of plants. There are exhibits on primitive plants in a reconstructed Jurassic landscape (which is sure to be of interest to kids who are serious about dinosaurs), an oasis, plants of the desert, and a Japanese meditation garden.

The former Palm House has been redesigned as a jungle, representing the reclaiming of an abandoned plantation by the surrounding tropical rain forest. The former Subtropical House has turned into an expanded exhibit of economic plants, focusing on crops that are used to make cosmetics, fiber, food, and industrial products.

The brand-new national garden features a rose garden, a butterfly garden, a First Ladies Water Garden, and a lawn terrace for outdoor events.

Bartholdi Park

Bartholdi Park, located across the street from the U.S. Botanic Gardens at Independence Avenue, is a serene, formally landscaped oasis within the city. It features the botanic gardens home-gardening demonstration landscape, which displays plants that are suitable for urban growth. Among the displays are:

- **The all-seasons garden**, where plants that have four seasons are on display
- **The heritage garden**, which features North American plantings
- **The romantic garden**, which features beautiful roses and a secluded park bench
- **The rock garden**, which features unusual plants in raised rock beds

≡FAST FACT

Within Bartholdi Park you'll find the meticulously restored Bartholdi Fountain. Combining electricity and water, it was a marvel for its time. Does the name sound familiar? The park and the fountain are named in honor of Frédéric Auguste Bartholdi, the sculptor of the Statue of Liberty.

Location and Hours

The U.S. Botanic Gardens are located at 100 Maryland Avenue and First Street SW, at the east end of the Mall. Bartholdi Park is located across the street, with entrances on Independence Avenue,

Washington Avenue, and First Street. Both are accessible from the Federal Center SW or Capitol South Metro station (Orange or Blue Line).

Admission to all public areas of the U.S. Botanic Garden is free. The conservatory is open from 10 A.M. to 5 P.M. daily, including weekends and holidays. Visitors are welcome in Bartholdi Park from dawn until dusk. There are no eating facilities.

The U.S. National Arboretum

✉ 3501 New York Ave. NE
🚇 Metro: Stadium Armory (Orange or Blue Line),
    then transfer to B2 bus
📞 202-245-2776
🖰 www.usna.usda.gov

The National Arboretum is a 446-acre preserve dedicated to research, education, and conservation of trees, shrubs, flowers, and other plants. Among the highlights are the National Bonsai and Penjing Museum, which includes fifty-three miniature trees given to the United States by Japan as part of its bicentennial gift.

The arboretum also features a conservatory for tropical bonsai trees that includes a Japanese garden. Across the road from the bonsai collection, the National Herb Garden features an extensive spread of antique roses and ten specialty herb gardens sorted by their functions, from fragrance herbs to herbs used by Native Americans.

The largest planting of azaleas in the nation can be found at the arboretum, as well as a historic rose garden and the Franklin tree, which is a species of tree now extinct in the wild, discovered by a botanist friend of Benjamin Franklin in 1765. There is also a national grove of state trees.

The arboretum also has a lovely gift shop with all sorts of books about plants, as well as planting and gardening-related paraphernalia. If you call ahead, you can find out about any special workshops or lectures that may be offered on the day of your visit.

Location and Hours

The Arboretum is located on New York Avenue, NE. To get there, take the Metro to Stadium Armory station (Orange or Blue Line), then transfer to the B2 bus to get to the intersection of Bladensburg Road and R Street, NE.

Hours of operation are 8 A.M. to 5 P.M. daily. The arboretum is closed on December 25. The National Bonsai and Penjing Museum is open from 10 A.M. to 3:30 P.M. Admission and parking are free. There are water and restrooms, but no food service. Picnicking allowed in the National Grove of State Trees.

Tram tours are available on Saturday and Sunday from April through October. The forty-minute, narrated, open-air tram tour of the entire site starts at 10:30 A.M., 11:30 A.M., 1 P.M., 3 P.M., and 4 P.M. You can buy tickets at the ticket kiosk in the administration building. Tours are $4 for adults, $3 for seniors, and $2 for children ages four to sixteen.

Other Gardens and Botanical Exhibits

Washington D.C. is a planned city and its architect, Pierre L'Enfant, made sure that there would be plenty of gardens and parks to decorate its streets. The many flowers—daffodils, tulips, roses, and the famous cherry blossoms—that line the city's thoroughfares provide wonderful natural beauty in an urban setting.

Enid A. Haupt Garden

✉ 10th St. and Independence Ave. NW
🚇 Metro: Smithsonian or L'Enfant Plaza (Orange or Blue Line)
✆ 202-357-2700

Enid Haupt, the donor after whom this garden was named, was an avid horticulturist who also has a conservatory named after her in New York's Botanical Gardens. These four acres of gardens, enclosed by the National Museum of African Art, Smithsonian Castle, the Arts and Industries Building, the Sackler and Freer galleries, and the Ripley center, provide a wonderful respite for kids after a long day of touring museums. While most children won't appreciate the central floral bed that copies the rose window design of the Smithsonian Castle, they will enjoy the fountain garden outside the African Art Museum and the large signs explaining various botanical experiments throughout the garden.

Location and Hours

Located in the inner courtyard of the Smithsonian museums on the Mall, the garden is accessible from Smithsonian and L'Enfant Plaza Metro stations (Orange or Blue Line). You can visit the Enid A. Haupt Garden from 7 A.M. Closing is determined seasonally. Admission is free.

Kenilworth Park and Aquatic Gardens

✉ 1550 Anacostia Ave. NE

🚇 Metro: Deanwood (Orange Line)

✆ 202-426-6905

🖰 www.nps.gov/nace/keaq

Kenilworth Aquatic Gardens, a twelve-acre garden devoted to water-living plants, is considered one of D.C.'s greatest natural wonders. There are more than 100,000 water plants, and more than forty ponds are filled with water lilies, lotus flowers, and other aquatic flora. Cattails and yellow flag irises edge the ponds. Completing this watery world is an interesting ecosystem of turtles, snakes, frogs, and ducks.

Bordering all this is the Kenilworth Marsh, the last remaining tidal marsh in the District. Walk the garden's River Trail for spectacular views of the marsh, the Anacostia River, and nearby wooded swamps.

Location and Hours

Not far from the U.S. National Arboretum, Kenilworth Aquatic Gardens is open to the public free of charge. Visitors are welcome to picnic in designated areas. The gardens are open daily from 7 A.M. to 4 P.M. The best time to visit is June and July to see the hardy water lilies, and July into August for tropical plants and lotuses. Take the Metro Orange Line to Deanwood.

Washington National Cathedral Gardens
✉ Massachusetts and Wisconsin Avenues NW
🚇 Tenleytown-AU (Red Line)
✆ 202-537-6200
🖰 www.cathedral.org

The Washington National Cathedral features fifty-seven acres of gardens above the city. There is a small herb garden, where visitors can purchase herbs, and the Bishop's Garden, which features magnolias, orchids, and other exquisite flowers.

═FAST FACT

The Cathedral Gardens are home to the English Tree, which, according to legend, blooms only on Christmas Day—or when British royalty visits. The tree, grown from a cutting of "The Holy Thorn of Glastonberry," has lived up to its legend. It has bloomed every Christmas and three other times: in 1951 and 1957, when Queen Elizabeth visited, and in 1981 when Prince Charles was in town.

Location and Hours
The cathedral is located at the intersection of Massachusetts and Wisconsin Avenues NW and is accessible from Tenleytown-AU Metro station (Red Line), though you should expect a fairly long walk along Wisconsin Avenue or to catch the bus.

You can stroll around the gardens on your own from 10 A.M. until sundown. For more information about visiting the cathedral, see Chapter 11.

Brookside Gardens
✉ Wheaton Regional Park, MD
🚇 Glenmont (Red Line)
✆ 301-962-1400
🖰 www.brooksidegardens.org

Just north of the city, this is a fifty-acre botanical garden with both indoor and outdoor gardens and two conservatories. Kids will love the annual summer butterfly show. There is also an annual chrysanthemum show featuring the city's landmarks, as well as animals, sculpted out of flowers.

Location and Hours

The gardens are accessible from the Glenmont Metro station (Red Line). You can visit the Gardens from sunrise to sunset any day of the year except December 25. The Visitors Center is open 9 A.M. to 5 P.M.; the Conservatories from 10 A.M., including Thanksgiving and January 1. Admission is free of charge, although fees do apply to some special programs and events.

Constitution Gardens

✉ 900 Ohio Drive SW
🚇 Metro: Farragut West (Orange or Blue Line)
✆ 202-426-6841
🖥 www.nps.gov/coga

The Constitution Gardens are composed of fifty acres of landscaped grounds, which include a lake and an island and are considered to be one of the prime picnic spots in the capital. Located near the Vietnam Veterans Memorial on the Mall, the gardens are home to 5,000 oak, maple, dogwood, elm, and crabapple trees spread over fourteen acres. The gardens also include a memorial to the signers of the Declaration of Independence. Open dawn to dusk year round. You can reach the Constitution Gardens from the Farragut West Metro station (Orange or Blue Line).

Franciscan Monastery Garden

✉ 1400 Quincy St. NE
🚇 Metro: Brookland-CUA (Red Line)
✆ 202-526-6800
🖥 www.myfranciscan.com

The Franciscan Monastery features forty acres of land planted with daffodils, flowering dogwood, cherry, and tulip trees. The garden pathways are lined with authentic replicas of Holy Land shrines. The monastery's greenhouse features hibiscus, lantanas, tiger lilies, giant caladiums and palms, and banana trees.

Location and Hours

Visit the monastery Monday through Saturday from 10 A.M. to 5 P.M. and Sunday from 1 to 4 P.M. Tours of the monastery and gardens are offered Monday to Saturday hourly (except noon) from 10 A.M. to 3 P.M., on Sunday from 1 to 3 P.M. Donation appreciated. The monastery is about three-quarters of a mile away from the Brookland/CUA Metro station (Red Line).

TRAVEL TIP

Here's another off-the-beaten-track option. Visit Gunston Hall Gardens, located just south of D.C., overlooking the Potomac. The 550 acres of gardens and wooded countryside are home to plants and shrubs that were found there during Colonial times! Open 9 A.M. to 5 P.M. For more information, call 703-550-9220 or visit *www.gunstonhall.org*.

Lady Bird Johnson Park and Lyndon Baines Johnson Memorial Grove

Metro: Arlington National Cemetery (Blue Line)
703-285-2600
www.nps.gov/lyba

The Lady Bird Johnson Park is an island in the Potomac that was built from material dredged from the river in 1916. The resulting park was named after the former first lady in 1968 in honor of her efforts to revamp Washington D.C.

The island sits at the Virginia end of the Memorial Bridge. In the spring, more than a million daffodils bloom throughout the park and along the highway. It's a great place for a picnic and view of the D.C. monuments. At the south end of the park, a fifteen-acre grove of trees was planted in honor of President Johnson and marked by a large block of pink Texas granite.

Location and Hours

To get to the island, you'll need to take the George Washington Memorial Parkway. You can also take the Blue Line Metro to the Arlington National Cemetery station (the Lyndon Baines Johnson grove is located adjacent to the Arlington National Cemetery). The park is open from sunrise to sunset. Restroom facilities are available from 7 A.M. to 10 P.M.

D.C.'s Parks

In addition to the many beautiful gardens, D.C. offers quite a few options to visitors who are interested in visiting a park—whether to see the memorials, to have a picnic, or to play frisbee with the kids.

Fort Dupont Park

✉ Minnesota and Massachusetts Avenues, SE
🚌 Metro: Potomac Avenue, then transfer to a V4 or V6 bus
✆ 202-426-7745
🖱 www.nps.gov/fodu

One of Washington's largest parks, Fort Dupont offers 376 acres of wooded land, which serve as a friendly haven for picnics, nature walks, and various outdoor sports. Although the Civil War fort itself is no more, earthworks and an explanatory plaque mark the former site. Runaway slaves found safety within its walls; Dupont was one of sixty-eight forts encircling Washington in the 1860s.

Today, the grounds feature a sizable garden, a skating rink, and a sports complex, among other amenities. A hiking-biking trail surrounds the park, while an activity center includes workshops and walks led by park rangers, nature studies, and Civil War exhibits. Most presentations are free, but there is a small charge for the ice rink and sports complex activities. Summers feature weekend jazz concerts at an outdoor stage, free to all.

🧳 TRAVEL TIP

The ruins of some of the other sixty-eight forts may be seen while walking the marked trails that make up the Fort Circle Parks. Maps are available showing the approximate location of the various forts in the ring; call the National Park Service or 202-426-7745 or see *www. nps.gov/rocr/ftcircle* for more information.

Location and Hours

The park is located between Minnesota and Massachusetts Avenues at Randle Circle. Take the Metro to Potomac Avenue station and transfer to a V4 or V6 bus. The activity center's hours are 8 A.M. to 4 P.M. Monday to Friday, Tuesday through Saturday in the summer. Best to call ahead.

Potomac Park

📞 202-426-6841

💻 *www.nps.gov/nama*

Potomac Park consists of the 722 acres of land around the Tidal Basin, surrounding most of the presidential memorials, and it's here that you will find all the lovely Japanese cherry trees. Potomac Park is divided into East Potomac and West Potomac Park.

West Potomac Park includes Constitution Gardens as well as the Vietnam Veterans, Korean War, Lincoln, and Jefferson Memorials and the reflecting pool. East Potomac Park has picnic grounds, three golf courses, a swimming pool, and biking and hiking trails overlook-

GARDENS, PARKS, AND RECREATION

ing the Potomac. At the southern tip of the park is Hains Point, which features ball fields, a golf course, picnic grounds, and *The Awakening*, the famous sculpture of a giant emerging from underground.

Rock Creek Park

✉ 5200 Glover Road NW

🚃 Metro: Friendship Heights (Red Line), transfer to E2 bus

☎ 202-895-6239 (headquarters)

☎ 202-895-6070 (Nature Center and Planetarium)

☎ 202-895-6070 (Peirce Mill)

☎ 202-426-6851 (Old Stone House)

🖱 *www.nps.gov/rocr*

Rock Creek Park, established in 1890, is one of the oldest national parks in the country and one of the largest forested urban parks in the United States. The park offers an undisturbed 1,754-acre expanse of urban forest, open fields, and creeks with running water. According to some locals, parts of it are still so wild that you can occasionally see deer in the fall and winter.

The main visitor center is the nature center and planetarium (5200 Glover Road, NW) where much of the information on the history of the park is located. You can view exhibits about the park's wildlife, visit a hands-on discovery center for children, view an observation beehive, and get your kids to participate in many child-oriented workshops and activities. The planetarium has many showings: every Wednesday at 4 P.M., "Young Planetarium," for ages two to ten; or, for the whole family, Saturday and Sunday is "The Night Sky" at 1 P.M. Also on weekends is "Exploring the Universe" at 4 P.M., best for adults and kids over seven. Programs last between forty and sixty minutes. From April through November there are meetings of the National Capital Astronomers, who hold a once-a-month evening stargazing session called "Exploring the Sky."

≡ FAST FACT

Rock Creek Park contains the Old Stone House, the oldest house in Washington D.C., and Peirce Mill (currently closed for renovations), which was once an active gristmill where corn and wheat were ground into flour using water power from Rock Creek. The park also contains Fort Stevens, the site of the only battle within the District of Columbia during the Civil War.

The park's grounds contain a wealth of hiking and biking trails, picnic facilities, tennis courts, a skating rink, horseback riding, and a golf course. Call ahead for fees and reservations.

Location and Hours

You can reach Rock Creek Park via public transportation. Take the Metro Red Line to Friendship Heights, then transfer to E2 bus, which should take you to the intersection of Glover and Military Roads.

The park is open seven days a week during daylight hours. The nature center and planetarium are open Wednesday through Sunday from 9 A.M. to 5 P.M. The Old Stone House is open Wednesday through Sunday from 9 A.M. to 4 P.M. These features are all closed New Year's Day, Fourth of July, Thanksgiving, and Christmas.

Admission to the planetarium is free, but you must pick up tickets at the nature center in advance.

The Discovery Creek Children's Museum

✉ 4954 MacArthur Blvd.

🚌 D6 Metrobus only

✆ 202-337-5111

🖥 www.discoverycreek.org

Located in the only remaining one-room schoolhouse in Washington D.C., this children's museum's focus is on interacting with nature, since it lies in the beautiful Glen Echo Park. The museum's events change seasonally, especially since so much of the program is based on interacting with nature.

Location and Hours

The children's museum is located on MacArthur Boulevard. Take the D6 Metrobus to Silbey Hospital, and get off at the intersection of MacArthur and Ashby Avenues. You can tour the schoolhouse on Saturday and Sunday from 10 A.M. to 3 P.M. and on Sunday from noon to 3 P.M. Admission is $5, $3 for seniors, and free for children under two.

Theodore Roosevelt Island

🚊 Metro: Rosslyn (Blue or Orange Line)

📞 703-285-2598

✉ www.nps.org/this

✉ www.theodoreroosevelt.org/modern/trisland.htm

Roosevelt Island is a memorial to the conservation efforts of President Teddy Roosevelt. Soon after his death in 1919, a memorial association was put together to purchase the ninety-one-acre island for this purpose.

Roosevelt Island is one of the locals' favorite places to picnic and just enjoy the wooded outdoors. There are a number of trails through the marsh, swamp, and forest where visitors can see birds and small mammals. There is also an outdoor memorial with a statue of Roosevelt, with quotes about his conservation beliefs. You can also rent canoes at Thompson Boat Center.

Location and Hours

The park is open seven days a week during daylight hours. The nearest Metro station is Rosslyn (Blue or Orange Line). Get off there, then walk across the pedestrian bridge at Rosslyn Circle. By car, take the George Washington Memorial Parkway exit north from the Theodore Roosevelt Bridge.

Sports and Recreation

D.C. is an active city where you can indulge in a variety of sports as a spectator or participant. There are hiking and biking trails, good boating of all kinds, tennis courts, golf courses, horseback riding, and more.

Hiking Paths

There are many hiking paths throughout the urban area and, therefore, many local hiking clubs. *The Washington Post* weekend section always lists hiking activities of the local clubs, which you can usually join. In addition, the C&O Canal in Georgetown has an eighteen-mile hiking path, which is fairly easy, so you can take slightly older children.

Both Rock Creek and Theodore Roosevelt Island have extensive hiking trails, but they are slightly more rugged. The hiking paths along East Potomac Park are fairly easy to navigate. There are also hiking trails in Mount Vernon.

Bike Paths

Again, check *The Washington Post* weekend section for bicycling tours, or call one of the many organized bicycling tours. (Bike the Sites, 202-966-8662, is the best known.) If you want to rent bikes and ride through a park, you can do so at Fletcher's Boat House at the C&O Canal, 202-244-0461, or at Thompson Boat Center, 202-333-9543, in Rock Creek Park. You can also rent bikes at Big Wheel Bikes, 1034 33rd Street, NW, 202-337-0254, in Georgetown, which is right near the C&O Canal and its extensive bike path.

There is also a new seven-mile bike path that takes you from Georgetown to Bethesda, Maryland, along an abandoned railroad track on the Potomac known as the Capital Crescent Trail.

Canoes and Paddle Boats

Thompson Boat Center (202-333-9543) in Rock Creek Park rents canoes, kayaks, rowing boats, and paddle boats, as long as you leave a photo ID and a credit card with your rental fee. Fletcher's

Boat House (202-244-0461) on the C&O Canal also rents canoes and rowboats and sells fishing licenses, with bait and tackle.

📖 TRAVEL TIP

You can rent a two-seater or four-seater paddleboat at the Tidal Basin. At the other end of the spectrum, you can ride the rapids of Great Falls (or watch from the shore). Info is available at 703-285-2966.

Tennis

There are public tennis courts at Rock Creek Park (202-722-5949) and East Potomac Park (202-554-5962), but you should call ahead for availability and fees. The D.C. Department of Parks and Recreation (202-673-7647) will also give you a list of other outdoor tennis courts in the district.

Ice Skating

The National Gallery of Art Sculpture Garden (202-737-4215) offers ice skating on the fountain pool in the winter. You can also skate on the C&O Canal in the winter (301-739-4200), but you must bring your own skates. Pershing Park at 14th Street and Pennsylvania Avenue (202-737-6938) also features outdoor skating.

Horseback Riding

The stables at Rock Creek (202-362-0117), near the nature center, offer a one-hour guided trail tour on Tuesday, Wednesday, and Thursday.

Fishing

Fishing in D.C.? Yep. The Potomac River is a great place for freshwater fishing with a good catch of smallmouth bass, rainbow trout, and perch. There are several fly-fishing shops and guides in Georgetown, Arlington, and Alexandria.

Sailing

The Potomac and Anacostia are relaxing and picturesque rivers for sailing. There are several marinas on the southwest waterfront, as well as in Old Town Alexandria and Arlington. Lessons and rentals are available at the Washington Sailing Marina (703-548-9027), just south of Reagan National Airport on US 1.

JUST FOR PARENTS

Golfers have a choice of three public courses in town: Rock Creek Park (202-882-7332), East Potomac Park (202-554-7600), and Langston Golf Course (202-397-8638). Call ahead for fees and information.

Professional Sports

Washington and professional sports—used to be a joke. But that was then and this is now. The District now has a wealth of strong teams of every sort, which makes for exciting sports if sometimes scarce tickets. All the teams have exciting Web sites where you may also purchase tickets, and some even let you print them out at home!

Washington Nationals

✉ Venue: RFK Stadium (until 2008)

🚇 Metro: Stadium-Armory (Orange or Blue Line)

✆ 888-632-NATS (6287)

✎ www.nationals.com

The former Montreal Expos played their first season as the Washington Nationals in 2005 with the promise of a state-of-the-art stadium within three years. That promise is rising now, a gorgeous facility in southeast D.C. on the Anacostia River. It is due for completion in 2008 at a probable cost of more than $600 million.

Washington Redskins

✉ Venue: FedEx Field, Landover, MD

🚇 Addison Road (Blue Line) or Landover or Cheverly
(Orange Line) then FedEx Shuttle

☎ 301-276-6050

🖝 *www.redskins.com*

The Redskins play football at FedEx field in nearby Landover, Maryland. Tickets are hard to come by for regular season games, but preseason games are generally available. Alternatives are ticket services like Ticketmaster or StubHub.com.

Washington Capitals

✉ Venue: Verizon Center

🚇 Gallery Place–Chinatown (Yellow, Green, or Red Line)

☎ 202-266-2350

🖝 *www.washingtoncaps.com*

Hockey fans can watch the Washington Capitals at the Verizon Center. It is possible to get tickets at the box office, over the phone, or on their Web site.

Washington Wizards

✉ Venue: Verizon Center

🚇 Gallery Place–Chinatown (Yellow, Green, or Red Line)

☎ 202-661-5100

🖝 *www.wizards.com*

If you're lucky, you might be able to catch a game with Michael Jordan's former home team at the Verizon Center.

Washington Mystics

✉ Venue: Verizon Center

🚇 Gallery Place–Chinatown (Yellow, Green, or Red Line)

☎ 202-661-5050

☎ 877-DCHOOP1

🖝 *www.washingtonmystics.com*

The Mystics are a female basketball team in the WNBA league. They share the Verizon Center with the Wizards. Supernatural!

D.C. United
✉ Venue: RFK Stadium
🚊 Metro: Stadium-Armory (Orange or Blue Line)
📞 202-587-5000
🖱 www.dcunited.com

Four-time MLS Cup champions (and counting), D.C. United play their soccer games at the RFK Stadium, but they are promoting a new 27,000-seat stadium as part of a redevelopment effort in the Poplar Point neighborhood.

Washington Freedom
✉ Venue: SoccerPlex, Germantown, MD
📞 443-259-0020

This popular women's soccer team plays in the beautiful Soccer-Plex in Germantown, MD. FanFest, their pregame promotions, are a crowd-pleaser with food, gifts, and entertainment. They start ninety minutes prior to the game.

CHAPTER 13

Shopping in D.C.

SHOPPING IN THE NATION'S capital is surprisingly diverse and exciting. Of course, there's a wealth of souvenirs available from street vendors, museum shops, and tourist attractions, but D.C. itself has a number of terrific outdoor flea markets, which offer everything from handmade jewelry to ceramics, and fabulous consignment shops, where you can buy slightly worn designer clothing. Georgetown features a wealth of trendy shops, and D.C. and the surrounding areas have a number of malls, shopping centers, and three great outlet centers. Also, Dupont Circle features an incredible collection of first-rate art galleries, offering works by local artists and internationally famous ones, as well as bookstores with a great selection of new and used books.

Markets and Fairs

Washingtonians are lucky urban dwellers. They have some of the best year-round markets and craft and food fairs in the country because of the mostly mild weather and the many farms that surround the city in neighboring Virginia and Maryland.

Eastern Market

✉ 225 7th St., SE

🚇 Metro: Eastern Market (Orange or Blue Line)

✆ 202-544-0083

✍ www.easternmarketdc.net

This is an all-week indoor market with a weekend crafts fair. Outside there are arts-and-crafts vendors (many of whom take MasterCard and/or Visa), from whom you can buy homemade jewelry, soaps, ceramics, and clothing and even get a tarot card reading. Indoors is Market Lunch, a fantastic sit-down counter with famously good blueberry buckwheat pancakes and crab cakes, and specialty meat-and-cheese shops that rival the best that New York and Paris have to offer. The market is open on Tuesday through Friday from 11 A.M. to 5 P.M., Saturday and Sunday from 8 A.M. to 5 P.M. The food merchants are open Tuesday to Saturday from 7 A.M. to 6 P.M. and Sunday from 9 A.M. to 4 P.M. The Saturday Arts & Crafts Fair and Sunday Flea Market are open 10 A.M. to 5 P.M.

Dupont Market

✉ 20th St., between Q St. and Massachusetts Ave. NW

🚇 Metro: Dupont Circle (Red Line)

✍ www.freshfarmmarket.org

This is a wonderful farmer's market with grand floral displays and wonderful homemade organic fare (sausages and cheeses) and homemade specialties (jams and even chocolates), and there are usually free samples.

Dupont Market is open every Sunday, from April through December, from 9 A.M. to 1 P.M.; and from 10 A.M. January to March.

Arlington Flea Market

🚇 2100 Clarendon Blvd., Arlington, VA

✆ 703-528-6748

Georgetown Flea Market
✉ Arlington City Courthouse Parking Lot, Arlington, VA
🚇 Metro: Court House (Orange Line)
✆ 202-775-3532
✍ www.georgetownfleamarket.com

The famed Georgetown Flea Market has moved across the Key Bridge to the nearby Arlington County (VA) Court House Metro parking lot, and is next to its sister market. They share many of the same vendors. You can browse through antiques and collectibles, from home furnishings to old records and vintage clothing, as well as nosh at the food, candy, and dessert vendors. Open year-round, weather permitting; the Saturday Arlington Flea Market is open 9 A.M. to 4 P.M. The Sunday Georgetown Flea Market opens an hour earlier. Free parking at 2100 Clarendon Blvd.

Shopping for Souvenirs

It's fun to shop for Washington souvenirs. You can bring home an array of mementos, from an FBI baseball cap purchased from a street vendor to a Hard Rock T-shirt. But it's also a lot of fun to visit the souvenir shops and see what they have to offer in terms of miniature Washington monument paperweights or commemorative plates.

Capitol Coin and Stamp
✉ 1001 Connecticut Ave., NW, Suite 745
🚇 Farragut West (Blue or Red Line)
✆ 202-296-0400
✍ http://capitolcoin.com

This is a shop that specializes in political paraphernalia, so it's perfect for the nation's capital. The merchandise here is unique and reasonably priced (the owner is nice, too), mainly post–World War II objects, although there are items going as far back as Lincoln's time. The offerings include buttons, bumper stickers, and presidential items, as well as autographs, photos, coins, and a lot more. Capitol Coin and Stamp is open Monday to Friday, 10 A.M. to 6 P.M.

💼 TRAVEL TIP

T-shirt wagons and souvenir stands line the side streets of the Mall and the streets along 10th and F Streets surrounding Ford's Theatre and the Petersen House. If you are planning on taking T-shirts and hats to the folks back home, these street vendors offer a good selection at a fraction of the cost of more expensive locations.

Destination D.C.
✉ 50 Massachusetts Ave. NE
🚇 Metro: Union Station (Red Line)
✆ 202-789-2365

Destination D.C. offers everything your heart could desire in T-shirts and sweats and D.C.-related souvenirs such as postcards, buttons, and sports bottles. Most items are under $15. Destination D.C. is located at Union Station; another branch can be found at the Fashion Center, Pentagon City, in Arlington, Virginia (703-415-4115).

Museum Shops

For some people, shopping the museum stores can be one of the high points of their trip to Washington. You can find unusual items, at fairly low prices, for just about everyone on your holiday gift list, no matter what time of the year you're shopping. For details on operating hours and directions, check the main museum listings.

The National Building Museum
✉ 401 F St. NW
🚇 Metro: Judiciary Square (Red Line)

☎ 202-272-7706 (shop)
🖰 *www.nbm.com*

Why did *The Washington Post* vote this the best museum gift shop in D.C.? It offers a mind-blowing selection of unique children's gifts, items for home and office, books, posters, and accessories you never knew existed. Many of these are available on the Internet as well.

👥 JUST FOR PARENTS

Adams Morgan and Capitol Hill are the two neighborhoods known for their antiques, even if they're less than fifty years old. You can't possibly go home empty-handed. And you'll have a great time exploring.

The International Spy Museum
✉ 800 F Street NW
🚇 Metro: Gallery Place–Chinatown (Red, Yellow, or Green Line)
☎ 202-393-7798
☎ 866-779-6873
🖰 *www.spymuseum.org*

The International Spy Museum gift shop has a fun array of spying gadgets for kids and grownups, as well as clever spy-related jewelry, apparel, items from classic television shows, home and office accessories, books, electronics, toys and games, and lots more.

The National Gallery of Art
✉ 6th Street and Constitution Ave. NW
🚇 Metro: Archives (Yellow or Green Line)
☎ 202-737-4215
🖰 *www.nga.gov*

The National Gallery of Art's gift shops feature calendars, note cards, journals, wall plaques, scarves, and jewelry based on the permanent collection, and there are always some items on sale. Don't miss the Children's Shop in the Concourse.

The Corcoran Gallery of Art

✉ 500 17th St. NW
🚇 Metro: Farragut West (Orange or Blue Line)
✆ 202-639-1700
✐ www.corcoran.org

The Corcoran gift shop offers a wonderful, somewhat wacky collection of art-related jewelry (often connected to a show), as well as a great selection of pop art dishes and glassware, and fun children's art projects. The Corcoran Gallery is located on 17th Street NW, between E Street and New York Avenue.

The Phillips Collection

✉ 1600 21st St. NW, at Q Street
🚇 Metro: Dupont Circle (Red Line)
✆ 202-387-2151
✐ www.phillipscollection.org

If you're interested in things like Man Ray teacups and a great bag with Marjorie Phillips's impressionist painting of American baseball, be sure to stop at the Phillips eclectic gift shop when you visit the museum.

The National Museum of Women in the Arts

✉ 1250 New York Ave. NW
🚇 Metro: Metro Center (Red, Orange, or Blue Line)
✆ 1-877-226-5294
✆ 202-783-5000
✐ www.nmwa.org

The gift shop of the National Museum of Women in the Arts has a well-stocked Just for Kids selection. Its forte is an interesting selection of jewelry, women-empowering note cards and journals, glassware, handbags, and lots of hard-to-find books about female artists. There is an annual sidewalk sale in August.

The Smithsonian Institution Museums

✆ 202-633-1000 (general)

✍ www.si.edu

And then, of course, there are the fabulous Smithsonian Institution museums, including the National Air and Space Museum, the National Museum of Natural History, and the National Museum of American History (which has been closed for renovation). Each of them is a shopper's delight, and you could easily spend an hour browsing in each one. Air and Space (on 6th Street and Independence Ave.) is a three-floor museum, and has the astronaut ice cream and every *Star Trek*–related model you could ever want.

≡FAST FACT

The Smithsonian Institution offers a wide variety of unique merchandise for sale, some based on its collections (want George Washington's wine bottle coaster?). You can order directly from them through its extensive four-color catalog or Web site. You'll find everything from toys and games to furniture reproductions, jewelry, prints, and clothing. You can order the catalog by calling 1-800-322-0344, or going to *www.smithsonianstore.com*.

The Museum of American History (between 12th and 14th Streets on Constitution Avenue) sells an excellent array of toys and crafts, historic reproductions (famous newspapers are popular), clothing, accessories, books, CDs, furniture, and home accents. Plans are to keep the shops operating as much as possible during the museum's renovation. You can buy dinosaur-fossil-making kits at the National Museum of Natural History (on 10th Street and Constitution Avenue), as well as those fantastic Smithsonian science-project kits. But the jewel of the place is a replica of the Hope diamond for *considerably* less than the real thing.

Malls and Department Stores

Most D.C. department stores are located in malls throughout the city and suburbs; the one exception is Macy's (which recently merged with the fifty-year-old local independent Hecht's and changed its name), the only D.C. department store that stands on its own. Its store, located at 12th and G Streets, has been at that location for more than fifty years, and from there its holiday display windows have delighted city residents for decades.

Cady's Alley
✉ 3318 M St. NW, Georgetown
✑ www.cadysalley.com

Cady's Alley is a group of converted nineteenth-century buildings that are home to seventeen home furnishing and décor shops.

Chevy Chase Pavilion
✉ 5355 Wisconsin Ave. NW
✆ 202-686-5335
✑ www.ccpavilion.com

Mazza Gallerie
✉ 5300 Wisconsin Ave. NW
🚊 Metro: Friendship Heights (Red Line)
✆ 202-966-6114
✑ www.mazzagallerie.com

These upscale malls are neighbors in the shopping neighborhood of Friendship Heights and include more than forty-five specialty shops. There is a Georgette Klinger spa and Filene's Basement, a wonderful discount store. You'll find browsing fun at places like

Villeroy & Boch, Krön Chocolatier, and Neiman Marcus. There's also a movie theater. Open Monday to Friday, 10 A.M. to 8 P.M., Saturday to 7 P.M., and Sunday, noon to 5 P.M.

Fashion Centre at Pentagon City
✉ 1100 Hayes St., Arlington, VA
🚇 Metro: Pentagon City (Yellow or Blue Line)
☎ 703-415-2401
🖰 www.fashioncentrepentagon.com

This is a mega-mall, located near the Pentagon. There are more than 160 shops here, with Macy's and Nordstrom as the anchors. There is a food court here as well. Open Monday to Saturday, 10 A.M. to 9:30 P.M.; Sunday, 11 A.M. to 6 P.M.

The Shops at Georgetown Park
✉ 3222 M St. NW
🚇 Metro: Foggy Bottom (Orange or Blue Line)
☎ 202-298-5577
🖰 www.shopsatgeorgetownpark.com

This is a lovely mall inside a rehabbed former Colonial-era tobacco warehouse. There are full-service restaurants and snack spots where you can get pretzels and coffee, and wonderfully original stores as well as chain store offerings, such as Benetton and J. Crew. Hours are Monday to Saturday, 10 A.M. to 9 P.M.; Sunday, noon to 6 P.M.

Union Station
✉ 50 Massachusetts Ave. NE
🚇 Metro: Union Station (Red Line)
☎ 202-371-9441
🖰 www.unionstationdc.com

There are at least 150 stores here, from 9 West and B. Dalton to GuGuGaGa and a Discovery Channel store. If you go to the Web site, there is a printable coupon for 15 percent off at many of the stores.

Keeping the kids happy are a forty-kiosk food court on the lower level and a nine-screen cinema. Open Monday to Saturday, 10 A.M. to 9 P.M.; Sunday, noon to 6 P.M.

Outlet Shopping

One of the best things about outlet shopping is that if you are a truly savvy shopper, you'll come prepared with coupons to save money on already marked-down merchandise. If you can't find your own coupons, locate the customer service desk and ask if it has any. Sometimes all you have to do is show your AAA membership card.

Leesburg Corner Premium Outlets
✉ 241 Fort Evans Rd., Leesburg, VA
✆ 703-737-3071
🖱 www.outletsonline.com

This outlet, just past Dulles Airport, offers more than 100 popular designer shops at up to 70 percent off, such as Calvin Klein, Tommy Hilfiger, a Gap outlet, and an Off Saks Fifth Avenue store. There are also a limited number of specialty shops selling children's toys (K-B Toy Outlet), clothes, and shoes.

Take Route 267 (Dulles Toll Rd./Greenway) or Route 7 to Route 15 North. Follow the signs, and turn right at the top of Fort Evans Road. Stores are open Monday through Saturday from 9 A.M. to 9 P.M. and on Sunday from 10 A.M. to 7 P.M.

🧳 TRAVEL TIP

Most outlet centers have a Web site where you might be able to download a certificate for a coupon book or an individual store. There might be a coupon for additional discounts in a local magazine or tourist guide. Also ask at the outlet information desk.

Prime Outlets, Hagerstown

✉ 495 Prime Outlets Blvd., Hagerstown, MD

✆ 301-790-0300

✆ 1-888-883-6288

☞ www.primeoutlets.com

Seventy-five minutes outside D.C., this outlet and discount center houses more than 100 designer and specialty stores, many of the same stores as Leesburg, and many specializing in children (Gymboree, Children's Place Outlet, Gap Kids/BabyGap, K-B Toys). Go to the Web site or find a customer service booth for discount coupons.

Take I-495 to I-270, which leads to I-70, and exit 29 will get you to Hagerstown Outlet Center. The outlets at Hagerstown are open Monday through Saturday from 10 A.M. to 9 P.M. and on Sunday from 10 A.M. to 7 P.M. Closed Easter, Thanksgiving Day, and Christmas.

Tyson's Corner Center

✉ 1961 Chain Bridge Rd., McLean, VA

✆ 703-847-7300

✆ 1-888-2TYSONS

☞ www.shoptysons.com

Tyson's Galleria

✉ 2001 International Dr., McLean, VA

✆ 703-827-7700

☞ www.tysonsgalleria.com

With more than 400 stores within seven miles of the city, Tyson's is where D.C. goes to shop. These two malls are not connected, and you can't walk from one to the other. The major department stores at Tyson's Corner are Bloomingdale's, Nordstrom's, and Lord & Taylor as well as The Gap, L.L. Bean, Coach, and a ton of children's shops, including a Disney Store. There are many places to eat, covering fast food, ethnic, and family-friendly restaurants. The Galleria is smaller and more upscale (its kids' stores are Jacadi and Oilily), and the anchors are Macy's, Neiman Marcus, and Saks Fifth Avenue.

Restaurants include the Cheesecake Factory, Legal Seafoods, and several ethnic eateries.

If you e-mail or call, you may be able to get a coupon book to use at various stores, depending on what promotion is running. Visit their Web sites for sales and events news. Take the Capital Beltway (I-495) to exit 46A or 47A. Tyson's Center is open Monday through Saturday from 10 A.M. to 9:30 P.M. and Sunday from 11 A.M. to 6 P.M. The Galleria is open Monday to Saturday, 10 A.M. to 9 P.M., and Sunday, noon to 6 P.M.

Bookstores

If you love books, Washington D.C. is your town. It has some terrific bookstores, from the serious to the quirky.

A Likely Story Children's Books

✉ 1555 King St., Alexandria, VA

🚇 Metro: King Street (Yellow or Blue Line)

✆ 703-836-2498

✍ www.alikelystorybooks.com

Child magazine called this store the best children's bookstore in the country. It's well stocked and has a regular series of readings and character presentations. Call or see the Web site for programs. You can get to the bookstore via the Metro; get off at King Street (Yellow or Blue Line) and walk two blocks east. Open Monday to Saturday, 10 A.M. to 6 P.M.; Sunday, 1 P.M. to 5 P.M. It has extended summer hours.

Chapters: A Literary Bookstore

✉ 445 11th Street NW

🚇 Metro: Federal Triangle (Orange or Blue Line)

✆ 202-737-5553

✍ www.chaptersliterary.com

This is a national monument to the importance of reading books and a dying breed. Chapters is a very literary bookstore (*literary* meaning fiction, poetry, belles lettres, foreign language) where authors frequently come to give free readings—check with the bookstore or the Web site about the schedule. Every July, Chapters holds a birthday party for Proust, and on Fridays there are free cookies, tea, and sherry.

Idle Time Books

✉ 2467 18th St. NW
🚇 Metro: Woodley Park (Red Line)
✆ 202-232-4774
🖰 www.abebook.com/home/idletime

Located in Adams Morgan, here are three floors containing 50,000 quality used paperback and hardcover books of every description, including children's. You can get former bestsellers for a few dollars. You'll have to hunt, but it's worth your time (and fun, too).

Kramerbooks and Afterwords Café & Grill

✉ 1517 Connecticut Ave. NW
🚇 Metro: Dupont Circle (Red Line)
✆ 202-387-1400
🖰 www.kramers.com

This has been a Washington institution since 1976. Some people spend the better part of their day at this cyber café, bookstore, and restaurant in Dupont Circle. The food's good and moderately priced; the people-watching is the best; the books, of course, are wonderful. A caution is that the ambiance (the menus and promo posters) tend to be a bit risqué—you should check the Web site before visting. It serves daily breakfast, lunch, dinner, and late supper; there's brunch on the weekends. Open daily 7:30 A.M. to 1 A.M.; open twenty-four hours on Friday and Saturday nights.

Lantern Bryn Mawr Bookshop

✉ 3241 P St. NW
✆ 202-333-3222
🖰 www.his.com/~lantern

This Georgetown used bookstore is a favorite for local university students, because you can purchase slightly worn hardcovers for as little as $3 and paperbacks for $1. Old records (lots of '70s rock) and used CDs are also available. Open weekdays, 11 A.M. to 4 P.M.; Saturday to 5 P.M.; Sunday, noon to 4 P.M.

Politics and Prose Bookstore and Coffeehouse

✉ 5015 Connecticut Ave. NW

🚊 Metro: Van Ness (Red Line), and walk 1 mile north or take the L1 or L2 bus

✆ 1-800-722-0790

✆ 202-364-1919

✍ www.politics-prose.com

Another Dupont Circle institution, even D.C. politicians come here to shop for books on history, political theory, and scandal. The store daily, and sometimes twice daily, features heavy-duty political speakers and heated discussions, so call or check the Web site for events and scheduling. Also see the site's children's page. Open Monday to Thursday, 9 A.M. to 10 P.M.; Friday and Saturday to 1 P.M.; Sunday, 10 A.M. to 8 P.M. Take the Red Line to Van Ness, walk one mile (fifteen minutes) north, or take the L1 or L2 bus from the Metro.

Consignment Shops and Thrift Stores

If you have a teenager who's looking for "retro" clothing, or if you're interested in finding a classic Coach bag for yourself, D.C.'s consignment shops and thrift stores are gold mines.

Clothes Encounters of a Second Kind

✉ 202 7th St. SE

🚊 Metro: Eastern Market (Orange or Blue Line)

✆ 202-546-4004

This is a great consignment shop where you can find bags and shoes and designer suits for a fraction of their original cost. The shop is located across the street from the Eastern Market and is accessible from the Eastern Market Metro station (Orange or Blue Line). Hours are Tuesday to Friday, 11 A.M. to 7 P.M.; Saturday, 10 A.M. to 6 P.M.; Sunday, noon to 5 P.M.

Funk & Junk

✉ 106½ N. Columbus St., Alexandria, VA
🚇 Metro: King Street station (Yellow or Blue Line)
📞 703-836-0749
🖱 www.funkandjunk.com

This store has an amazing assortment of collectibles of every kind. There are thousands of pieces of men's and women's vintage clothing alone—jeans, shirts, shoes, coats. They also have action figures, collectible toys, you name it. Funk & Junk is located in Alexandria, but you can reach it via the Metro (King Street station on the Yellow or Blue Line). Open Thursday to Saturday, 1 P.M. to 6 P.M.; Sunday, 1 P.M. to 6 P.M.

Secondi Consignment Clothing

✉ 1702 Connecticut Ave. NW
🚇 Metro: Dupont Circle (Red Line)
📞 202-667-1122

Secondi is a store that specializes in secondhand designer clothing, shoes, and accessories. It's open Monday, Tuesday, Thursday, and Saturday, 11 A.M. to 6 P.M.; Wednesday and Friday to 7 P.M.; Sunday, 1 P.M. to 5 P.M.

Toy Stores

Washington D.C. has a number of delightful independent toy stores that are thriving because the chain toy stores are located in the malls on the outskirts of the city. Many of the stores have a regular program of readings and milk and cookies, so call before you visit.

🧳 TRAVEL TIP

Although the District has so many museums and museum stores, even in airports and locations throughout the city, it's hard to find a regular chain toy store in the city itself. You have to go to the suburbs to find a Toys R Us or K-B Toys.

Child's Play

✉ 5536 Connecticut Ave. NW
🚇 Metro: Friendship Heights (Red Line)
☎ 202-244-3602

Located in the Friendship Heights neighborhood, this toy store features building toys, computer software, art supplies, and games. Winter hours are 9:30 A.M. to 7 P.M. daily, Thursdays to 8 P.M. Summer hours are shortened slightly. It's about six blocks from the Metro. Call for alternate directions and current hours.

Sullivan's Toy Store

✉ 4312 Wisconsin Ave. NW
🚇 Metro: Tenleytown (Red Line)
☎ 202-362-1343

This is a terrific little store for younger children featuring learning games, costumes, stickers, and a great selection of books and stuffed animals. There is an art-supply store next door that might be of interest to slightly older children. Open Monday, Tuesday, and Saturday from 10 A.M. to 7 P.M.; Wednesday to Friday, to 7 P.M.; Sunday, noon to 5 P.M.

Tree Tops Toys

✉ 3301 New Mexico Ave. NW
🚇 Metro: Farragut West (Orange or Blue Line)
☎ 202-244-3500

This store specializes in plush dolls, European toys, books, and even children's clothing. Open Monday to Saturday, 10 A.M. to 5 P.M.

Other Specialty Shops

From a magic shop your kids are sure to enjoy to a comics store and vegan products center, here are a few other shops worth a visit.

Barry's Magic Shop
✉ 11234 Georgia Ave., Wheaton, Maryland
🚇 Metro: Wheaton (Red Line)
✆ 301-933-0373
🖰 *www.barrysmagicshop.com*

Visiting Barry's is an entertainment in itself. Barry and Susan Taylor have held sway here since 1974. They carry a full range of magic supplies, from the simplest to the most cutting-edge. You'll also find new and out-of-print books, videos, props, and rare, hard-to-find tricks. Open Tuesday to Saturday, 11 A.M. to 6 P.M.

💼 TRAVEL TIP

You don't have to spend big bucks just because you're a tourist. Like any big city, Washington D.C. is home to numerous dollar stores. They come and they go, but you can find a current list at *http://localdc.com/dollaritems.htm*.

Big Planet Comics
✉ 3145 Dumbarton Ave., NW
✆ 202-342-1961

If you're in Georgetown and interested in comic books, this store is a classic. You can get the latest graphic novels and comics, as well as back issues of the old DC and Marvel comics here. Open Monday to Friday, 11 A.M. to 7 P.M., Wednesday to 8 P.M., Saturday to 6 P.M.; Sunday, noon to 5 P.M.

Pangea

✉ 2381 Lewis Ave., Rockville, Maryland

🚇 Metro: Twinbrook (Red Line)

📞 301-816-8955

📞 1-800-340-1200

🖱 www.veganstore.com

If any of your family are vegetarians or vegans, this is the place to shop, with animal-friendly products you never thought existed: non-leather shoes, belts, wallets, jackets; vegan foods and candy; body care products; and books. Open Saturday and Sunday only, from 11 A.M. to 6 P.M. Call or see their Web site for full directions.

CHAPTER 14

Family Dining

WASHINGTON D.C. IS NOT often known as a restaurant town, but don't kid yourself—it is a great place to eat. There are more than 2,000 restaurants in the capital, and with so many to choose from there is a restaurant for every palate, from haute cuisine to Japanese teahouses to cafeterias. The museum restaurants can also be surprisingly good, and many of the hotel restaurants are family-friendly.

The restaurants in this chapter are geared toward sit-down family dining with slightly older children, ages seven and up. For families with younger children, the chain or hotel restaurants are probably your best bet for dinner. Of course, the iron-clad rule applies—*call ahead.*

Downtown D.C.

Andale
✉ 401 7th St. NW
🚊 Metro: National Archives (Yellow or Green Line)
✆ 202-783-3133

At publication, this trendy hotspot was closed for renovation. Washington D.C. Chef Alison Swope made the top lists serving up contemporary Mexican food that was original and creative. Call to check when it reopens. Reservations are suggested.

Arena Cafe

✉ 521 G St. NW

🚇 Metro: Gallery Place (Red, Yellow or Green Line)

📞 202-789-2055

Near the Verizon Center, this restaurant that looks like a diner from the outside is a real treat. It is known for its excellent salads, great crab cake sandwiches, and a full selection of beers. Entrees run $12 to $20. Major credit cards are accepted.

Bistro Bis

✉ 15th E St. NW (in Hotel George)

🚇 Metro: Union Station (Red Line)

📞 202-661-2700

🖱 www.vidaliadc/bistro

Located in the trendy Hotel George, part of the Kimpton Hotel chain, Bis has been one of the hottest restaurants in town for the past few years, so make reservations. Its food is Parisian bistro with an American flair, as evidenced by such entrees as calamari with chorizo or duck breast with olives and citrus fruit. Still, the hotel chain is exceedingly family-friendly, and there should be items on the menu for all age groups. Entrees range from $22 to $32. Major credit cards are accepted.

💼 TRAVEL TIP

Special attire recommendations (now rare—"business casual" has become the new "jacket and tie") or no shorts are noted in the reviews. Otherwise, you should be able to wear whatever you have on while sightseeing.

Capital Grille

✉ 601 Pennsylvania Ave. NW
🚇 Metro: National Archives (Yellow or Green Line)
📞 202-737-6200
🖰 *www.thecapitalgrille.com*

This is a popular bar and restaurant, part of a multicity chain, where locals eat and hang out. Noted for its steaks and dry-aged cuts of beef, there's an aging room on the premises with sides of beef hanging on display. It also serves lobster, large portions of fish, and generous side dishes. Some seats have a view of the Capitol building. Entrees run $31 to $39. Jacket and tie are strongly suggested. Major credit cards are accepted.

Coeur de Lion

✉ 926 Massachusetts Ave. NW (in the Henley Park Hotel)
🚇 Metro: Metro Center (Red, Orange or Blue Line)
📞 202-414-0500 or 202-638-5200
🖰 *www.henleypark.com/dining.htm*

Located in the Henley Park Hotel, this restaurant is ideal for romantic couples, which is precisely why older children (especially teenage girls) might like it. Coeur de Lion is a local favorite because of its romantic, elegant décor and cozy atmosphere, and it serves a wonderfully rich continental cuisine with an American flair. The cognac-flavored lobster bisque is a favorite, and so are the crab cakes, but the menu changes seasonally, and there are a lot of lighter entrees. Desserts are a specialty, so save room for the cheesecake, crème brulée, or a seasonal winner like the chocolate pecan tart. Entrees run $22 to $35. For men, a jacket is required. This is an intimate restaurant with candlelight tables, so reservations are recommended. Major credit cards are accepted.

D.C. Coast

✉ 1401 K St. NW
🚇 Metro: McPherson Square (Orange or Blue Line)

✆ 202-216-5988
✍ www.dccoast.com

This is one of the hottest restaurants in town, so don't even think about going without making reservations. Set in the Tower Building, the art deco interior with its two-story dining room and glass-enclosed balcony make the place airy, and the bronze mermaid at the door lets you know you're in for some fun, too. Seafood is a specialty here—if they are available, try the crab cakes, tuna tartare, or Chinese smoked lobster—and there are also some hearty entrees like the double-cut pork chop. Entrees run $19 to $29. Major credit cards are accepted.

ESPN Zone

✉ 555 12th Street NW, at E Street
🚇 Metro: Metro Center (Red, Orange, or Blue Line)
✆ 202-783-3776
✍ www.espnzone.com/washingtondc

There are enough sports activities here to satisfy any fan-atic. Everything here is over-the-top—200 sports-tuned TVs, even in the restrooms, including a 15-foot projection screen; 10,000 sq. ft. of interactive games and attractions. Oh, and the food . . . six chefs prepare a huge menu of some fifty items with enough choice to make everybody happy: steak, chicken, shrimp, salads, pizza, and a separate kids' menu.

Equinox

✉ 818 Connecticut Ave. NW
🚇 Metro: Farragut West (Orange or Blue Line)
✆ 202-331-8118
✍ www.equinoxrestaurant.com

Founded by Todd Gray, one of chef Roberto Donna's disciples, this is another hot restaurant. The food is American bistro fare with a wide variety of creative choices, but this is an exciting place with a changing menu. Currently, the big thing is a tasting menu with three, four, or six courses . . . quite an adventure. A flavored butter is served with your bread basket, and homemade cookies are served after the meal, so you don't need any other dessert. Entrees run $28 to $34, but lunch is cheaper. Major credit cards are accepted.

Georgia Brown's
✉ 950 15th St. NW
🚇 Metro: McPherson Square (Orange or Blue Line)
✆ 202-393-4499
🖰 *www.gbrowns.com*

This restaurant offers Southern cooking that everyone loves (entrées range from $15 to $36 for filet mignon). Signature dishes include shrimp and grits, Southern fried chicken, and bourbon pecan pie, and there are also vegetarian selections. The brunch is considered one of the best in the city ($32.95 per person; $21.95, children twelve and under). Major credit cards are accepted. Parking is available.

≡FAST FACT

We would have recommended the seafood restaurant Grillfish (1200 New Hampshire Ave. NW, Metro: Foggy Bottom [Orange or Blue Line]) for its good food, casual atmosphere, and kids' and vegetarian menus, but the restaurant is dominated by a huge erotic painting (you can preview it at *www.grillfishdc.com*). Entrées go for $11 to $26, and the kids' menu for about $5.50.

Hard Rock Cafe
✉ 999 E St. NW
🚇 Metro: Metro Center (Red, Orange, or Blue Line)
✆ 202-737-7625
🖰 *www.hardrock.com*

The Washington branch of the famous Hard Rock chain calls itself "The Embassy of Rock and Roll." This theme restaurant is located right around the corner from Ford's Theatre and the Petersen House, and it might be a good lunch stop for children or teens who are tired of "ancient" history. It serves average American fare in a fun atmosphere jam-packed with rock memorabilia. Clever items on the menu include Tupelo chicken with barbecue sauce and honey mustard, the Jumbo Combo of rings, rolls, and chicken, Mad Anthony's (of Van Halen) grilled skirt steak, as well as burgers, chili, and pizza. The kids' menu includes macaroni and cheese, pizza, hot dogs, fresh breaded chicken fingers, or a cheese sandwich for $6.99, with a souvenir cup.

≡FAST FACT

The kids will love this rock-stuffed place, and so will you. Some of the memorabilia on view is an outfit worn by Gene Simmons of KISS, complete with fangs and leather cape; signed guitars by Jimmy Page (Led Zeppelin), Pete Townshend, Gidget Gein (bassist for Marilyn Manson), Bob Dylan, Lenny Kravitz, and Seal; and tons of other interesting items.

An amusing painting depicts George Washington in a Hard Rock T-shirt. Other items of interest include some of Elvis's gold records and the saxophone President Clinton played at his 1993 inauguration, signed by the president and many celebrities, including Michael Jackson. The souvenir shop on the premises sells a very cute D.C. T-shirt featuring the Capitol and the Washington Monument ($24). Major credit cards are accepted. There is a coupon in various hotel handouts for a free souvenir with the purchase of an entree.

Legal Seafoods
⊠ 704 7th St. NW
🚇 Metro: Metro Center (Red, Orange, or Blue Line)
✆ 202-347-0007
🖋 www.legalseafoods.com

Located on the outskirts of Chinatown, near Verizon Center, this is a Boston-based seafood chain that has won awards for its kids' menu, which offers macaroni and cheese, hot dogs, hamburgers, and a kid's portion of steamed lobster, popcorn shrimp, or a small fisherman's platter of shrimp, clams, and scallops. The kids' menu runs from $1.50 to $16.95 on the upper end for the 1-pound lobster.

The clam chowder is highly regarded, and the fresh fish is always good. Boston cream pie is always served. Dinner runs anywhere from $12 to $43. Major credit cards are accepted.

🧳 TRAVEL TIP

Another branch of Legal Seafoods is located at 2020 K Street NW, (202-496-1111). It was actually the first to open, in 1995, and the eatery proved so successful that four more followed (on 7th Street; at Tyson's Galleria in McLean, VA; in Crystal City, VA; and in Bethesda, MD).

Les Halles
✉ 1201 Pennsylvania Ave. NW
🚆 Metro: Federal Triangle (Orange or Blue Line)
✆ 202-347-6848
🖊 www.leshalles.net/washington.php

This is an offshoot of rogue-chef Anthony Bourdain's famous restaurant of the same name, classic French with an emphasis on beef and desserts. The décor is authentically French, with lace curtains, a homey wooden interior, and popular French songs playing in the background. The fare is mainly beef, which is well prepared—the filet with béarnaise sauce is divine—but there are also other traditionally French items on the menu, such as cassoulet and a marvelous onion soup, which is a meal in itself. It also features rich and wonderful desserts, such as a chocolate souffle. The children's menu is $8.50–$9.50 and they can order an appetizer. Entrées go from $15.50–$26 ($48 for a big double ribeye for two). It runs a huge, day-long, don't-miss bash on Bastille Day (see Appendix A) as part of a Liberty Festival that starts July 4. Major credit cards are accepted.

M & S Grill

✉ 600 13th St. at E St. NW

🚇 Metro: Metro Center (Red, Orange, or Blue Line)
   or Gallery Place (Red, Yellow, or Green Line)

📞 202-347-1500

🖥 www.McCormickandSchmicks.com/DC

This is the surf-and-turf sister restaurant of McCormick & Schmick's (see below), and it's right near Verizon Center. This one is a little more relaxed and much heavier on the meat (ribs and steaks abound). There's a weekday happy-hour special of $2 appetizers and plenty of sandwiches from $10 to $15. Entrées run $15.85 to $30.75. Major credit cards are accepted.

McCormick & Schmick's Seafood Restaurant

✉ 1652 K St. at Connecticut Ave. NW

🚇 Metro: Farragut North (Red Line)
   or Farragut West (Orange or Blue Line)

📞 202-861-2233

🖥 www.McCormickandSchmicks.com/DC

Part of an Oregon chain, this is one of the better restaurants in town. It features linen tablecloths and fancy chandeliers, but dress is casual. People come here for the oyster bar and the crab cakes, and the desserts are highly recommended. There is an all-day light-fare menu with entrees under $10; otherwise, entrees are priced from $12.95 to $42. A weekday happy hour from 3:30 to 6:30 P.M. offers appetizers for about $2 (with a two-drink minimum), which makes this a very popular after-work hangout. Another branch is at 901 F Street NW, 202-639-9330, Metro: Gallery Place (Red, Yellow, or Green Line). Major credit cards are accepted

Morrison-Clark Historic Inn Restaurant

✉ 1015 L St. NW, at L Street

🚇 Metro: Metro Center (Red, Orange, or Blue Line),
  but be prepared for a bit of a walk

✆ 1-800-332-7898

✎ www.morrisonclark.com

This is a class act, with award-winning creative cuisine served amid Victorian décor in a historic landmark. The menu changes seasonally; some past winners are goat cheese and phyllo rolls or wild mushroom fritters ($9), as well as the many delicious desserts such as the homemade chocolate napoleon and Martha Washington Pear-Gingerbread Cake with white chocolate mousse and roasted pears ($8). Entrees also change from season to season, but the menu offers a full array of fish, beef, duck, rabbit, pork, and lamb on a regular basis, and runs $20 to $36. All the ice cream is made on the premises.

Reservations are strongly suggested since the dining area only seats about forty people, and this restaurant is popular with the local crowd for business lunches and romantic dinners. Major credit cards are accepted.

Old Ebbitt Grill

✉ 675 15th St. NW

🚇 Metro: McPherson Square (Orange or Blue Line)
  or Metro Center (Red, Orange or Blue Line)

✆ 202-347-4800

✎ www.ebbitt.com

Now part of the Clyde's chain, this very old Washington watering hole is still a popular place for the power lunch crowd and is well known for its brunches. Because of its location, this is a great place to catch a sit-down meal, especially if you are touring the White House.

Clyde's was opened as a saloon in 1856 and has moved several times since, but it retains its venerable patina, with etched-glass partitions and paneled wooden booths surrounded by political memorabilia, such as Teddy Roosevelt's animal trophies and Alexander Hamilton's wooden bears. While a restaurant this old has standards that regulars return for—the burgers, the New England clam chowder, and the Maryland crab cakes—the menu does vary seasonally, and it is said that this is the only place in Washington where you can get fresh Alaskan halibut when it's in season.

Kids can choose from the $6 kids' menu (price includes tons of choices plus milk or soft drink and ice cream or fresh fruit), and the sandwiches are generous. Lunch runs $8.95 to $15.95. Entrees are $10 to $24. This is one of the few restaurants downtown that serves breakfast ($9.95 to $13.95); Sunday brunch is $4.95 to $18.95. Major credit cards are accepted.

═FAST FACT

Old Ebbitt Grill has been a favorite watering hole of presidents, political insiders, journalists, celebrities, and theater-goers during its many moves since 1856. Its clientele has included: Presidents Grant, Cleveland, Harding, Theodore Roosevelt, and Clinton; and celebs such as Clint Eastwood and the Rolling Stones.

Oval Room

✉ 800 Connecticut Ave. NW
🚇 Metro: Farragut West (Orange or Blue Line)
✆ 202-463-8700
🖥 www.ovalroom.com

The Oval Room is located within walking distance of the White House. Inside, you'll find some charming murals of Washington D.C., past and present (presidents and Hollywood stars). The restaurant's soups are highly recommended, and so are the tuna tartare and crab-cake appetizers; there's also a wide selection of meat and seafood entrees. Entrees run $14 to $29. Major credit cards are accepted. Casual dress. Complimentary valet parking is available with dinner.

Palette

✉ 15th and M Streets NW
🚇 Metro: Metro Center (Red, Orange, or Blue Line)
📞 202-587-2700
🖱 www.palettedc.com

The Palette offers modern American cuisine to rave reviews, but it's not a place for younger kids. Diners enjoy signature dishes while viewing art exhibits on loan from private galleries. The ever-changing and smartly creative menu can be viewed at their Web site. Creativity expands to the drink menu as well. The signature drink, Palette, is mixed from Grey Goose l'Orange Vodka with Chambord and a splash of pineapple juice. Meals run $12 to $32, but there is lighter fare in the lounge area. Major credit cards are accepted.

Pier 7

✉ 650 Water St. SW (in the Channel Inn Hotel at Maine Ave. and 7th St., Waterfront)
🚇 Metro: Waterfront (Green Line)
📞 202-554-2500
🖱 www.channelin.com

This restaurant offers a wonderful waterfront dining experience with panoramic views of the Potomac and various monuments. Pier 7 is known for its seafood, such as the crab cakes and bouillabaisse, but there is also a wide selection of pastas and meat dishes on the menu, as well as a pretheater prix fixe menu. Entrees run $19 to $32. Live jazz Sunday nights. Major credit cards are accepted.

🧳 TRAVEL TIP

When traveling, and even in your own hometown, lunch is a good way to experience some of a city's more expensive or trendy restaurants without having to pay top dollar.

Poste

✉ 558 8th St. NW
🚇 Metro: Gallery Place–Chinatown (Red, Yellow, or Green Line)
📞 202-783-6060
💻 www.postebrasserie.com

Located in the trendy Hotel Monaco, former home of the Tariff Building, Poste is an American brasserie that features a wonderful selection of seasonal meals for breakfast, brunch, lunch, pretheater, and dinner. There's a select choice of meat, poultry, fish, and game beautifully prepared by Chef Robert Weland, formerly of New York's Guastavino's. The desserts are magnificent and seasonal. For adults there might be a raspberry rhubarb soup with lemongrass tapioca and spiced tuiles, and for the kids an ice cream cone sampler, or ice cream, cookies, and a bunch of chocolate goodies. There is a menu of delicious house cocktails, and a lounge menu of lighter fare.

Dinner runs between $18 and $28; salads and lighter fare are available. This is a nice treat for youngsters who enjoy a fancier meal. Major credit cards are accepted, and valet parking is available.

Red Sage

✉ 605 14th St. NW, at F Street
🚇 Metro: Metro Center (Red, Orange, or Blue Line)
📞 202-638-4444
💻 www.redsage.com

Ask anyone who's been here, and they'll refer to this restaurant as "a Wild West fantasy." Think of it as an upscale theme restaurant, with unique Western touches such as buffalo horn chandeliers. The menu offers many creative Southwestern opportunities, but it's best when you stick to traditional Western food like chili, burritos, or the fabulous homemade sausage. Reservations are recommended for the main dining area (a very popular tourist draw in the summer), but the Border Café doesn't accept them. Meals run $25 to $36 in the main room, $10 to $17 at the café, and cheaper at lunch. Major credit cards are accepted.

Willard Room
✉ 1401 Pennsylvania Ave. NW
✆ 202-637-7440
🖱 *www.washington.interconti.com*

The Willard Room in the Willard Hotel is the very best that D.C. dining has to offer, so it might not be appropriate for your children. The setting is palatial, restored to its turn-of-the-century grandeur with chandeliers, wood paneling, and columns. It is considered one of the most romantic settings in town, and many marriage proposals have been made in this dining room.

══FAST FACT

The Willard Room is known as the "residence of the presidents" because it has served most presidents dinner the night before their inauguration. Lincoln is said to have come here for the corned beef and blueberry pie, and Henry Clay is said to have invented the mint julep at Willard's bar.

For such a spectacular, historical setting, the food is reasonably priced. The menu changes daily, but the seafood is especially wonderful, as are the desserts. Main courses run $31 to $45. Major credit cards are accepted. Jacket and tie are suggested but not required, and reservations are a must. Complimentary valet parking with dinner is also available.

Zola
✉ 800 F St. NW
🚇 Metro: Gallery Place–Chinatown (Red, Yellow, or Green Line)
✆ 202-654-0999
🖱 *www.zoladc.com*

Zola is located next door to the International Spy Museum and a stone's throw from the National Portrait Gallery (and the American

Museum of Art, when it reopens). This is a surprisingly affordable sit-down restaurant that runs between $7 and $17 for lunch and $7 to $24 for dinner. Major credit cards are accepted.

Capitol Hill

America
✉ 50 Massachusetts Ave. NE
🚇 Metro: Union Station (Red Line)
📞 202-682-9555

This is a great spot for a leisurely meal after getting off the train at Union Station. As you eat, you can watch passersby head to and fro, and the fourth floor offers a view of the Capitol building.

The food offered at America is supposed to be traditional American, and there are dishes from all fifty states, with selections like roast turkey and stuffing, macaroni and cheese, and spaghetti and meatballs. Meals run $7.95 to $19.95 for dinner, and lunches are less expensive. Major credit cards are accepted.

B. Smith's
✉ 50 Massachusetts Ave. NE
🚇 Metro: Union Station (Red Line)
📞 202-289-6188
🖱 www.bsmith.com/restaurant_dc.php

This is the most expensive restaurant in Union Station and is a branch of a New York restaurant founded by model Barbara Smith (the Oil of Olay beauty). It is built in a beautiful Beaux Arts building and former presidential waiting area, where presidents once greeted visiting dignitaries.

The food is creative Southern, Creole, soul food with a French flair, which means wonderful Chesapeake crab cakes, Cajun red beans and rice, fried green tomatoes, catfish, jambalaya, and pecan-and-sweet-potato pies. Weekend brunch is outstanding ($29.95, $15 for kids 12 and under, including limitless orange juice, champagne, or Mimosas). Jazz on Friday and Saturday nights. Entrées run $17.95 to $32.95. Major credit cards are accepted.

Thunder Grill
✉ 50 Massachusetts Ave. NE
🚇 Metro: Union Station (Red Line)
✆ 202-898-0051
🖰 www.arkrestaurants.com

This high-concept Southwestern restaurant with a beautiful wooden interior and portraits of Native Americans on the walls is also located at Union Station. Entrees include traditional Southwestern fare such as fajitas and quesadillas, as well as crabmeat-stuffed Virginia trout, or grilled New York steak or bison. The menu includes sandwiches, pasta, and salads as well, from $7.95 to $19.95. The children's menu runs $3.95 to $7.95. There's a selection of twenty-three tequilas on the menu, and happy hour (weekdays 3:30 to 8:30 P.M.) features a different frozen margarita every day and $4 appetizers. Major credit cards are accepted.

Adams Morgan/Woodley Park

Cashion's Eat Place
✉ 1819 Columbia Rd. NW
🚇 Metro: Woodley Park (Red Line)
✆ 202-797-1819

This is an all-American-style restaurant decorated with owner Ann Cashion's family photos. It's small and always crowded; some people love it, some don't. The menu changes daily, but there's a variety of comfort food like roast chicken and steak and wonderful garlic mashed potatoes, as well as some pretty exotic fare such as buffalo steak and roasted duck breast with beets. The goat cheese ice cream is always recommended if it's on the menu, and locals say the desserts are not to be missed, so save room. It's also a local choice for Sunday brunch.

Dinner runs between $19 and $35, and Cashion's takes Master-Card and Visa only. Open Tuesday through Sunday for dinner, and for Sunday brunch. Valet parking is also available.

New Heights

✉ 2317 Calvert St. NW, at Connecticut Ave.
🚇 Metro: Woodley Park (Red Line)
✆ 202-234-4110

This two-story restaurant with large windows is popular because you can order any selection in appetizer or meal sizes, and the menu is creative but dependable. Full entrees run from $19 to $29, but appetizer portions are about half that. Major credit cards are accepted. Free valet parking is available.

Perry's

✉ 1811 Columbia Rd. NW
🚇 Metro: Woodley Park (Red Line)
✆ 202-234-6218
✐ *www.perrysadamsmorgan.com*

Perry's is a former disco; today it's a hip, fun restaurant with cozy sofas around tables and a funky, bizarre, alienlike chandelier. Perry's serves Asian fusion food in the evenings, and there's a rooftop dining area open in the spring and summer where you can eat sushi or beef loin with sweet espresso crust. Most meals run between $17 and $24, but you can make a meal out of sushi (big menu) and an appetizer. Sunday brunch. Major credit cards are accepted. Take the Metro to Woodley Park station.

JUST FOR PARENTS

Perry's hosts a famous and fabulous drag-queen brunch every Sunday that serves up a display of pan-Asian and American breakfast treats with a wicked cocktail. It may not be appropriate for children between the ages of five and the late teens, but there are plenty of baby boomers with strollers and toddlers in attendance every Sunday.

Georgetown

1789 Restaurant
✉ 1226 36th St. NW
✆ 202-965-1789
🖱 *www.1789restaurant.com*

This upscale restaurant, named for the year that Georgetown was founded, is located in an old townhouse with working fireplaces and old maps of Washington D.C., on the walls. The food is based on traditional American cooking, with an updated twist by Chef Nathan Beauchamp, who varies the menu according to what's available seasonally.

There's a full range of seafoods, meats, game, vegetarian dishes, and poultry, and the desserts are rich. Entrees run from $21 to $34, but there is a pre-theater prix fixe menu that offers three courses for $35. Jackets are required for men, and free valet parking is available. Major credit cards are accepted.

🧳 TRAVEL TIP

It used to be that Georgetown was a hassle to get to because the Metro bypassed this popular spot. Now there's the DC Circulator that connects Union Station and Georgetown and many other stops in between.

Old Glory Barbecue

✉ 3139 M St. NW
☎ 202-337-3406
🖱 www.oldgloryBBQ.com

Ample American barbecue with a Southern flair is served here. Although there's an excellent children's menu, portions are so wonderfully generous that you might want to order family-style and share. There's a terrific appetizer sampler, the Whole Lotta Glory, which features a little bit of everything—fried green tomatoes, buffalo wings, oak-grilled chicken wings, and St. Louis–style spareribs. And the entire shebang costs a mere $12.95! Entrees include ribs, of course, and even barbecued lamb, as well as pulled pork. There's hand-carved brisket, country steak, Old Glory Jalapeno Hotty pork sausage, and oak-grilled catfish Creole style. Major credit cards are accepted.

Sea Catch

✉ 1054 31st St. NW
☎ 202-337-8855
🖱 www.seacatchrestaurant.com

Conveniently located in a courtyard of art galleries in the Georgetown mall, Sea Catch overlooks the C&O Canal and features a fireplace and tables on a deck. The raw bar features oysters and clams, and Sea Catch also serves up great shrimp and lobster and fresh fish in numerous forms, but nothing is ever fried or breaded. Entrees run from $22 to $34. Major credit cards are accepted, and parking is free.

Sequoia

✉ 3000 K St. NW, at 30th St.

🚊 Metro: Foggy Bottom (Orange or Blue Line)

✆ 202-944-4200

🖃 *www.arkrestaurants.com*

Sequoia is located at Washington Harbor, and it's one of the most spectacular view-with-a-meal dining experiences in D.C. Most people come for the view of the Potomac (especially for drinks after work), but the food is decent, too—crab cakes, calamari, pizza, catfish, and salads. Meals run $15 to $29. If you want a table with a view, it's a good idea to make a reservation. Major credit cards are accepted.

Dupont Circle

Al Tiramisu

✉ 2014 P St. NW

🚊 Metro: Dupont Circle (Red Line)

✆ 202-467-4466

🖃 *www.altiramisu.com*

This is a good Italian restaurant that has a variety of pastas as well as seafood and meat and fish. Entrées range from $19 to $22. Major credit cards are accepted.

Capital Café

✉ 1919 Connecticut Ave. NW, in the Hilton Washington

🚊 Metro: Dupont Circle (Red Line)

✆ 202-483-3000

Buffet-style dining here is perfect for families. Breakfast, lunch, and dinner are served from 6:30 A.M. to 11:30 P.M. seven days a week. It's known for its homemade soups, and there is also a full à la carte menu, if you prefer. It offers entrées, sandwiches, salads, and desserts, including healthy selections. Lunch buffet is $16, dinner $20.95.

Dupont Grille

✉ 1500 New Hampshire Ave. NW

🚇 Metro: Dupont Circle (Red Line)

✆ 202-939-9596

💻 www.jurysdoyle.com

Situated right on Dupont Circle, this a great location for people-watching, which makes it a terrific summer brunch site. The fish dishes are excellent, from the crab cakes to the vanilla duck and leg confit, and the menu offers a variety of chicken, lamb, pork, fish, and beef. Dinner runs between $12 and $28, but the appetizer portions are large enough for smaller appetites. Breakfast is served every day, and the brunch is $22. This restaurant also serves wonderful waffles and French toast. Major credit cards are accepted.

Firefly

✉ 1310 New Hampshire Ave. NW

🚇 Metro: Dupont Circle (Red Line)

✆ 202-861-1310

💻 www.fireflyrestaurant.com

Located in the Hotel Madera, this is a one-of-a-kind dining experience that should entrance children and adults alike. The interior features a replica of a tree festooned with summer lights, and birch trunks lining the wall give the atmosphere of a summer evening, even in the dead of winter. The menu varies with the seasons and has won universal praise. Dinner entrées run from $17 to $24. If the pumpkin pudding is on the menu, order it.

The bill is presented in a mason jar with holes in the lid. A brunch is also offered, and major credit cards are accepted. Firefly is a small restaurant, so make a reservation, especially on the weekend.

Nora

✉ 2132 Florida Ave. NW, at R St.

🚊 Metro: Dupont Circle (Red Line)

✆ 202-462-5143

🖅 www.noras.com

This is one of the best restaurants in Washington D.C., in spite of the fact (or because of it, depending upon your culinary tastes) that all the food is organically grown. The setting is lovely, in a private townhouse with a skylight and a restored stable as the main dining room, with quilts and local art on the walls. This is not your tofu-and-bean-sprout burger restaurant but, rather, haute cuisine for the culinary correct. There's an emphasis on seafood, but there's also free-range chicken and even kidney on the menu. Desserts are wonderful, especially the pies and homemade ice cream, and there's a varied wine list. Of course, a restaurant like this varies the menu depending on seasonal produce, so there is always something new and different to try. Entrees range from $27 to $33. Reservations are strongly recommended. Nora takes MasterCard, Visa, and Discover only.

Smith & Wollensky

✉ 1112 19th St. NW (between L and M Streets)

🚊 Metro: Farragut West (Orange or Blue Line)

✆ 202-466-1100

Because Washington D.C. is a town that loves its red meat, this is just the restaurant that the city needs. This branch of the renowned New York steakhouse, with its famous green-and-white exterior, serves lots of steak (even a double porterhouse for $66), as well as lamb chops and lobster. Open until 1 A.M. Entrees run $25 to $65. Major credit cards are accepted. Dress is business casual.

Vidalia

✉ 1990 M St. NW

🚇 Metro: Dupont Circle (Red Line)

✆ 202-659-1990

🖂 www.vidaliadc.com

Considered one of the most creative Southern restaurants in D.C., Vidalia has been a popular favorite for a long time. The dining room is down a flight of stairs and has no windows, but people don't seem to mind as they slap vidalia marmalade on the delicious corn bread and try the new ways that the chef has come up with to flavor his fish, beef, lamb, and game. There are many interesting and mouth-watering entrees on the menu, but many may be too much for kids to take, so check the menu at the Web site. Desserts are superb, too. Try the pecan pie. Entrees run $26 to $36. Most major credit cards are accepted.

Foggy Bottom/West End

Aquarelle

✉ 2650 Virginia Ave. NW

🚇 Metro: Foggy Bottom (Orange or Blue Line)

✆ 202-298-4455

🖂 www.thewatergatehotel.com

Here's your chance to get inside the infamous Watergate Hotel and see how the other half lives or eats. If you're going to the Kennedy Center, this is actually a good place to go for an exquisite pretheater meal (prix fixe $42, which is a bargain at this upscale restaurant) and some fabulous views of the Potomac. (Call ahead for a reservation if you want a good table with a view.)

The menu includes such upper-crust entrees as quail, rack of lamb, squab, and sweetbreads, all wonderfully prepared. Entrees run $24 to $33. Free valet parking is available. Men are requested to wear business casual at dinner. Major credit cards are accepted.

Dish

✉ 924 25th St. NW

🚇 Metro: Foggy Bottom (Orange or Blue Line)

✆ 202-338-8707

🖥 *www.dishdc.com*

Dish is located in the River Inn, near the Kennedy Center and Georgetown. At this casual and friendly restaurant, the attention to detail—whether it's the playful sizes and shapes of the Crate & Barrel dishes or the eight-foot diptych of a Weimaraner dog photograph by William Wegman—sets the tone. During the winter months, a gaslit fireplace warms the guests.

Menu favorites include crispy fried chicken, blackened pork chops, and a New England clambake. At lunch, hearty sandwiches such as meatloaf and Colorado turkey melt are big enough to share. The brown cow ice-cream float is a perfect ending. Dinner entrees run between $19 and $28. Breakfast is served daily. Major credit cards are accepted.

🧳 TRAVEL TIP

A growing number of restaurants have Web sites, and it's a good place to start in helping to decide if a menu would be appropriate for your family. If you are a micro-planner, you can even make reservations online ahead of time and get to eat in some of the most popular places in town.

Galileo

✉ 1110 21st St. NW (between L and M Streets)

🚇 Metro: Foggy Bottom (Orange or Blue Line)

✆ 202-293-7191

🖥 *www.robertodonna.com*

This was one of the most talked-about restaurants of the late 1980s, because it was the first restaurant in chef Roberto Donna's Italian eatery empire (others include the Il Radicchio chain and Pesce). Executive chef Amy Brandwein has taken it to new levels. It's so popular you cannot get in for dinner without a reservation, and some book weeks in advance. The food is mind-blowingly rich, complex, and inventive. Pasta dishes start at $24, and entrees run from $25 to $35, but it's worth it. Major credit cards are accepted.

Teatro Goldoni

✉ 1909 K. NW

🚊 Metro: Farragut North (Red Line)

✆ 202-955-9494

🖎 *www.teatrogoldoni.org*

This place is a trip. It's theatrical to say the least, with exuberant designs and colors and lighting effects and graphics. You'll have a hard time concentrating on the food . . . until you take your first bite. It's complex and wonderful—lots of light sauces and intricate food layering. The desserts are supreme. Pasta is $23.50 to $26.50, and entrees run from $29.50 to $43.50. Major credit cards accepted. Valet parking is available.

👥 JUST FOR PARENTS

If there's a restaurant you're dying to try, but you think the food's too highfalutin for the kids, call ahead and explain your situation. Most real chefs welcome the opportunity to strut their stuff and prepare something not on the menu. They'll do that for you too.

Kinkead's

✉ 2000 Pennsylvania Ave. NW
🚇 Metro: Foggy Bottom (Orange or Blue Line)
📞 202-296-7700
🖰 www.kinkead.com

This is a popular American brasserie just a few blocks west of the White House. It is known for its seafood entrees, such as the grilled squid and polenta appetizer, and the signature dish of a pepita-crusted salmon with shellfish and chili ragout, but there is always at least one meat and poultry entree on the menu. There is live jazz every night of the week. Dinner entrees run $19 to $36; lunch is less expensive. Major credit cards are accepted.

Roof Terrace Restaurant/KC Café

✉ The Kennedy Center, New Hampshire Ave. NW
🚇 Metro: Foggy Bottom (Orange or Blue Line)
📞 202-416-8555
🖰 www.kennedy-center.org/visitor/restaurant_terrace.cfm

This is an excellent restaurant with fabulous panoramic Potomac views located at Rock Creek Parkway in the Kennedy Center. It requires a reservation—but the lighter-fare KC Café doesn't. Let's make it easy—everything is recommended, and there's always a daily special. The bounteous Country Kitchen Sunday brunch beggars the imagination and costs $33.95. It always attracts a crowd.

Hours of operation are really geared around performances, so call to make sure that the restaurant is open. The recently renovated KC Café on the roof terrace level is a better bet for families. It has a quick service line that offers gourmet sandwiches, a salad bar, vegetables, and antipasto. The Chef's Table has daily specials of pasta, fish, and meat, all prepared to order. Major credit cards are accepted. There is garage parking, but you have to pay for it.

CHAPTER 15

Cheap and Exotic Eats

WHAT INCREDIBLE VARIETY THIS city has when it comes to places to eat! Because Washington has a very diverse population, there are wonderful affordable ethnic restaurants, with great Chinese fare in D.C.'s small Chinatown, as well as Greek, Indian, Japanese, Thai, and Vietnamese restaurants, and more Ethiopian restaurants than in any other American city. In this chapter, you'll also find good options for an inexpensive breakfast or lunch, with most meals running under $12. The majority of these places would also be a good choice to eat dinner, and many are located downtown or in the Dupont Circle area.

Eating on the Cheap

There are so many wonderful restaurants, diners, cafes, and cafeterias throughout Washington D.C. that breakfast and lunch should never put you over the top of your budget. Since you'll be on the go from morning until the sun sets, look for something along your route during the day and then splurge on one of the city's unique dining experiences for dinner, when you'll need to get off your feet. Or, if you want a midday break, eat lunch at a stylish restaurant you couldn't afford in the evening, and have a simpler meal at night.

There are fabulous breakfasts throughout the city, but your best bet is likely to be a diner around the corner (check out your hotel restaurant first—some can be very pricey). Ask the hotel staff if there's a good, inexpensive breakfast place nearby. Many hotels offer a continental breakfast with the hotel room price. If you are going to be in town on Sunday morning and have the time to dine leisurely, you might want to schedule a Sunday brunch, because the city hosts a phenomenal variety of truly unique brunch experiences.

💼 TRAVEL TIP

There are many unique and exotic options listed in this chapter, but there are days when you may prefer to stop at the nearest fast-food chain restaurant. If you're looking for a Burger King or McDonald's, ask your hotel desk clerk or concierge for the one closest to you.

You will most likely eat lunch on the go, and if you are touring one of the city's major museums, you should consider eating in either its restaurant or cafeteria. They all offer a good variety of kid-pleasing menu items, and some are truly exceptional dining experiences, such as the Corcoran Gallery or the restaurant in the National Gallery of Art. Because of security concerns, it is now almost impossible to bring food into a museum or interior in a knapsack, as all bags must be checked when you enter.

Downtown D.C.

Cheap Eats

The Bread Line
✉ 1751 Pennsylvania Ave. NW
🚇 Metro: Farragut West (Orange or Blue Line)
📞 202-822-8900
✍ www.breadlinedc.com

This market and lunch place is a fave of Washingtonians, so it gets a bit hectic midday. But the fresh and tasty fare is worth it because there is something here to please all of the clan at low prices. The menu changes daily, but you can count on an array of gourmet sandwiches, comfortable standbys (BLTs), falafel, pizza, soups, and salads from $4.90 to $9.95 for combos with soup. Sandwiches are $6.90. Closed Saturday.

Fadó Irish Pub
✉ 808 7th St. NW
🚇 Metro: Gallery Place (Red, Yellow, or Green Line)
✆ 202-789-0066
🖰 *www.fadoirishpub.com/washington*

If you're touring Chinatown or Verizon Center, this is a good bet. The menu features such Irish staples as corned beef and cabbage, and there are some interesting deviations such as salmon, plus a wide selection of Irish beer and whiskey. Entrees are very reasonably priced, with most under $20. Major credit cards are accepted.

Full Kee
✉ 509 H St. NW
🚇 Metro: Gallery Place (Red, Yellow, or Green Line)
✆ 202-371-2233
🖰 *www.fullkeedc.com*

This is one of the best little Chinese restaurants in town (named as one of the top 100 in the country), with a daily menu of specialties (featuring a lot of fish and shellfish in the summer) that includes everything from short ribs to frog to jellyfish if your taste runs that way. Lunch specials start at $4.50, but they can whip up an exotic abalone with black mushrooms for $38.50. The restaurant accepts cash only.

National Museum of Natural History
✉ 10th St. and Constitution Ave. NW
🚇 Metro: Smithsonian (Orange or Blue Line)
✆ 202-633-1000
🖱 *www.si.edu/dining*

The Atrium Café, located on the ground floor, is a food court with signs that point you to the hamburgers, pizza, homemade soups, hot food, salads, and personally prepared sandwiches, desserts, coffee, and tea. Meals can run up to $10 with a drink. The Fossil Café on the first floor corner of Dinosaur Hall serves salads, sandwiches, desserts, and beverages amid tabletop exhibits. Major credit cards are accepted.

The National Museum of American History
✉ 14th Street and Constitution Ave. NW
🚇 Metro: Smithsonian (Orange or Blue Line)
✆ 202-633-1000
🖱 *www.si.edu/dining*

As this is being written, the museum was about to close for an extensive renovation, scheduled for completion in 2008. The original, old-fashioned ice cream parlor and three other restaurants in the museum were popular because you didn't have to leave the premises for lunch or dinner. Major credit cards are accepted.

The National Museum of the American Indian
✉ 4th St. and Independence Ave. SW
🚇 Metro: Federal Center SW (Orange or Blue Line)
✆ 202-633-1000
🖱 *www.si.edu/dining*

Here's something different. In line with its mission of exposing people to the cultures of Native Americans, the Mitsitam Café features native-inspired sandwiches, soups, entrées, desserts, and beverages from five regions of the Western Hemisphere.

Ollie's Trolley

✉ 425 12th St. NW

🚇 Metro: Federal Triangle (Orange or Blue Line)

✆ 202-347-6119

A neighborhood institution and a real kid-pleaser, Ollie's Trolley is a restaurant shaped like an old trolley. Everyone comes for the ten-ounce burger with unique herbs and spices on a sesame bun, as well as Ollie's fries with special spices and the excellent milk shakes; other sandwiches are available. Most sandwiches and combo meals are under $10. The restaurant accepts cash only.

TGI Friday's

✉ 2100 Pennsylvania Ave. NW, at 21th St.

🚇 Metro: Foggy Bottom (Orange or Blue Line)

✆ 202-872-4344

✍ *www.tgifridays.com*

The Washington location of this popular and often very crowded restaurant reflects the chain's effort to "kick it up a notch." Basic lunch items of the Tex-Mex variety have been regally supplemented by such specialties as Bruschetta Chicken Parmesan and Tortilla-Crusted Tilapia. There's something for everyone—vegetable grill, salads, a low fat and low carb menu, and a new $10 menu. It is kid-friendly with a good and inexpensive kids' menu. Entrees run $7 to $15, less for lunch and appetizers, from which you can easily make a meal. There is a Sunday brunch as well. Most major credit cards are accepted.

Tony Cheng's Mongolian Barbecue

✆ 202-842-8669

Tony Cheng's Seafood Restaurant

✉ 619 H St., NW

🚇 Metro: Gallery Place (Red, Yellow, or Green Line)

✆ 202-371-8669

Two floors, two restaurants, one owner. Downstairs is the Mongolian Barbecue for an all-you-can-eat feast running $10.50 for lunch and $16.95 for dinner. Upstairs, the menu features traditional Chinese seafood specialties. Lunch runs from $10.50 for chicken dishes to $11.50 for seafood, more for lobster; dinner is $13 to $16, again, more for lobster. Chef and owner Tony Cheng is usually on the premises, and you can see pictures of him with presidents of the past thirty years, from Carter to Bush. American Express, MasterCard, and Visa are accepted.

Waffle Shop
✉ 522 10th St. NW
🚇 Metro: Metro Center (Red, Orange, or Blue Line)
✆ 202-638-3430

A neighborhood institution for more than fifty years, this counter-service, cash-only, all-day breakfast spot is a real find. Steak and eggs, huge pancakes, and eggs with sausage and bacon are all about $10, and meals can be served with delicious grits. Lunch is served as well, also at extremely reasonable prices. Be prepared to wait a bit on weekends, but it's worth it. This is a great location for breakfast and/or lunch while you're visiting Ford's Theatre and the Petersen House, which are on the same block.

The Wright Place Food Court
✉ National Air and Space Museum
   Independence at 4th St. SW
🚇 Metro: Smithsonian (Orange or Blue Line)
✆ 202-633-1000
✐ www.si.edu/dining

When you tour the National Air and Space Museum, stop at the Wright Place Cafeteria. Recently remodeled and taking up a large space on the first floor of the museum, this cafeteria offers McDonald's, Boston Market, and Donato's Pizza. The McDonald's Happy Meal has a little space shuttle in it. Credit cards are accepted.

🧳 TRAVEL TIP

Because it's a tourist town, there are many kid-friendly Washington eateries, even in unexpected places. Some that come to mind are: Legal Seafoods, TGI Friday's, the Austin Grill, ESPN Zone, and the Old Ebbitt Grill.

Moderate Options

Bombay Club

✉ 815 Connecticut Ave. NW

� Metro: Farragut West (Orange or Blue Line)

✆ 202-659-3727

🖰 www.bombayclubdc.com

The Clintons often dined at this very popular upscale Indian restaurant. The setting is very British colonial, with ceiling fans and wicker chairs. The food is often very hot and spicy, but it's well done, and many of the seafood entrees are unique to this restaurant. Entrees run $19.95 to $24. There's a pretheater prix fixe meal at $25, as well as a Sunday brunch for $20. Major credit cards are accepted.

Café Atlantico

✉ 405 8th St. NW

🚈 Metro: Archives (Green or Yellow Line) or Gallery Place (Red Line)

✆ 202-393-0892

🖰 www.cafeatlantico.com

A popular Latin three-level restaurant and nightclub, this place is usually packed, so make a reservation. The décor is colorful with art-work on the walls. The restaurant has a number of signature drinks to choose from, and your server will make guacamole at your table right in front of you. There are many great appetizers on the menu, and many people make a meal out of them. You can also choose the tasting menu. Desserts are rich and creative.

Entrees run $15 to $28; lunch is less expensive, and the appetizers start at $9. Most major credit cards are accepted.

Jaleo
✉ 480 7th St. NW
🚇 Metro: Metro Center (Red, Orange, or Blue Line)
📞 202-628-7949
💻 www.jaleo.com

This popular tapas bar is named after a John Singer Sargent painting of a Spanish dancer, El Jaleo, which is re-created on the back wall. The sangria is refreshing, and the tapas (a small plate of food) selection is wide—Spanish cheeses, sausages, gazpacho, the traditional torta omelet, and lots more. There is also paella for two (really for four). Tapas are $3.95 to $9.95, entrées $14.95 to $16.95. A meal for one (two tapas with a half carafe of sangria) should run about $20. Homemade bread, Spanish olive oil, and a dish of olives are served with your meal. Major credit cards are accepted. Call for reservations—this place is popular with the locals (also right next door to the National Shakespeare theater), and you might have to wait up to an hour without a reservation in the summer months. It's a great restaurant for kids who like to eat, because they can choose from the various tapas for a main meal.

Zaytinya
✉ 701 9th St. NW
🚇 Metro: Gallery Place–Chinatown (Red, Yellow, or Green Line)
📞 202-638-0800
💻 www.zaytinya.com

A marvelous and skillful Greek restaurant that is surprisingly affordable, with a crisply contemporary blue-and-white interior. This is a great restaurant for children with an adventurous palate.

Make a meal of the mezza (small plates of different foods) and desserts; they are all delicious, and prices run between $4.95 and $10.95. The main course is a kebab platter for $24.95. Order the platter and maybe two mezza to feed the family. Have the dessert wine from Samos—it's surprisingly sweet and strong. Warning: it's very popular and there are no reservations. Major credit cards are accepted.

Capitol Hill

Cheap Eats

Market Lunch
✉ 225 Seventh St. SE
🚇 Metro: Eastern Market (Orange or Blue Line)
✆ 202-547-8444
✍ *www.easternmarketdc.net*

Eastern Market is an indoor-outdoor marketplace that thrives with arts and food vendors on the weekend. Inside the south hall of the marketplace is Market Lunch, a great sit-down (outdoor) diner where you can get fabulous blueberry buckwheat pancakes on Saturday or egg sandwiches for breakfast, and lunches of crab cakes and soft shell crab sandwiches, all under $10. Market Lunch is popular with the locals, so be prepared to wait about half an hour. The restaurant accepts cash only.

Monocle
✉ 107 D St. NE
🚇 Metro: Union Station (Red Line)
✆ 202-546-4488
✍ *www.themonocle.com*

If your kids like crab cakes, this is the place for them. There's also a good selection of sandwiches and salads. Lunch runs between $9 and $22, dinner from $15 to $30. Major credit cards are accepted.

👥 JUST FOR PARENTS

If you have access to the Internet, you might want to visit the various Web sites that review restaurants and those that issue savings coupons, as well as the restaurant sites themselves (if they have one). Just be wary of the dates of the reviews; some are very old. A site that issues coupons for different cities is *www.urbansavings.com*.

Oodles Noodles
✉ 1120 19th St. NW
🚊 Metro: Dupont Circle (Red Line)
✆ *202-293-3138*

There's always a big lunch crowd for this pan-Asian noodle shop featuring all sorts of noodle dishes, as well as curries and teriyaki. Prices run from $8 to $12. Major credit cards are accepted.

Union Station Food Court
✉ 50 Massachusetts Ave. NE
🚊 Metro: Union Station (Red Line)
✆ 202-371-9441
✑ *www.unionstationdc.com*

Located on the lower level of Union Station, the food court is an entire floor of fast-food establishments that offer everything from burgers to burritos, salads to souvlaki, curry to cookies. Most meals are around $7.

Uno Chicago Grill
✉ 50 Massachusetts Ave. NE
🚊 Metro: Union Station (Red Line)
✆ 202-842-0438
✑ *www.unos.com*

Home of the Chicago deep-dish pizza, Uno also features hot wings and appetizers that can make a meal, as well as burgers, sandwiches, and salads. Kids love this place because they can make their own pizzas with provided ingredients. Kids' menu prices run under $5. Major credit cards are accepted.

Moderate Options

Lebanese Taverna
✉ 2641 Connecticut Ave. NW
🚇 Metro: Woodley Park (Red Line)
✆ 202-265-8681
✎ www.lebanesetaverna.com

This is a mainstay of the Woodley Park dining zone since it opened almost thirty years ago. (An American success story, owner Toni Abi-Najm came to this country in 1975 with $700 and today owns four restaurants and three cafés.) The Lebanese Taverna is deservedly a very popular Lebanese restaurant, and it is usually packed on the weekends (reservations are accepted only for lunch, 11:30 A.M. to 3:30 P.M., and dinner before 6:30 P.M.). The interior is decorated with prints of Old Lebanon and prayer rugs; Lebanese music plays in the background.

The big hit on the menu is the selection of almost forty demi mezza, small plates of various "appetizers," made with an amazing variety of things (meats, vegetables, cheeses). Don't worry, this extended Lebanese family didn't forget the kids. Their "little ones" menu has something to please them as well, for $5. There are also homemade breads, pies, and pizza, Lebanese style, cooked in the wood-burning oven and a wonderful selection of main courses, such as kabobs, falafel, fish, and vegetarian dishes. Meals run from $13 to $19. Across from the Woodley Park Metro station. Free parking is available at a nearby garage. Most major credit cards are accepted.

Meskerem
✉ 2434 18th St. NW
🚊 Metro: Woodley Park (Red Line)
✆ 202-462-4100

Some say that this is the best Ethiopian restaurant in the city. Its spicy fare of lamb, chicken, beef, and vegetables is served with the traditional Ethiopian bread (*injera*) by a staff dressed in Ethiopian clothing. Ethiopian wine and beer is served, and live Ethiopian music is performed 11 P.M. to 3 A.M. on Friday and Saturday nights. Meals run from $9.25 to $12.25, less for vegetarian. Their special Meskerem Messob platter of foods feeds adults for $11.25 each, but kids can nibble along for free. Major credit cards are accepted.

Adams Morgan/Woodley Park

Cheap Eats

Julia's Empanadas
✉ 2452 18th St. NW
🚊 Metro: Woodley Park (Red Line)
✆ 202-328-6232

Julia's is a great little lunch place where you can get a variety of meat or vegetable empanadas for about $3 each. Soups are sometimes offered as well. There are only three chairs, so have a backup seating plan. The restaurant accepts cash only.

🧳 TRAVEL TIP

Julia's Empanadas has three other locations in the city. These have more seating and offer soup as well: 1000 Vermont Ave. NW, 202-789-1878; 1221 Connecticut Ave. NW, 202-861-8828; and 2452 18th St. NW 202-387-4100.

Al Crostino

✉ 1324 U St. NW

🚇 Metro: Woodley Park (Red Line)

☎ 202-797-0523

🖥 www.alcrostino.com

From the owner of Al Tiramisu, this is an increasingly popular neighborhood place serving finely honed Italian dishes representing many regions of the country. Locals praise the wait staff and chef. Entrées go for $12 to $17.50. Open Tuesday to Thursday, 6 P.M. to 10 P.M.; to midnight on Friday and Saturday; and to 9 P.M. on Sunday.

Santa Rosa Seafood

✉ 2224 18th St. NW

🚇 Metro: Woodley Park (Red Line)

☎ *202-518-8100*

Great neighborhood place for inexpensive seafood (also beef and chicken) of all kinds. There are more than fifty items to choose from for dinner, from $11.95 to $19.95, and more than thirty for lunch, at $5.95 to $14.95. Dine inside or in the sidewalk terrace overlooking Adams Morgan. Happy hour is weekdays 4 to 7 P.M. Accepts Visa only.

Georgetown

Cheap Eats

Austin Grill

✉ 750 E St. NW

🚇 Metro: Federal Triangle (Orange or Blue Line).

☎ 202-393-3776

🖥 *www.austingrill.com*

Austin Grill is part of a chain that features a big menu of good, inexpensive Tex-Mex fare, and the emphasis here is on chili and ribs. This is a kid-friendly restaurant with a good kids' menu featuring burgers, tacos, enchiladas, and nachos, all under $5, drink included. It also has vegetarian dishes. Major credit cards are accepted.

Café Deluxe
✉ 3228 Wisconsin Ave. NW
✆ 202-686-2233
⌨ *www.cafédeluxe.com*

Ask Washingtonians what their favorite restaurants are, and after they try to impress you with the fact that they've been to the latest hot spot, they will all mention Café Deluxe. It's always packed and full of lively energy. The food is consistent and never expensive. The interior is fairly plain, with white tablecloths and simple white plates—a step up from a diner—but the beef and tuna burgers are excellent, and so is the meat loaf. The desserts are homemade, as are the soups. There is a $3.95 kids' menu. Lunch runs $6.95 to $17.95 (if you really want to get fancy); dinner from $7.95 to $21.95. Amex, Visa, and MasterCard are accepted.

≡FAST FACT

It seems as if D.C. has more Ethiopian restaurants than any other American city, and that might be the case. According to D.C.'s tourist office, Washington D.C. was very open to Ethiopian refugees after the fall of Haile Selassie's regime in the 1980s, and many of these immigrants set up family-run restaurants, which have become quite well known.

Café Divan
✉ 1834 Wisconsin Ave. NW
✆ 202-338-1747
⌨ *www.cafedivan.com*

Go to Georgetown and visit Turkey, if you want to (try to) expand your kid's dining vocabulary. The Divan serves up authentic and delicious Turkish food at rock-bottom prices. The menu is huge—you can be as safe or experimental as you want to be. The kebab sandwiches are a good introduction to Turkish cooking for the kids. They'll like the baklava or kazan dibi dessert, a sweet pudding. Entrées run $5.95 to $16.

Ching Ching Cha
✉ 1063 Wisconsin Ave., NW
✆ 202-333-8288

Okay, you'll make fun of the name, but maybe you'll appreciate the authentic tea room tranquility. Guess not, but you will love the food and ambience after a hectic vacation day. Linger, if you can, over an exotic tea; there are close to fifty to choose from. Load the kids with dumplings while you sample more exotic fare elegantly served. Everything here is $11 or less.

Clyde's of Georgetown
✉ 3236 M St. NW
🚆 Metro: Foggy Bottom (Orange or Blue Line)
✆ 202-333-9180
🖱 www.clydes.com

Founded in 1963 as a faux-Victorian pub for Georgetown University students, this has become a popular chain of local restaurants (including the venerated Old Ebbitt Grill and several other Clyde's locations) where you can always get good American saloon food. The standard selection includes a juicy burger, buffalo wings, crab cake sandwich, hearty soups, and a surprisingly excellent cheese platter that pairs blackberries with your four cheese selections. Most people order from the appetizer menu, which is varied and creative. Of course, there's a wide selection of beers on tap and a good wine list.

Weekend brunches have become a tradition (especially because this restaurant is located in the Shops at Georgetown Park). Meals run from $4.50 to $22, and lunch is less expensive. Validated parking is available in the nearby mall. Major credit are cards accepted.

Shops at Georgetown Park Food Court
✉ M St.

This is restaurant row. There are at least a dozen or so fast-food establishments located here, offering pizza, Philly cheese steaks, pretzels, ice cream, gyros, and other light fare, all reasonably priced. There is also a string of restaurants—Indian, French, Chinese, vegetarian, Afghani, you name it. Stroll down the street and menu shop.

Dupont Circle

Cheap Eats

Helix Lounge
✉ 1430 Rhode Island Ave. NW
🚇 Metro: McPherson Square (Orange or Blue Line)
✆ 202-462-9001
🖱 www.hotelhelix.com

One of the restaurant lounges in the Kimpton Hotel chain, this small, hip lounge offers great burgers and a terrific array of hearty appetizers. You could actually order a few appetizers and feed the whole family. Every day there's a happy hour from 5 until 7 P.M., when food and drink are half-price and the burgers are only $5. Wonderful creative drinks are available too, even for kids. Have them ask for the fruitini, which is mixed fruit juices and 7-Up served in an adult martini glass. Preteens and teens will love the beaded curtains and the flashing lights. This place is very older-child-friendly. Major credit cards are accepted.

👥 JUST FOR PARENTS

Happy hour is always a special time at the Kimpton Hotels. For guests, there's a wine reception every night; for outsiders, three of the hotels—Hotel Helix, Hotel Rouge, and Hotel Topaz—hold a great happy hour from 5 P.M. to 7 P.M. drinks are half price and there are food specials.

Kramerbooks & Afterwords Café & Grill

✉ 1517 Connecticut Ave. NW, at Q St.

🚇 Metro: Dupont Circle (Red Line)

📞 202-387-1400

🖱 www.kramers.com

This is a good restaurant, and it's located in one of the late-night bookstores and cybercafes in town (with a free fifteen-minute e-mail check available). The menu is pages long, featuring a variety of dishes from vegetable chili to lamb chops to quesadillas, with a wide selection of beers. Saturday and Sunday brunch (served all day) is very popular here and runs $14.50 to $16.95. Dinner entrees go from $11.75 to 16.75, lunch $8.25 to $10.75. Breakfast is $5.95 to $9.75. It has a "Sharezies" menu—pick three entrées for $18. Major credit cards are accepted. A caution is that the ambiance (the menus and promo posters) tend to be a bit risque—check the Web site.

🧳 TRAVEL TIP

With so much to do and see in the city, you don't want to be walking through the streets looking for a good or affordable place to eat when the museum closes. So it's a good idea to plan your meals in conjunction with your sightseeing, and if the place is highly recommended, make a reservation just in case.

Luigi's
✉ 1132 19th St. NW
🚇 Metro: Dupont Circle or Farragut North (Red Line)
📞 202-331-7574
🖱 www.famousluigis.com

Great pizza with lots of options for toppings is only part of the attraction of Luigi's, a restaurant that has been in existence since 1943. Great pasta is offered here, too—including cheese ravioli, lasagna, and manicotti. Dinners run from $10.75 to $17.95. Kids can order sides or split dishes. Major credit cards are accepted.

Mark's at Mark and Orlando's
✉ 2020 P St. NW
🚇 Metro: Dupont Circle (Red Line)
📞 202-223-8463
🖱 www.markandorlandos.com

Here's a story to tell back home: a restaurant with a split personality. Downstairs is the formal dining room, upstairs the kid's dorm . . . well, not really that bad. If it's haute cuisine (but with one foot on the ground) and starched linens and entrées for $18–$24 you crave, downstairs is the place. If the kids want cheeseburgers (albeit on a brioche) and wings, step up to Mark's, where no entrée is more than $9, and the atmosphere is definitely relaxed. The food is great on both floors.

Teaism

✉ 800 Connecticut Ave.

🚇 Metro: Dupont Circle (Red Line)

✆ 202-835-2233

🖥 *www.teaism.com*

This might be a stretch for kids, but this wonderful Asian restaurant serves a wide selection of personal potted teas, ice creams (green tea and ginger are first-rate), and meals, including Japanese bento boxes, kebobs, curries, salads, and even a buffalo burger. Most meals are under $6 to $12. Breakfast runs $1.95 to $9, and there's an afternoon tea for $20. Most credit cards are accepted. There are two more branches, both of which also serve dinner: one at 2009 R Street NW, 202-667-3827, and another at 400 8th Street NW, 202-638-6010.

Topaz Bar

✉ 1733 N St. NW

🚇 Metro: Dupont Circle (Red Line)

✆ 202-393-3000

🖥 *www.topazhotel.com*

Another of the restaurant-bars in the Kimpton Hotel chain, Topaz Bar offers a pan-Asian appetizer spread that can serve as a meal (half-price every day between 5 and 7 P.M.). The food is delicious, and there are some kicky signature drinks. Because this is a bar atmosphere, it is inappropriate for younger children. Major credit cards are accepted.

Zorba's Cafe

✉ 1612 20th St. NW, at Connecticut Ave.

🚇 Metro: Dupont Circle (Red Line)

✆ 202-387-8555

🖥 *www.zorbascafe.com*

This inexpensive Greek restaurant is located on Dupont Circle's main drag. It features a wonderful selection of fast Greek food, from dips to fried cheese to a souvlaki plate and baklava for dessert. Entrees run $7.95 to 10.50; all sandwiches are less than $7. Some credit cards are accepted.

Moderate Options

Buca di Beppo
✉ 1825 Connecticut Ave. NW
🚇 Metro: Dupont Circle (Red Line)
✆ 202-232-8466
✍ www.bucadibeppo.com

Family-style, large portions of Southern Italian cuisine are this restaurant chain's claim to fame, which was designed to resemble a 1950s supper club. Platters of pasta, oversize pizza, and standards such as chicken cacciatore are featured on the menu. Entrees run $13.95 to $33.95, but they are meant to be shared. Most major credit cards are accepted.

══FAST FACT

Although hotel restaurants are a good bet for breakfast, show your kids some real Americana and wolf down a real American breakfast at the Waffle House downtown, where you can sit at a counter and order a filling meal of eggs and bacon, or pancakes, waffles, and even steak and eggs, all for under a ten-spot, bub.

The Levante's
✉ 1320 19th St. NW
🚇 Metro: Dupont Circle (Red Line)
✆ 202-293-6301
✍ www.levantes.com

This pleasant, inexpensive Mediterranean restaurant (Turkish cuisine via Europe) has an outdoor patio and features a terrific appetizer plate of fried cheese, salad, and dolmathes (stuffed grape leaf rolls); their spinach pie is so good, even the kids might like it. Entrees run $9.50 to $10.50. For $24, you can get a mixed grill plate to feed the whole family. Most major credit cards are accepted.

Urbana

✉ 2121 P. St. NW
🚇 Metro: Dupont Circle (Red Line)
📞 1-877-866-3070
📞 202-956-6650
🖱 www.hotelpalomar-dc.com

Not only has Kimpton made waves with its hip and creative approach to hostelry, but its in-house restaurants have set the pace as well. The Urbana reflects the upscale and contemporary flavor of its parent hotel, The Palomar. The cuisine is Mediterranean-inspired, with pastas, pizza, meats, and seafood to satisfy your whims and the kids' pickiness, all at really reasonable prices. Dinners run $8 to $30, lunches a bit cheaper. The clan will love to watch the chefs prepare their meal in the exhibition kitchen.

Foggy Bottom/West End

Cheap Eats

Malaysia Kopitiam

✉ 1827 M St. NW
🚇 Metro: Farragut North (Red Line)
📞 202-833-6232
🖱 www.malaysiakopitiam.com

Okay, this might take some persuasion, but the wonderfully authentic food here, coupled with low prices, has made this one of the most prized of Washington's ethnic restaurants. The illustrated menu will clue you in on the unfamiliar food and allow you to choose wisely. Don't be afraid to ask questions. You'll have a hard time deciding on the many delights offered. The kids might go for the noodle dishes, or skewered meat satays. Appetizers go for $2.95 to 6.95; entrées from $7.95 to $15.95.

Moby Dick House of Kabob

✉ 1070 31st St. NW

🚇 Metro: Cleveland Park (Red Line)

✆ 202-333-4400

✍ *www.mobysonline.com*

This is a very popular restaurant with the locals, featuring Persian food, mainly kabobs and grilled meat, laced with a secret house seasoning. Although it's near Georgetown Harbor, the name refers to the puffed pita, not the whale. There's hardly any seating, and it seems like it's always crowded, but there's a reason. Entrées cost $6 to $13 (for the super combo), sandwiches $5 to $7. Quiet the kids with hummus for $3. There are daily lunch specials. Only cash is accepted. There's another Moby's at Dupont Circle, 1300 Connecticut Ave. NW, 202-833-9788.

Nam Viet

✉ 3419 Connecticut Ave. NW, at Macomb St.

🚇 Metro: Cleveland Park (Red Line)

✆ 202-237-1015

This is one of the older and best Vietnamese restaurants in town. Everyone recommends the *pho* (beef noodle soup) and the fresh crispy fish, as well as the spring rolls and the shrimp toast. Entrees run $12 to $15. The kids will be happy with an appetizer. Most major credit cards are accepted.

Moderate Options

Circle Bistro

✉ One Washington Circle NW (in the One Washington Circle Hotel)
🚇 Metro: Foggy Bottom (Orange or Blue Line)
☎ 202-293-5390
🖰 www.thecirclehotel.com/circle_bistro.htm

Located near the Kennedy Center and Georgetown, this stunning American bistro with a Mediterranean flair serves up signature dishes including Moroccan-style lamb with figs, caramelized plantains and couscous, curried veal with grilled papaya and pineapple, ravioli with lobster and jumbo lump crabmeat, and vegetable strudel with zucchini, squash, eggplant, and peanut essence.

The pretheater menu offers three courses for $30. The lounge, with its oversize sofas and widescreen TV, features tempting cheese and chocolate fondues, a favorite among kids who can handle a skewer. Also available are sandwiches and appetizers. Dinner runs $19 to $26, but the appetizer portions are large enough for smaller appetites. Breakfast runs $8 to $11; lunch, $12 to $17. Several items are offered at $1 apiece during the 5 to 7 P.M. happy hour. Major credit cards are accepted.

▮ TRAVEL TIP

Combine sightseeing with a cultural connection by visiting Washington's small Chinatown, visiting the shops (great souvenirs), and then having a meal in one of the local restaurants.

U Street Corridor

Cheap Eats

Ben's Chili Bowl

✉ 1213 U St. NW

🚊 Metro: U Street (Green Line)

✆ 202-667-0909

Ben's may be off the beaten path, but the restaurant is a D.C. landmark nonetheless. This seventy-year-old establishment was made famous on *The Cosby Show* in the late 1980s, and people have been lining up for Ben's delicious and ample chili dogs (with or without cheese and onions) for years. There are chili burgers, and just plain chili as well; vegetarian chili is also available. Almost everything is $5 to $12 tops. Only cash is accepted.

Love Cafe

✉ 1501 U St. NW

🚊 Metro: U Street (Green Line)

✆ 202-265-9800

🖱 *www.cakelove.com*

Owner Warren Brown told his story of making cakes from scratch and selling them in a tiny U Street storefront on *The Oprah Winfrey Show*, and before you know it, everyone in Washington D.C. was going to the Love Cafe for these delicious cakes. Then he gets his own TV show on the Food Network. Has success spoiled a good thing? The original storefront is closed now, but there is a sit-down café serving breakfast and lunch seven days a week. Available are soups, salads, sandwiches, and, of course, baked goods. (The famous cupcake combinations are still available, but for $3, they're no longer the bargain they used to be.) Breakfast fare goes from $1 (dry bagel) to $7.95 (french toast); lunch $4.50 to $6.95. Not bad. There is a live DJ on Tuesday and Wednesday nights from 5 P.M. to 11 P.M.; on Wednesday evening, all chocolate goods are 30 percent off. Brunch is served on the weekends. If you buy any baked goods on your way out of town, they'll pack them for you. Amex, Visa, and MasterCard are accepted.

Brunches and Afternoon Teas

Afternoon tea and Sunday brunch are a big dining to-do in this town, and some of these are spectacular or at least unique: The National Cathedral's afternoon tea is legendary, although it has been pared down and is not intended as a full meal. Here are a few suggestions.

Best Brunches

Washingtonians love Sunday brunch, so you'll find it offered at most hotel restaurants and most of the chain restaurants. Of course, not all brunches are equal. Some are opulent food extravaganzas that offer everything but the kitchen sink, including unlimited champagne; others are so quirky they seem like something out of *Alice in Wonderland*. The following is a list of the standouts in town:

- The Federalist Restaurant at the Madison Hotel
- Georgia Brown's
- The Corcoran's gospel brunch
- Dupont Grill
- Poste
- Roof Top Terrace at the Kennedy Center
- The Morrison-Clark Hotel Restaurant
- Perry's
- Old Ebbitt Grill
- B. Smith's
- Firefly

Other good brunch locales are the Jefferson Hotel, the Beacon Hotel, Willard Intercontinental, Kramerbooks, TGI Friday's, Bombay Club, Clyde's of Georgetown, and Westfields Marriott in Chantilly, VA.

Afternoon Tea

Afternoon tea is a big deal in Washington. You'll find it offered at most of the better hotel restaurants. There are a handful of truly stellar afternoon tea experiences in the city, and if you like a late lunch or a little something before dinner, you should really try to fit them into your schedule.

The Tea we mentioned at the National Cathedral is elegant, but they'll tell you to eat lunch beforehand. You must make a reservation because it's very popular with tourists and regulars. The Tour and Tea is held on Tuesdays and Wednesdays only at 1:30 P.M. and costs a flat $22, for which you are offered a selection of tea sandwiches, cookies, scones, and tea. A tour of the cathedral comes with the tea. Call 202-537-8993 or go to *www.cathedral.org/cathedral/visit/tourandtea tours.shtml*. Teaism is a Washington restaurant that specializes in tea, and so does the Tea Cellar at the Park Hyatt Hotel. Other hotel restaurants that feature afternoon tea include the Lafayette in the Hay-Adams Hotel; the Wilkes Room at the elegant Henley Park Hotel; The Garden Terrace Lounge in the Four Seasons Hotel; Peacock Alley at the Willard; the Jefferson restaurant; Potomac Lounge at the Watergate Hotel; and the lobby lounge of the Westfield Marriott in Chantilly, Virginia (near Tyson's Corner).

CHAPTER 16

Where to Stay under $100

THERE ARE HUNDREDS OF hotels in Washington D.C., from those that cater to the family to some of the most luxurious suites in the nation. While this chapter features the budget hotels—under $100, if you get a special—there may be moderate-, high- or even luxury-priced hotels listed in the following chapters that are very near in price on a deal. Remember that sometimes it's worth it to pay a little more for location. Otherwise, you'll be paying to park the car all day and/or paying Metro or cab fares for the whole family, when you could have been just walking from a downtown hotel.

How to Save

There are many ways to cut the cost of your hotel stay. See if you can use Automobile Association of America (AAA) and the American Association of Retired Persons (AARP) discounts, which are usually around 10 percent. Make sure these discounts are not off the "rack" price—you may do better with Internet booking sites, where many chains now guarantee you the lowest price available. You can also look for hotels that offer free continental breakfast or even have kitchenettes. There are often discounts for business travelers, as well as summer, weekend, and promotional specials and family rates, so ask for the lowest rate when you call for reservations.

≡FAST FACT

The average room runs about $145 for double occupancy during the week and drops to $95 on the weekend, according to the Washington Convention & Tourism Corporation. Hotel taxes are 14.75 percent a night, and parking charges can be as high as $25, even $35, a night.

Always try the variety of Internet travel search engines that offer hotel rooms (some offer discounts, too), because they often have the best rates available and make a deluxe hotel very affordable for the family. The following is a good selection of travel-related sites.

Washington D.C. Convention and Visitor's Corporation
✎ www.washington.org

This site offers information on special visitor promotions and searchable hotel listings prepared by the Washington D.C. Convention and Tourism Corporation. The information here is organized by price and location, offering listings from hotels, bed and breakfasts, hostels, and even campgrounds. It has a special weekend-rate search engine too.

Fodors.com
✎ www.fodors.com

The travel guide site offers a similar hotel index that you can use to search by name or category, as well as its own list of best hotels.

Priceline
✎ www.priceline.com

This travel Web site offers two ways to order your travel. You can make all the choices yourself, using its information to comparison shop, or you can name your price and it will book you a discounted hotel room in D.C. Priceline says that all its hotels are members of major chains, and you can probably get a very good rate this way, but just be aware that there are parts of downtown Washington that you have to take a cab to once the sun sets.

🧳 TRAVEL TIP

The travel-booking Web sites—Expedia, Orbitz, Travelocity, Hotels .com, and TripAdvisor—are a boon to travelers, invaluable for price shopping. Just make sure that the locations they quote are not in or adjacent to the seedier parts of town.

Expedia.com
✑ *www.expedia.com*

This site will give you a listing of hotels by location and price, and you can even see photos. Expedia also offers a best-price guarantee.

Orbitz
✑ *www.orbitz.com*

This travel Web site has a hotel search engine with hotel photos. Like Expedia, Orbitz offers a low-price guarantee.

TripAdvisor
✑ *www.tripadvisor.com*

This great Web site will give you travelers' reviews as well as the best price on the Web for any hotel you are searching for.

Travelocity
✑ *www.travelocity.com*

Another good Web site with cheap last-minute deals, it has printout games to take with you.

The Washington Post
📖 www.washingtonpost.com

Among the many services offered by the newspaper is a search engine that lists hotels by neighborhood.

Hotels.com
📖 www.hotels.com

Easy-to-use Web site that lists hotels with deals in any order you want. Partners with all the players in the field.

🧳 TRAVEL TIP

In tourist-happy Washington D.C., most hotels are kid-friendly. But some may meet your needs better than others. Many hotels now offer in-room video games (most for a fee), some have a pre-screened list of child caretakers, and most have computer data ports. Loew's and Holiday Inn also offer free meals to kids.

Hotel/Motel Chains
📖 www.holidayinn.com
📖 www.radisson.com
📖 www.daysinn.com
📖 www.courtyard.com
📖 www.bestwestern.com

These hotel chains have Internet sites, and you can sometimes find good packages and last-minute deals there. If there is a chain not listed you that personally like, go to the site and check it out.

Downtown D.C.

Hampton Inn
✉ 901 6th St. NW
🚇 Metro: Gallery Place/Chinatown (Red, Green, or Yellow Line)
📞 1-800-HAMPTON (426-7866)
📞 202-842-2500
🖱 *www.washingtondc.hamptoninn.com*

This has upscale features for a great bargain when you get a deal. Contemporary rooms offer family-friendly amenities like a fridge, microwave, iron and board, coffeemaker, safe, cable TV, video-on-demand (for a fee). Also free are a hot buffet breakfast, local calls, and high-speed Internet. There's an indoor pool with spa, a laundry room, and an exercise room.

Holiday Inn Capital at the Smithsonian
✉ 550 C St. SW
🚇 Metro: L'Enfant Plaza (Yellow, Orange, Green, or Blue Line)
📞 1-800-HOLIDAY (465-4329)
📞 202-479-4000
🖱 *www.holidayinncapitol.com*

Location, location, location. This newly renovated, 529-room hotel is a block away from the Smithsonian's National Air and Space Museum, the most popular museum in the Smithsonian Institution, as well as the other Smithsonian museums and the National Archives. Rooms are designed in traditional hotel-chain style, with hair dryers and irons available. There's a rooftop pool and a health club. On-site dining includes Smithson's Restaurant, the Shuttle Express Deli, and a hip and trendy lounge for cocktails. Kids under twelve eat free, and it is serviced by Pizza Hut Express and Starbucks. Published room rates are as much as $329 per night, but Internet specials often list rooms for under $100, so ask how you can get a room at that price. Parking is an additional $22 per night. All major credit cards are accepted.

The Quincy

✉ 1823 L St. NW

🚇 Metro: Farragut North (Red Line)
   or Farragut West (Orange or Blue Line)

📞 1-800-424-2970

📞 202-223-4320

Formerly the Lincoln Suites Downtown, this is an all-suite, ten-story hotel with ninety-nine suites. Many guests stay for weeks or longer when doing business in the city because it is only five blocks from the White House and central to most of the capital's attractions. Great for families, about one-third of the suites feature full kitchens; others have microwaves, refrigerators, and coffeemakers. Other amenities include video games (fee charged), a wet bar, hair dryer, complimentary milk and cookies in the evening, and an expanded continental breakfast in the morning. There is a "DC for Kids" package deal, which includes the above room amenities plus a Metrocard, a bag full of snacks, and a coloring book. There are two restaurants on site. Recession II is a secluded, hideaway, and Mackey's Pub serves traditional Irish food and drink. Suites are listed at $89 to $250. Major credit cards are accepted. Parking is an additional $22 per day in the adjoining garage.

═FAST FACT

Here's some D.C. trivia: The classic movie *Mr. Smith Goes to Washington* was filmed at the Hotel Washington. And did you know that Albert Einstein once lived at the St. Regis Hotel?

Red Roof Inn

✉ 500 H St. NW

🚇 Metro: Gallery Place (Yellow, Green, or Red Line).

✆ 1-800-THE-ROOF (1-800-733-7663)

✆ 202-289-5959

🖱 *www.redroof.com*

A newly renovated, ten-story hotel in the heart of the capital's Chinatown, right across the street from one of the best Chinese restaurants in town (Full Kee), the Red Roof is also within walking distance of many of the city's major attractions, such as the Verizon Center, Ford's Theatre, and the Convention Center. Rooms are spacious and decorated in contemporary hotel decor, with pay-per-view movie service, as well as Nintendo for children (fee charged). The hotel's restaurant serves an inexpensive breakfast and lunch, and there is a washer and dryer on the premises, as well as a health club and sauna. Weekday rates are $120 to $170 for a double, and weekend rates are considerably less. Outdoor parking is $20 per day. Major credit cards are accepted.

Swiss Inn

✉ 1204 Massachusetts Ave. NW

🚇 Metro: Metro Center (Red, Orange, or Blue Line)

✆ 800-955-7947

✆ 202-371-1816

🖱 *www.theswissinn.com*

This is an affordable hotel in a former brownstone within walking distance to almost everything you'll need, but it's a small hotel, so book in advance. Rooms are simple, in the traditional European tradition, but nicely decorated with a kitchenette in each room. Pets are allowed. Room rates are $89 to $139. Most major credit cards are accepted. Parking is available at five nearby parking facilities ranging from $9 to $25.

Homewood Suites by Hilton
✉ 1475 Massachusetts Ave. NW
🚇 Metro: McPherson Square (Orange or Blue Line)
✆ 202-265-8000
🖰 www.homewoodsuites.com

Another great find if you can get one of the Internet deals (or ask on the phone). Upscale amenities abound in this elegant but homey downtown hotel with 175 two-room suites and fully equipped kitchens. There is a free hot breakfast buffet and evening manager's reception (salad bar, entrées, beverages) every Monday to Thursday, as well as grocery shopping, fitness room, high-speed Internet, and more.

Capitol Hill

Best Western Capitol Skyline Hotel
✉ 10 "I" St. SW
🚇 Metro: Navy Yard (Green Line)
✆ 1-800-458-7500
✆ 202-488-7500
🖰 www.bestwesterncapitolskyline.com

The family-style hotel was recently completely renovated. There are 196 guest rooms and 7 suites in its seven floors. The hotel is walking distance to many of the major attractions, and there is also a free shuttle to the Metro, Navy Yard, Union Station, and Smithsonian. It offers family dining in the Skyline Diner (three meals a day). Rooms have wireless high-speed Internet, dataports, free local calls and long-distance access, cable TV movies, iron and board, and coffeemaker. There is also a gym and outdoor seasonal pool. A family-plan room rate is available if the kids want a separate room. Parking is $15 a day.

Adams Morgan/Woodley Park

Windsor Park Hotel
✉ 2116 Kalorama Rd. NW, at Connecticut Ave.
🚇 Metro: Woodley Park-Zoo (Red Line)
✆ 202-483-7700

This charming forty-three-room hotel is furnished with antiques and dried flowers, giving it a Victorian feel. Hotel amenities include a minibar, free newspaper delivery, and a continental breakfast buffet in the Tea Room. It's an easy walk to neighborhood services, embassies, and majestic homes. Parking is available on the street. Major credit cards are accepted.

💼 TRAVEL TIP

The old rule that rooms in the District are cheaper on the weekend because of the glut of business travelers on weekdays no longer holds true. Computers, the Internet, and increasing tourist travel have all allowed hotels to finely hone their pricing, to the point where rates vary almost day to day. Your best travel bet is to use one of the travel sites listed earlier.

Adams Inn
✉ 1746 Lanier Place NW
🚇 Metro: Woodley Park-Zoo (Red Line)
✆ 1-800-578-6807
✆ 202-745-3600
🖱 www.adamsinn.com

This bed-and-breakfast, located between Calvert Street and Ontario Road, is composed of three turn-of-the-twentieth-century townhouses that have been combined to make a total of twenty-six rooms, some of which do not have bathrooms of their own. This is a charming Old-World inn furnished in a faux Victorian style. In keeping with that décor, the rooms do not have televisions or phones, but there is a pay phone in the lobby, and the hotel will take messages for you. There is also a communal television room and a refrigerator and microwave for guest use. There is a washer and dryer for guest use, and a free continental breakfast is offered in the morning.

Room rates are $89 for a double without a bathroom, $99 to $129 for rooms with a bathroom, but are due for an increase. Weekly rates are available. Major credit cards are accepted. Parking is an additional $10 per night, depending on availability. The closest Metro stop is a hike.

Kalorama Guest House at Kalorama Park

✉ 1854 Mintwood Place NW

✆ 202-667-6369

Kalorama Guest House at Woodley Park

✉ 2700 Cathedral Ave. NW

✆ 202-328-0860

🚊 Woodley Park-Zoo (Red Line)

✑ www.kaloramaguesthouse.com

The Mintwood Place location, between 19th Street and Columbia Road, is composed of four townhouses. The Cathedral Avenue branch is housed in two townhouses.

Though small by hotel standards, these charming inns both offer a great location for a great price. They are a good option if you don't mind sharing a bathroom (this is actually perfect for families or friends traveling together, and there *are* rooms with private baths) and possibly not having a television or phone in your room. Show the kids what life used to be like. There are a limited number of rooms with TVs, and only rooms in Mintwood have phones, but there is a communal television room for those who just can't live without the tube, and there is a phone in the lobby where you can make free local calls (the inn will take messages for you). A free continental breakfast is served every morning as well as lemonade, cookies, and sherry each afternoon, and an evening sherry to help you relax. Children must be six years of age or older. Room rates are $100 for a double with a shared bathroom, $115 for a double with bathroom. Parking is an additional $15. Major credit cards are accepted.

Dupont Circle

Jurys Normandy Inn
⊠ 2118 Wyoming Ave. NW
🚇 Metro: Dupont Circle (Red Line)
📞 1-800-424-3729
📞 202-483-1350
✍ www.jurysdoyle.com

This is a lovely small hotel (seventy-five rooms) near Connecticut Avenue in the midst of Embassy Row, so many travelers are here on foreign affairs business. The hotel has a European air (it's run by an Irish company) and serves afternoon coffee, tea, and cookies in the appropriately named Tea Room. The Tea Room is also where the complimentary continental breakfast is served every morning, and Tuesday nights there is a wine and cheese reception. In-room amenities include a small refrigerator and a coffeemaker, and the hotel charges a mid-rate of $225, but Internet discounts are generous, bringing the daily rate to $89 at publication. The hotel also guarantees it will give you the lowest rate available. Parking is an additional $20. Major credit cards are accepted.

Windsor Park Hotel

✉ 2116 Kalorama Road NW
🚇 Woodley Park-Zoo or Dupont Circle (Red Line)
📞 1-800-247-3064
📞 202-483-7700
🖋 www.windsorparkhotel.com

This charming bed-and-breakfast-style hotel is housed in a 1926 building. Rooms are gracious, but have all the modern conveniences—mini-refrigerator, modem port, cable TV, and the expected amenities. There's no restaurant in the hotel, but a free breakfast is served every morning, vending machines offer snacks and beverages, and the neighborhood has many restaurants of all kinds.

Brickskeller Inn

✉ 1523 22nd Street NW
🚇 Metro: Dupont Circle (Red Line)
📞 202-293-1885
🖋 www.thebrickskeller.org

Housed in a 1912 building overlooking Rock Creek Park, the Brickskeller is a Washington institution with rock-bottom hotel rates and an inexpensive, award-winning restaurant. The rooms are large and comfortable, some have a shared bath, some have private baths. Rooms with private bath have air-conditioning and television, all rooms have a telephone, and guests have the use of a washing machine and dryer. The desk is staffed 24 hours a day. The Brickskeller Restaurant, which occupies the first two floors of the building, serves lunch and dinner weekdays, and dinner only on the weekends. It has won awards as the city's best cheap eats. The Brick's bar has also won a Guinness award for its 1,000-beer selection. Rates run from $62 for a single with shared bath to $99 for a double with private bath.

Foggy Bottom/West End

The River Inn
✉ 924 25th St. NW
🚇 Metro: Foggy Bottom (Orange or Blue Line)
📞 1-800-424-2741
📞 202-337-7600
🖥 *www.theriverinn.com*

The River Inn is located between K and I Streets., within walking distance to the Kennedy Center and to Georgetown (a long walk). This is a newly renovated, very affordable boutique hotel offering guests fully stocked kitchens and microwave ovens. The kids will appreciate the in-room video games (fee charged), and those rooms with DVD and CD players. You can also get a free shoeshine. The newly opened Dish restaurant serves up excellent American classics with a fresh twist at affordable prices. Hotel amenities include a free continental breakfast, a health club, and newspaper delivery. Major credit cards are accepted. Parking is an additional $20 per night.

Georgetown

George Washington University Inn
✉ 824 New Hampshire Ave. NW
🚇 Metro: Foggy Bottom (Red Line)
📞 1-800-426-4455
📞 202-337-6620
🖥 *www.gwuinn.com*

Housed in what started in life as a luxury apartment building, GWU Inn is usually classified as a luxury hotel, but generous promotions often put it in the budget category. It's a great opportunity to experience one of Washington's most delightful boutique hotels. Inspired by historic Williamsburg, Virginia, the rooms are furnished with reproduction antiques but deliver all the amenities of a modern hotel. These include two-line phones with data port, CD players, cable TV, and other goodies, such as free access to the local Bally Total Fitness, and umbrellas if it rains. The efficiencies and suites have fully equipped kitchenettes, and a new restaurant, just being planned as this is being written, is sure to be a winner. The GWU Inn just barely makes the Georgetown listing (it's ½-mile away), but it's the only hotel in this price range nearby. And happily, it's only two blocks from the Kennedy Center—so check out the free performances while you're there.

CHAPTER 17

Moderately Priced Hotels ($100–$150)

THIS CHAPTER FEATURES THE moderately priced family hotels, in which Washington D.C. really seems to specialize. When traveling with a family, remember that how close your hotel is to the attractions you want to see is a consideration if your children need to nap or take a midday pool break. Also check to see if the hotel has pay-per-view movies and Nintendo or a game room, as well as a pool.

Downtown D.C.

Beacon Hotel and Corporate Quarters

✉ 1615 Rhode Island Ave. NW

🚇 Metro: Farragut North or Dupont Circle (Red Line)

📞 1-800-821-4367

📞 202-296-2100

🖝 www.beaconhotelwdc.com

The Beacon shines forth out of a $20-million renovation of the Governor's House, a hotel built in the refurbished home of a former governor of Pennsylvania. This elegant hotel now boasts 139 deluxe rooms, 52 "corporate," and 8 deluxe suites. The hotel has the kinds of amenities you'd expect in an upscale hotel, plus fee-based video-games, high-speed Internet, DVD players, and a fitness center. It is within walking distance of many of the city's popular attractions. The hip, new on-site restaurant, The Beacon Bar & Grill, features "playful" nouvelle cuisine, serving three meals a day and a Champagne Sunday Brunch. Families note: The bar and restaurant are discreetly separated. Now here are the surprises: Despite the name, the Beacon is a great hotel for families, and it courts leisure travelers as much as road warriors. Second surprise: Although you will see rates quoted from $139 to the stratosphere, the Beacon is an aggressive marketer and constantly offers promotions of every kind. In the summer, it offers rooms for $1 a day with one day at listed rate. That brought it down to the budget category. It has also offered discount coupons on the Web site. Valet parking is an additional $24 a day.

Henley Park Hotel
✉ 926 Massachusetts Ave. NW
🚇 Metro: Metro Center (Red, Orange, or Blue Line) or Mt. Vernon Sq./7th St.–Convention Center (Yellow or Green Line)
✆ 1-800-678-8946
✆ 202-638-5200
✐ www.henleypark.com

Once an elegant apartment building, the Henley Park is now a gracefully restored ninety-six-room hotel with 118 gargoyles on its façade (including the faces of the architect and his wife). The rooms are large and nicely decorated, with two-line speaker phones, cable TV, and nonsmoking floors, as well as a terry bathrobe, coffeemaker, hair dryer, and iron. Other hotel amenities include free newspaper and shoeshine, nightly turndown service with chocolates, and a free limousine service in the morning. The hotel restaurant, Coeur de Lion, serving New American fare, is one of the best hotel restaurants in the city, and hors d'oeuvres are served along with live entertainment Friday and Saturday night at the Blue Bar. There is also a fireside afternoon tea in the Wilkes Room, which has stained-glass windows and original Mercer tile floors.

The hotel is within walking distance of the National Gallery, Ford's Theatre, the National Museum of Women in the Arts, and Chinatown. Published rates start at $175 for a single and $195 for a double, but there is a $93 summer promotion rate. Major credit cards are accepted. The closest Metro station is about five blocks away.

🧳 TRAVEL TIP

You may be able to save even more money if you book a reservation directly with a hotel by asking if it has package deals and/or if it can offer you a meal plan.

Hotel Helix
✉ 1430 Rhode Island Ave. NW
🚇 Metro: McPherson Square (Orange or Blue Line)
✆ 1-866-508-0658
✆ 202-462-9001
🖱 www.hotelhelix.com

This Kimpton hotel is a great place for families with teens and preteens; in fact, kids are encouraged—there's even a special "Bring 'em Along" package offered. It's unbelievably hip, with a giant painting of Magritte's businessman in a bowler hat on the outside of the building. There's a great lounge that serves up a contemporary menu *in shareable portions*, along with terrific burgers for the kids. In the living room, there's a "Bubbly Hour" with free champagne every day from 5 to 6 P.M. An outdoor patio is open in the summer. Rooms are stylish, with green gauze canopies over the bed with faux fur bedspreads, a flat-screen television, Nintendo, Wi-Fi, and a CD player in every room. Amenities include bathrobes and the fabulous Aveda soaps and shampoos.

JUST FOR PARENTS

Although there is plenty of nightlife in Washington, most of the better hotels have highly recommended lounges where you can hear piano and/or jazz, and some even have dancing. Among those that stand out are the Grand Hyatt, Henley Park, Channel Inn Hotel, Bethesda Marriott, Kinkead's, One Washington Circle Hotel, the Phoenix Park Hotel, and the Hilton Mclean Tyson Corner.

There's a continental breakfast in the morning with bagels and cereal. Room rates are about $125, slightly more for a king and more for the bunk suite, but there are always specials. There are terrific "bunk bed" suites that have a second room for the kids, but these are limited, so reserve ahead. All Kimpton hotels are pet-friendly; parking is an additional $27 per night. All major credit cards accepted.

Hotel Harrington
✉ 436 11th St. NW
🚊 Metro: Gallery Place (Red, Orange, or Green Line)
📞 1-800-424-8532
📞 202-628-8140

The last of its kind in Washington D.C., this family-owned and -operated hotel has been serving traveling families since 1914. It has a great location and good rooms at an affordable price. No problem with food: There's an Ollie's Trolley, a hotel restaurant, and a sandwich and snack place in the building. It is right in the heart of things, easy walking to most of the city's main attractions. The Harrington offers adjoining family rooms for $169. Doubles are $125, and underground parking costs $10 a day. There are often price promotions, so check. The Web site is great and offers a free activities guide for kids and parents. Major credit cards are accepted.

Morrison-Clark Inn

✉ 1015 L St. NW
🚇 Metro: Metro Center (Red, Orange, or Blue Line)
📞 1-800-222-8474
📞 202-898-1200

This hotel was once two separate townhouses, which have been joined to create this unique inn, the only city inn to be listed in the National Register of Historic Places. From 1923 until the 1980s, the site was the Soldiers, Sailors, Marines and Airmen's Club. Some rooms are small, but they are elegantly detailed and furnished with wonderful antiques. There are transformed carriage houses on the first floor, which offer spacious accommodations, and some rooms feature fireplaces, pier mirrors, and wrought-iron ceiling medallions. Hotel amenities include nightly turndown service with chocolates, free morning newspaper, complimentary small fitness center (open twenty-four hours with your room key), and a minibar in every room. Babysitting service is available. The hotel restaurant is nationally acclaimed and offers fabulous contemporary American cuisine, including great desserts.

🧳 TRAVEL TIP

The two most important elements in choosing your accommodations in D.C. should be location and price. Of course, if you are traveling as a family or visiting the city on business, there might be additional amenities that you will want (such as a pool or Wi-Fi). Even if you are coming by car, try to find a hotel near a Metro station.

The Morrison-Clark is within walking distance of the National Gallery, Ford's Theatre, Verizon Center, and the Convention Center. Published room rates are $175 for a deluxe double room and $325 for an exquisite Victorian double room, but there is a summer rate. Major credit cards are accepted.

Washington Plaza

✉ 10 Thomas Circle NW, at 14th St.

🚇 McPherson Square (Orange or Blue Line)

✆ 1-800-424-1140

✆ 202-842-1300

✑ www.washingtonplazahotel.com

A little off the beaten track, but trying to be family-friendly, the Washington Plaza offers many family-oriented activities in the summer, such as periodic Friday night poolside barbecues (check on dates). Originally a resort, the Plaza was recently renovated, and this large hotel (339 rooms) brings back the international style of the 1960s in its lobby furnished with Mies van der Rohe chairs. Rooms are large, with in-room coffeemakers. Other amenities include twice-daily maid service, twenty-four-hour room service, and a morning paper.

═FAST FACT

Winter is a wonderful time to see Washington because the city has gone all-out to make it a tourist delight with their Holiday Homecoming promotion. From December 1 (the lighting of the national tree) through the end of February, you can get 50 percent discounts and more on accommodations, attractions, tours, and performances. Plan early! For details, call 1-800-422-8644 or log on to www.washington.org.

There is nightly jazz in the plaza lounge, free American breakfast buffet, and a fitness center.

While the highest published rate is $299, in reality it ranges from $99 up, so check it out. Major credit cards are accepted. Self-parking is an additional $18 a night, $22 for valet.

Capitol Hill

Phoenix Park Hotel
✉ 520 N. Capitol St. NW
🚇 Metro: Union Station (Red Line)
☎ 1-800-824-5419
☎ 202-638-6900
🖰 www.phoenixparkhotel.com

This hotel is a block away from Union Station and two blocks from the Capitol and was once known as the Commodore Hotel. The Phoenix Park has an Irish restaurant and pub, the Dubliner, on the premises that offers live entertainment nightly. It has tried to make things Irish throughout, with Irish toiletries and linens and much green in the decor. The 150 rooms are comfortable and feature hair dryers and coffeemakers. Room rates start at $149 and go to $299 for a double in high season. Parking is $15.

Capitol Hill Suites
✉ 200 C St. SE
🚇 Metro: Capitol South (Orange or Blue Line)
☎ 1-888-627-7811
☎ 202-543-6000
🖰 www.capitolhillsuites.com

Its location on the House of Representatives side of the Capitol makes this a regular haunt of congresspeople, whose recent photos adorn the lobby walls. This is an all-suite hotel with 152 rooms, most of which have kitchens and dining rooms, so it is also a good family place to stay. There is no on-site restaurant, but there is a food court and many nearby restaurants about which the hotel staff will gladly inform you. Amenities include a continental breakfast, washer and dryer on premises, and use of a nearby health club. Suite rates are $125 to $219, but there are special offers during the year, and guarantee best available rate. Parking is $15 per night. Major credit cards are accepted.

Dupont Circle

Hotel Madera
✉ 1310 New Hampshire Ave. NW
🚊 Metro: Dupont Circle (Red Line)
✆ 1-800-430-1202
✆ 202-296-7600
🖃 www.hotelmadera.com

The Hotel Madera is a lovely, peaceful hotel a little off to the side in downtown Washington near the Heurich House. There's an utterly fabulous American bistro on the premises, so be sure to make a reservation to dine at Firefly, where the décor is that of a summer evening. Rooms are decorated in a rich brown-and-gold hue, there's a free wine-tasting every night at 6, and half the rooms have a balcony with a splendid view of the city's rooftops. Order room service in the morning and drag a chair out there. As in all Kimpton hotels, there's a large television, Nintendo, DVD and CD players, two phones, a dataport, free daily newspaper, and Aveda soaps and shampoos provided in each room. The Hotel Madera is also pet-friendly. Rooms start at about $149, but there are always specials, and be sure to check the Internet for deals. Parking is $27 per night. All major credit cards are accepted.

Topaz Hotel
✉ 1733 N St. NW
🚊 Metro: Dupont Circle (Red Line)
✆ 1-800-775-1202
✆ 202-393-3000
🖃 www.topazhotel.com

This site was once "The Little White House" when it was Teddy Roosevelt's private residence. Now it is one of the coolest hotels in D.C., as part of the hip Kimpton hotel chain. Every room in the hotel is decorated in turquoise and chartreuse, and the beds have canopy linens and pillows that are both plush and stylish. All rooms have a

27-inch television, high-speed Internet, a CD player, and a tea maker, among many other amenities. There are specialty rooms for yoga and fitness (as well as a free, in-room program), and every guest gets some healing stones on the pillow before bed. This is a great choice for a mother-daughter getaway. Amenities include an array of Aveda hair and soap products and a morning paper.

Prices run from $139, more for specialty rooms, but there are many "hot dates," weekend specials, and package deals. Free high-energy drinks are served in the morning. There's a great bar lounge with a terrific happy hour that offers appetizers and drinks from 5 to 7 P.M. daily. Live entertainment is Thursday at 8 P.M. Parking is $30. All major credit cards are accepted.

Hotel Rouge
✉ 1315 16th St. NW
🚇 Metro: Dupont Circle (Red Line)
📞 1-800-738-1202
📞 202-232-8000
💻 *www.rougehotel.com*

This is the red hotel in the Kimpton chain, with rooms decorated in rich red velvet and leopard fabrics. Most rooms have an ottoman, too, which kids love when sitting in front of the large flat-screen television or playing Nintendo. Kids also love the oversize zebra bathrobes (which can be purchased). At a good location off of Dupont Circle, near Embassy Row, the hotel's rooms are spacious, with desk work areas and a funky decor. Some rooms have balconies; others have kitchenettes. There is a lounge on site. Amenities include Aveda soaps and shampoos, daily newspaper delivery, and a minibar in the room. Monday to Friday there is a complimentary "first call" red wine and beer hour, and on weekends, complimentary "last call" Bloody Mary and cold pizza.

Room rates are $125 for "hot dates," more for suites and specialty rooms, such as the Chill room, which offers two TV-entertainment stations, so the kids can play while the parents relax. There are package rates and e-mail and Internet specials as well. Rouge is pet-friendly. Parking is $26 a night. Major credit cards are accepted.

💼 TRAVEL TIP

If you prefer cooking to restaurants, kitchenettes (great for leftovers) can be found at The Quincy, The Swiss Inn, Homewood Suites, Doubletree Guest Suites, The River Inn, the Georgetown Dutch Inn, Hotel Rouge, and the George Washington University Inn.

Foggy Bottom/West End

Hotel Lombardy
✉ 2019 Pennsylvania Ave. NW, at 21st St.
🚇 Metro: Foggy Bottom (Orange or Blue Line)
✆ 1-800-424-5486
✆ 202-828-2600
🖱 *www.hotellombardy.com*

This was once an elegant apartment building and has been recently refurbished into an elegant ten-story hotel (with a handful of apartment-like suites available for rental). The hotel still has an elevator operated by a human being. The rooms are individually decorated and have retained some of the apartment building flavor, such as crystal doorknobs and breakfast nooks. Hotel amenities include a coffeemaker, hair dryer, high-speed Internet, and complimentary newspaper. There's a fitness center and a very good European-style bistro restaurant on the premises. Cafe Lombardy serves breakfast, lunch, and dinner, and also contains The Venetian Room, an elegant dining area for wines, spirits, and small-plate appetizers.

The location of the hotel puts it within walking distance of both the White House in one direction and Georgetown in the other. Room rates vary wildly. On certain days you can get a double room for $121 a night, and the hotel also has online, e-mail, and special package deals. All major credit cards are accepted. Parking is $28 per night.

State Plaza Hotel
✉ 2117 E St. NW
🚇 Metro: Foggy Bottom (Orange or Blue Line)
📞 1-800-424-2859
📞 202-861-8200
✍ www.stateplaza.com

This all-suite hotel is located about five blocks from the White House and the Mall. From one of its two towers (which are connected through the garage) you can see the Mall and the Washington Monument. From the north tower, you can see downtown Washington. The newly renovated Garden Café—the quintessential neighborhood bistro—is in the north tower and serves three meals a day. Outside, the Garden Terrace is a tranquil refuge during the warmer months. The hotel has a fitness center and offers free coffee, local phone calls, and morning newspaper. All rooms have kitchens; one-bedrooms have a dining area.

Room rates vary considerably, with published rates of $178 to $275, but rooms can be as low as $109. There are a number of special promotions and deals, so call or visit the Internet. Parking is an additional $30 per night. All major credit cards are accepted.

Renaissance Hotel
✉ 1143 New Hampshire Ave. NW, at M St.
🚇 Metro: Foggy Bottom (Orange or Blue Line)
📞 1-888-803-1298
📞 202-775-0800

This hotel is the site of a former private hospital, then the Wyndham City Center and now, just renovated, it joins the Marriott family. Its 352 rooms are spacious and have some interesting decorative features. Rooms feature all the amenities you expect from a good modern hotel, including cable and satellite TV, videos, Internet browser and Web TV, and a coffeemaker. There is a fitness club on the premises and a good restaurant, Shula's Steakhouse.

≡FAST FACT

The old adage, "Never buy anything at retail" goes double for hotels. To get the best price, first research the travel sites listed earlier, then check the hotel, or chain owner's, Web site. Finally, if you go through a hotel's reservations desk, don't be afraid to haggle; sometimes a lower price magically appears on the computer screen.

Room rates start at $109 but are published at a higher rate. There are many ways to get a deal, including Marriott special promotions and discounts given to AAA, seniors, government employees, and certain corporations. Parking is $28 per night. Major credit cards are accepted

One Washington Circle Hotel
✉ One Washington Circle NW
🚇 Metro: Foggy Bottom (Orange or Blue Line)
📞 1-800-424-9671
📞 202-872-1680
🖥 www.thecirclehotel.com

This is an all-suite hotel with a variety of suite sizes and is said to be where President Nixon stayed when hiding out in town after the Watergate scandal. It has just emerged from a multi-million-dollar makeover. Despite its promotion as a business hotel, it is a family-friendly place that will treat you right. All suites include a kitchen, dining area, and a terrace. The on-site restaurant, Circle Bistro, under young chef Brendan Cox, serves wonderfully creative French and American food, but he'll do up an exquisite hamburger as well. It's hard to pin down the suite rates, but they seem to start at $159, and sometimes there are weekend specials and package deals; larger suites are more expensive. Valet parking is $24 per night. Major credit cards are accepted.

Georgetown

Hotel Monticello of Georgetown
✉ 1075 Thomas Jefferson St. NW
🚇 Metro: Foggy Bottom (Orange or Blue Line)
📞 1-800-388-2410
📞 202-337-0900
📧 *www.hotelmonticello.com*

This small, forty-seven-unit inn offers spacious studio and one-bedroom apartment-like suites. In-room amenities include computer-access, two-line phones, TVs, coffeemaker, wet bar with refrigerator, and microwave. The hotel offers a free continental breakfast and use of a nearby health club. Room rates average $249, but special deals have brought it down to $169, more for larger suites. Parking is $25. Major credit cards are accepted. The closest Metro service is about five to six blocks away.

CHAPTER 18

In Style—
Luxury Hotels

WASHINGTON HAS SOME OF the most historic hotels in the country. You can actually stay in rooms where presidents and royalty have slept, as well as famous rockers like U2 and the Rolling Stones. It is a city that has been putting out the red carpet for over 200 years, and many of its best hotels have both stories and traditions of their own. You could actually have a wonderful time just touring the city's best and oldest hotels (and you can, if you go to the Historic Hotels of America's Web site and request a tour of its D.C. properties, *www.historichotels.org*).

Downtown D.C.

Grand Hyatt Washington
✉ 1000 H St. NW
🚇 Metro: Metro Center (Red, Orange or Blue Line)
📞 1-800-233-1234
📞 202-582-1234
✎ *www.grandwashington.hyatt.com*

This is a luxurious mega-hotel with 900 newly renovated rooms. The lobby alone is stupendous, with a glass-enclosed atrium that is twelve stories high and features fountains and a waterfall; a baby grand piano floating on its own island in a "lagoon" surrounded by a bar; and two floors of shops and restaurants. The hotel is across the street from the Convention Center and near Verizon Center. Rooms are large but relatively standard with hair dryers, cable and satellite TV, high-speed Internet, coffeemaker, and a basket of toiletries. The health club is two stories high, with a lap pool and sauna.

The standard room rate is $379, but special rates can range down to $179, and Internet specials can be as low as $139, all depending on the day. There are a number of special packages available (such as the winter holiday package), so ask for specials when you make your reservations. Parking is $20 for self-parking (no in-and-out) and $26 for valet (come and go as you please). Major credit cards are accepted.

📖 TRAVEL TIP

Don't get scared off by published rates. Even the most expensive hotels have special summer and off-day pricing, so you may be able to stay at a luxury-class hotel for half-price if you ask for a summer or special rate.

Hotel Monaco
✉ 700 F St. NW
🚊 Metro: Gallery Place–Chinatown (Red, Yellow, or Green Line)
📞 1-800-649-1202
📞 202-628-7177
💻 www.monaco-dc.com

This is a one-of-a-kind hotel, and it's very kid-friendly. The Kimpton hotel chain bought this old post office building and converted it into a fun hotel. Rooms are large and have wonderful windows and high ceilings, and you can even request that a "companion" goldfish in a bowl be brought to your room. It's also near the International

Spy Museum, Ford's Theatre, and the newly reopened Donald W. Reynolds Center for American Art and Portraiture. Some rooms have vaulted ceilings and Jacuzzis, and there's a well-equipped health club on the premises. All rooms have Nintendo, a DVD and CD player, and the signature Aveda soap and shampoos. There is also complimentary morning coffee and an evening wine reception. The Poste Brasserie on the premises offers a terrific selection of bistro fare, and there's a lounge at the front of the restaurant for slightly faster and less expensive fare. Rooms run about $149 to $429 per night, if you add in super special deals, but there are numerous "hot dates" (25 percent off regular rate), specials, and package deals. Parking is $34 a night.

💼 TRAVEL TIP

During the summer months and at various times sprinkled throughout the year, when Washington empties its hotel rooms of lobbyists because the House and Senate are not in session and the tourists have gone home, some of the best hotels in the city offer incredibly reduced rates. It's worth the time to research these luxury hotels.

Hay-Adams Hotel
✉ 16th & H Sts. NW
🚇 Metro: McPherson Square (Orange or Blue Line)
☎ 1-800-424-5054
☎ 202-638-6600
🖰 www.hayadams.com

This hotel was built on the former land of John Hay and Henry Adams, two prominent Washington social and political bigwigs whose homes faced Lafayette Square and were across the street from the White House. When the hotel opened in 1927, such luminaries as Charles Lindbergh and Amelia Earhart stayed here. *W* magazine said of the recent restoration, "This is as close as one gets to staying at the White House, short of being invited by the president."

Rooms on the fifth through eighth floors on the H Street side have spectacular views of the White House with the Washington Monument behind it. Some rooms have fireplaces. Hotel amenities include bathrobes, nightly turndown service, a daily newspaper, and health club privileges. Rumor has it that the ghost of Hay's wife haunts the hotel's fourth floor.

The hotel's restaurant, The Lafayette, overlooking the White House and Lafayette Square, offers contemporary American cuisine as well as afternoon tea. Off the Record, a wine and champagne bar, serves cocktails and light fare. Room rates are $329 to $975, standard rack rate is $500, and suites run higher. Parking is $33 a day. Major credit cards are accepted.

Hotel Washington
✉ 515 15th St. NW
🚇 Metro: Metro Center (Red, Orange, or Blue Line)
✆ 1-800-424-9540
✆ 202-638-5900
🖱 www.hotelwashington.com

This elegant hotel, right across the street from the White House, has changed owners and has a new look following a $10 million renovation. Its 315 rooms and 26 suites have been given a fresh, contemporary look (no more Colonial-style antiques or four-poster beds), but the hotel's long tradition has not been abandoned. A new Hall of History has been added, and you can still sit in its lobby and look out over the White House and the Treasury Building. Sky Terrace, the rooftop deck, offers dinner and drinks and a stupendous view of the city, which you can always take in even if you are not staying here.

Rooms run from $135 to $400 for a single room. However, in the summer, when Congress is not in session, the hotel runs a super family sale for $155 per night. All major credit cards are accepted. Parking is $28 per day (in-and-out) in the on-site garage.

The Jefferson

✉ 1200 16th St. NW, at M Street

🚇 Metro: Farragut North (Red Line)

📞 1-866-270-8118

📞 202-347-2200

🖅 *thejeffersonwashingtondc.com*

The Jeff is now under the Kor Hotel Group banner. This former luxury apartment building was built in 1923 and was a hotel for military personnel during World War II. In 1986, it was restored and transformed into a 100-room hotel, which is now a popular hotel for dignitaries and celebrities. Both the lobby and some rooms feature some genuine Jefferson artifacts (on loan from Monticello), such as signed documents and letters, as well as a bust of Jefferson in the lobby and Jefferson prints in the restaurant.

≡FAST FACT

The Jefferson, opened in 1923, is one of D.C.'s finest and most exclusive hotels. It features an exquisite collection of fine art and antiques and is home to several original documents signed by Thomas Jefferson.

Hotel amenities include high-speed Internet, nightly turndown service with Godiva chocolate, a morning newspaper, VCRs, CD players, bathrobes, and a twenty-four-hour on-site health club. Some rooms have fireplaces and four-poster beds. The Restaurant at the Jefferson features American cuisine, as well as an afternoon tea, and an excellent Sunday brunch. It is located four blocks from the White House. Published hotel rates are $159 to $339 for a single or a double room, and special packages are available. Parking is $28. Major credit cards are accepted.

L'Enfant Plaza Hotel

✉ 480 L'Enfant Plaza SW
🚇 Metro: L'Enfant Plaza (Yellow, Orange, Green, or Blue Line)
📞 1-800-635-5065
📞 202-484-1000
🖰 www.lenfantplazahotel.com

This posh hotel is located a hop, skip, and a jump from the Mall, and it has a reputation for catering to visitors traveling with pets. (Being able to take your dog for a run on the Mall is a real treat. There is a one-time charge of $25 for your pet, plus a refundable deposit.) The hotel has a year-round rooftop pool and a fitness center and there's a gourmet coffee cart in the lobby.

Room rates can run from $109 to $389, and there are occasional specials. Parking is $28 a night for valet, $18 for self-park with no in-and-out. Major credit cards are accepted. The L'Enfant Plaza Metro station leads you right into the hotel.

Renaissance Mayflower Hotel

✉ 1127 Connecticut Ave. NW
🚇 Metro: Farragut North (Red Line)
📞 1-800-HOTELS1 (1-800-468-3571)
📞 202-347-3000
🖰 www.renaissancehotels.com

The Mayflower is one of the most historic and luxurious hotels in the city and offers 660 deluxe guest rooms. Located four blocks south of the White House, it was where Calvin Coolidge held his 1925 inauguration for 1,000 people, which was also the hotel's grand opening. It was designed by Warren & Wetmore, the same architectural firm that designed New York's Grand Central Station, and it is almost as big, taking up most of the block. Franklin Delano Roosevelt lived at the Mayflower between his election and inauguration; John F. Kennedy used to stay here when he was a congressman; and Jean Harlow was so fascinated by the switchboard that she played operator-for-a-day when she visited.

≡FAST FACT

The Renaissance Mayflower Hotel, built in 1925, has so much Washington D.C. history that a book has been written about it, which you can buy in the hotel lobby gift store. It has been the site of many inaugural balls and the makeshift home of most of our presidents while they waited to occupy the White House.

When it opened its doors, the Mayflower boasted more gold leaf than any other building in the city except the Library of Congress and was one of the capital's first air-conditioned buildings. Forty-six thousand square feet of Italian marble was used to create the hotel's bathrooms. A recent renovation uncovered a sixty-foot skylight that had been blacked out during World War II, as well as murals painted by Edward Lanning.

Hotel amenities include bathrobes, a morning newspaper, your own pot of coffee with wake-up call, a small television in the bathroom, and a fitness center.

Depending on the date, room rates can start at $169 and run higher for suites. Major credit cards are accepted.

The St. Regis
✉ 923 16th St. NW
🚇 Metro: Farragut West or McPherson Square (Orange or Blue Line)
📞 1-800-325-3535
📞 202-638-2626
🖰 www.stregis.com/washington

The St. Regis will be closed for extensive renovation until the middle of 2007. Now under Starwood Management, this ornate hotel is a favorite of celebrities of all sorts, from Queen Elizabeth to the Rolling Stones when it was The Sheraton Carlton. Designed to look like an Italian palazzo, the St. Regis' lobby features chandeliers and Empire furniture. Rooms are on the smallish side, but they are elegantly furnished, with desks set aside in alcoves, and marble bathrooms stocked with everything from cotton balls to mouthwash. There's also an umbrella tucked away inside the closet. Other amenities include bathrobes, hair dryers, personal safes, coffee with wake-up call, nightly turndown, and a fitness club. The St. Regis Library Lounge and Restaurant is book-lined, features a working fireplace, and allows cigar smoking after 10 P.M., something very hard to find in the city anymore.

Room rates are $225, single or double. Major credit cards are accepted. Valet parking is $28 per day. The St. Regis is within walking distance to the White House.

Willard Intercontinental

✉ 1401 Pennsylvania Ave. NW

🚊 Metro: Metro Center (Red, Orange, or Blue Line)

✆ 1-800-827-1747

✆ 202-628-9100

🖑 www.washington.interconti.com

This is one of the best hotels in D.C. because of its location near the White House, its fabulous restaurant, its luxurious rooms, and its historical importance. In 2006, the Willard celebrated the 150th anniversary of its founding and 20th of its reopening with a series of citywide cultural events hosted by many museums. Most U.S. presidents have stayed or dined here, from Lincoln to Clinton. Julia Ward Howe wrote "The Battle Hymn of the Republic" at the Willard in the same room that Martin Luther King Jr. later penned his "I Have a Dream" speech. Management has installed a photographic museum on the history of the hotel, with startling photos of how it was left abandoned in the 1980s and transformed to its current luster.

≡FAST FACT

President Grant was known to smoke cigars and sip brandy in the lobby of the Willard, where he was constantly sought out by those wanting something from him—and this is how the word *lobbyist* came into being.

The Willard was designed by the same architect who built the Plaza Hotel in New York. The lobby features seals of the forty-eight states on the ceiling, as well as chandeliers, marble columns, and gilt trim. Rooms are large and decorated in Empire or Federal style and feature an in-room safe, minibar, hair dryer, scale, and a telephone in the marble bathrooms. Other amenities include twice-daily maid service, bathrobes, and a complimentary newspaper and shoeshine. The Willard Room is a beautiful restaurant that features exquisite cuisine and fabulous desserts. There is a new "Taste of America" Sunday brunch for $65; kids five through twelve eat for $35, under five eat free. The room is also popular as a place where Washingtonians propose to one another because of its cozy, yet elegant ambiance of candlelight and chandeliers and consistently good food. The Round Robin Bar has quite a drinking history. It has been a popular drinking place for two centuries, with such luminaries as Mark Twain, Walt Whitman, and Nathaniel Hawthorne. It is said that Washington Irving brought Charles Dickens here for a drink. There is also the new Café 1401 that offers casual dining for breakfast and lunch, and the new Terrace at the Willard outdoor café. Also new is an elegant afternoon tea in Peacock Alley.

Room rates are $239 to $549, the rack rate is given as $579, and there are always specials. Valet parking is $28 per night. Major credit cards are accepted. This hotel is convenient to the Metro Center station.

Capital Hilton
✉ 1001 16th St. NW, at K St.

🚇 Metro: Farragut North (Red Line), also Farragut West or McPherson Square (Orange or Blue Line).

☎ 1-800-HILTONS (1-800-445-8667)

☎ 202-393-1000

🖝 www.capital.hilton.com

This is a mega-hotel (549 rooms) that is popular because of its location two blocks from the White House. Rooms feature three phones (one in the bathroom), coffeemaker, premium TV, complimentary newspaper, and secure door locking. The Tower floors (ten through fourteen) offer extra amenities such as complimentary breakfast, hors d'oeuvres, and evening refreshments. The on-premise restaurant is Twigg's Grill, serving contemporary American cuisine. It is open 6:30 A.M. to 10 P.M., and there are many neighborhood places as well.

Typical rack room rates are $269 to $319 for a double, but an Internet search brought up rooms for $142. Major credit cards are accepted. Parking is $28 per day.

🧳 TRAVEL TIP

In addition to hotels, Washington has many wonderful small inns and bed and breakfasts. Some are listed here, but you can get a full list at www.bedandbreakfastdc.com or by calling 1-877-893-3233 or 1-413-582-9888.

Renaissance Washington D.C. Hotel
✉ 999 9th St. NW

🚇 Metro: Gallery Place–Chinatown (Yellow or Green Line)

☎ 1-800-HOTELS1 (1-800-468-3571)

☎ 202-898-9000

🖝 www.dcrenaissance.com

This is another mega hotel (800 rooms) that caters to Washington business travelers visiting the nearby Convention Center. It is also within walking distance to D.C.'s Chinatown and Verizon Center. Rooms are spacious, with work areas and a dataport. Hotel amenities include coffeemakers, iron and board, cable and satellite TV, and video games (fee charged). There is a health club on the premises with an indoor pool. For dining, the hotel has Florentine, which serves American food; President's Sports Bar, open for lunch and dinner; Starbucks, open for lunch; and the Lobby Bar.

Rooms run $159 to $449, but a typical Internet rate showed $139. Valet parking is $27 per day, self-park is $22. All major credit cards are accepted.

The Madison
✉ 1177 15th Street NW, at M Street
🚇 Metro: McPherson Square (Orange or Blue Line)
✆ 1-800-424-8577
✆ 202-862-1600

After completing a ten-month, $40-million renovation, The Madison has set out to claim its original place along the stellar hotels of D.C. Opened in 1963, with the President and Mrs. Kennedy in attendance, it was one of the Camelot hangouts and was considered one of the most stylish hotels of the early '60s. The current renovation is a combination of classic styles—Federalist, Georgian, and American Empire, with contemporary flair. The 353 rooms feature 300-count Egyptian cotton sheets, CD players, and a heated towel rack in the bathroom. There is a fitness center on the premises, as well as three restaurants, the highly praised Palette, The Federalist (where there is a Sunday Jazz Brunch), and the PostScript Bar.

Listed room rack rate is $319 per night, but a Web check showed $150, and the hotel runs specials as well as weekend packages. Their summer package ran $159 a day. Major credit cards are accepted. Parking is available for $31.

Capitol Hill

Hyatt Regency Washington on Capitol Hill

✉ 400 New Jersey Ave. NW

🚇 Metro: Union Station (Red Line)

✆ 202-737-1234

🖰 www.hyattregencywashington.com

This mega-hotel (834 rooms) is located between First and D Streets and is the perfect location for travelers who need to be within walking distance of the Capitol, the Supreme Court, or the House or Senate, which is one of the reasons the renovated rooms may be so pricey if you don't do some shopping. The hotel offers a business plan, which includes twenty-four-hour access to a private business office, free local phone calls, a morning newspaper, and a buffet breakfast at the Park Promenade restaurant. Families will find a generous number of amenities as well. In addition to the fare at the Park Promenade, lighter meals are served at Perks, Coffee & More in the lobby, and kids will love the square pizzas from the Pizza Factory.

Rooms range from $119 to $1,300. Parking is $33 per day, $38 for SUVs and vans. All major credit cards are accepted.

Holiday Inn on the Hill

✉ 415 New Jersey Ave. NW

🚇 Metro: Union Station (Red Line)

✆ 202-638-1616

🖰 www.hionthehilldc.com

This hotel is down the street from the Capitol, near the Library of Congress and the Folger Shakespeare Library. Rooms are newly renovated and stylish with large work areas, hair dryers, minibars, and coffeemakers. It's very family-friendly. Kids eat and stay free, and they have Nintendo, TV, and a pool for diversions. They'll also love the unique lobby blue-bubble wall. The Senators Bar and Grill will fascinate with its memorabilia from the now-defunct D.C. baseball team. Room rates are $91 to $410 per night. Parking is $25 per night. All major credit cards are accepted.

≡FAST FACT

The Watergate Hotel is next door to the notorious apartment and office complex where the fateful burglary took place in the 1970s. The hotel itself has long been a favorite of celebrities, politicians, and performing artists.

Hotel George
✉ 15 E St. NW
🚇 Metro: Union Station (Red Line)
✆ 1-800-576-8331
✆ 202-347-4200
⌨ www.hotelgeorge.com

The Kimpton hotel chain has taken an old building and rehabbed it to an ultra-modern fantasy. The Hotel George presents itself as the hip hotel for those doing business on the Hill. Posters throughout the hotel depict images of George Washington in contemporary gear, without the wig. Rooms are spacious, with desks, hair dryers, coffeemakers, irons, and an audio speaker in the bathroom. The hotel restaurant, Bis, serves French bistro food. The hotel has a fitness club and steam rooms, as well as a billiard room. Other amenities include a morning newspaper, nightly turndown service, a video player, Nintendo, and T1 high-speed Internet access. Room rates are $149 to $454, but there are occasional special rates and packages, so ask when you call. Parking is $24 per night. Major credit cards are accepted.

Adams Morgan/Woodley Park

Marriott Wardman Park

✉ 2660 Woodley Rd. NW, at Connecticut Ave.

🚇 Metro: Woodley Park–Zoo (Red Line)

📞 1-800-228-9290

📞 202-328-2000

🖥 *www.marriott.com/wasdt*

The former site of the Sheraton Washington, this is the largest hotel in the city, sitting on a sixteen-acre plot of land a hop, skip, and a jump away from the National Zoo. Its more than 1,300 rooms have undergone a major renovation. Because of its size, the hotel tends to cater to convention-goers, but it's also a good place for families because of its heated pool and proximity to the zoo. There are reduced rates in the summer and when the hotel is not at capacity.

Wardman Park is a former apartment building for the rich and famous—for instance, Gore Vidal and Douglas Fairbanks Jr. once lived here—and the 200-odd rooms in this section retain a bit of its earlier charm with high ceilings and intricate moldings. In-room amenities include hair dryers, Internet browser and Web TV, cable and satellite TV, videogames and player for rent, refrigerator, coffeemaker, refrigerator, irons, and morning newspaper delivery. The hotel has a heated outdoor pool (seasonal), a fitness center, and a number of shops and services. Pets are allowed. On-site dining is available at Perle's; Harry's Pub is open for lunch and dinner; Woodley Market is a gourmet deli serving breakfast, snacks, and takeout sandwiches and meals; and Starbucks offers coffee and fresh baked goods. Room rates are about $189 to $309, but there are specials all year round. Self-parking is $23 per night, valet is $28. Major credit cards are accepted.

Omni Shoreham

✉ 2500 Calvert St. NW, at Connecticut Ave.

🚇 Metro: Woodley Park-Zoo (Red Line)

☎ 1-800-843-6664

☎ 202-234-0700

🖱 *www.omnishorehamhotel.com*

This is another mega-hotel (834 rooms) that serves the convention crowd. Set on an eleven-acre plot of land overlooking Rock Creek Park, it's within walking distance of the National Zoo. It was built in the 1930s and has been the site of many an inaugural ball. A suite on the eighth floor is said to be haunted and bears a plaque marked "Ghost Suite." Rooms are very spacious—some have marvelous views of Rock Creek—and nicely decorated. The hotel has an outdoor, heated swimming pool with poolside snack bar and a children's pool, fitness center (daily fee), steam room and whirlpool, spa facilities, and nearby jogging and bicycling paths.

The upscale restaurant serves elegant meals and overlooks the park. There is also a more casual dining spot and a convenience center for coffee and sandwiches. Unwind at the lounge or poolside bar. The beautifully landscaped grounds have an elliptical lawn (like the one in front of the White House but smaller) and a formal garden with fountains, which is a popular location for weddings and parties. Room rates are published at a low of $140 to $1,500 but average $459 to $2,100 without special deals or packages, of which many are offered. Parking is $28 for valet, $23 for self-parking. Major credit cards are accepted.

Dupont Circle

Washington Hilton & Towers

✉ 1919 Connecticut Ave. NW, at T St.

🚇 Metro: Dupont Circle (Red Line)

☎ 1-800-HILTONS (1-800-445-8667)

☎ 202-483-3000

🖱 *www.washington.hilton.com*

This is the hotel where John Hinkley Jr. tried to assassinate President Reagan. It has been a major stop for presidential events and continues to be one, with a new bulletproof side entrance added after the shooting. It has the largest ballroom on the East Coast and therefore has a steady stream of important shindigs, from inaugural balls to society events. The more than 1,100 rooms are designed in a contemporary décor. Above the fifth floor there is a panoramic city view from most hotel windows.

The hotel offers six on-site dining alternatives, from the more upscale 1919 Grill to casual poolside dining. There are children's and kosher menus available. There is a long list of family-friendly amenities, including the Vacation Station, which has toys the kids can borrow for free. The hotel features a heated outdoor pool and a children's pool, tennis courts, and a health club. Room rates are $99 to $329; tower rooms are slightly more expensive. Parking is $23 per night. Major credit cards are accepted.

Westin Embassy Row

✉ 2100 Massachusetts Ave. NW, at 21st St.

🚇 Metro: Dupont Circle (Red Line)

☎ 1-800-325-3589

☎ 202-293-2100

✎ www.starwoodhotels.com

Vice President Al Gore just about grew up in the Westin, which has been one of the places to stay in Washington for the rich, famous, and powerful since it opened in 1927. (It was once the Ritz Hotel, the Ritz-Carlton, and the Fairfax.) It was renovated in the '90s, and rooms are elegantly decorated, many featuring armchairs and ottomans and marble tubs. Some rooms have a view of Embassy Row. Views from upper floors include the Washington Monument and Georgetown. Rooms contain the expected amenities. The hotel has guest rooms fitted with workout equipment (extra fee), a fitness club with sauna, and provides maps for the jogging and walking route nearby. There's a Kids Club (where stories are told), and pets are allowed.

The Fairfax Lounge, which serves cocktails, has a working fireplace and a piano bar. Room rates are $129 and up for a double, with specials and packages offered. Valet parking is $28 a night. Major credit cards are accepted.

💼 TRAVEL TIP

If you've been to D.C. before, and you would prefer a more relaxing vacation this time around, perhaps with some golfing and spa treatments, you might want to consider Westfield's Marriott Resort in Chantilly, Virginia (703-818-0300, *www.westfieldsmarriott.com*), just twenty minutes from downtown. It is very family-friendly, with a terrific indoor pool as well as an outdoor pool in the summer.

The Mansion on O St.
✉ 2020 O St. NW
🚇 Metro: Dupont Circle (Red Line)
📞 202-496-2000
🖊 www.omansion.com

This combination hotel, museum, and gallery offers ultra-private and secure one-of-a-kind lodging. It is housed in a connected series of brownstones and run by probably the most imaginative staff in the city. Rooms are decorated in unique themes; you never know what you'll find (a teak bathtub, or maybe a shower made from a London telephone booth?). On reserving, you'll be asked your needs, preferences, and dreams, and they do their best to fulfill. The amenities are world-class. Rooms are equipped with the latest technology, from WiFi to XM radios. There is a 20,000-book library and a huge CD collection. There is a pool, and you also get free passes to Sports Club LA. Free breakfast comes with your stay, and you can order whatever you want. Room rates run from $250 to $1,000 (government rate is $188, if available). Parking is $25. All major credit cards are accepted.

Hotel Palomar

✉ 2121 P St. NW

🚊 Metro: Dupont Circle (Red Line)

📞 1-877-866-3070

📞 202-448-1800

✑ www.hotelpalomar-dc.com

Formerly the Radisson Barcelo, the Kimpton Hotel group has worked its magic, spent $32 million, and added another gem to its crown of kicky hotels. The outside presents an amazing façade reminiscent of old Europe, but once inside you are presented with a soaring, modern lobby and a chic, sophisticated ambience. Despite adding thirty rooms and a huge meeting space to this former apartment house, the Palomar still has some of the most spacious rooms in the city, averaging 520 square feet. It has great amenities for you and the kids, including a flat-screen TV, CD player and a library of DVDs, robes, and complimentary wireless Internet. The hotel also has a fitness center and pool, and there is a free evening wine reception. Dining is at the Urbana, an upscale, contemporary Mediterranean restaurant that has won plaudits. Room rates are from $169 to $469; there are many specials and package deals. The hotel is very pet-friendly (there is even a pet package offered). Parking is $32 per night.

═══FAST FACT

You'll see two telephone numbers in the hotel listings. The 800 number is the national reservations telephone, and its staff can usually answer all your questions. The local area code numbers are those of the hotel, for more specialized questions. If you call that and ask for reservations, you'll probably get transferred to the centralized reservations operator.

Courtyard by Marriott Northwest

✉ 1900 Connecticut Ave. NW

🚇 Metro: Dupont Circle (Red Line)

📞 1-800-321-2211

📞 202-332-9300

🖱 www.courtyard.com

This 147-unit hotel is operated by the same Irish company that runs the Normandy Inn and has brought many of the same European amenities to this hotel, such as coffee and tea served all day in the lobby and cookies in the afternoon. In-room amenities include cable and satellite TV, movies and videos, pay-per-view, refrigerator, Internet access (wired in-room, wireless in public areas), coffeemakers, and hair dryers, and the hotel has an outdoor pool and a fitness center. Freebies include a newspaper, toll-free phone calls, and dinner delivery from nearby restaurants. The on-site restaurant, Claret's, serves American food for breakfast and dinner, and The Lobby Lounge offers dinner. The best room rates are $94 to $189 for a double. Parking is $20 per night. Major credit cards are accepted.

Foggy Bottom/West End

Fairmont Hotel

✉ 2401 M St. NW

🚇 Metro: Foggy Bottom (Orange or Blue Line)

📞 1-800-441-1414

📞 202-429-2400

🖱 www.fairmont.com/washington

This 415-room hotel, formerly the Washington Monarch Hotel, went through a $12-million restoration and has become a mecca for celebrities. The big draw is its state-of-the-art fitness center, which is an additional $10 per person, although the pool, sauna, steam room, and whirlpool are free to guests. The hotel has a beautiful garden courtyard, which about one-third of the rooms overlook. In-room amenities include high-speed Internet in rooms (WiFi in lobbies), cable TV, bathrobes, three phones, and high-end toiletries. There is twice-daily maid service and nightly turndown service. Pets are pampered—treats given to dogs at check-in are handmade by the executive chef. Room rates can run from $159 to $769. Valet parking is $27. Major credit cards are accepted.

🧳 TRAVEL TIP

The difference between valet parking and self-park is more than just handing over your keys. Valet parking means you can come and go all day with no extra charge. If you self-park, you'll have to pay the daily rate every time you return.

Park Hyatt Hotel
✉ 1201 24th St. NW, at M St.
🚇 Metro: Foggy Bottom (Orange or Blue Line)
✆ 1-800-778-7477
✆ 202-789-1234
✍ www.parkhyatt.com

Designed as a luxury hotel by the famed New York architectural firm of Skidmore, Owings & Merrill, this 224-room hotel has just undergone a massive reconstruction and redesign by New York designer Tony Chi. There is a new mezzanine, a lobby bar, and an open kitchen restaurant. The design is mature, contemporary, and sophisticated. Rooms are dotted with authentic folk art, accompanied by books available for sale. In-room amenities include marble bathrooms with toiletries designed by Parisian perfumer Blaise Mautin, weekday newspaper delivery, nightly turndown service, and desks wired for broadband. Guests have complimentary use of a Tony Chi–designed Audi A8 L sedan. The health club is excellent, with a pool, but the separate kid's pool has been eliminated. The Blue Duck Restaurant is topnotch, with innovative New

American entrees, but it's not family-friendly in atmosphere or menu. Tea is served all day at the new Tea Cellar, with afternoon tea from 2:30 to 4:30 P.M. Room rates are $319 to $495. Parking is $35 per night. Major credit cards are accepted.

Watergate Hotel

✉ 2650 Virginia Ave. NW

🚇 Metro: Foggy Bottom (Orange or Blue Line)

📞 1-800-424-2736

📞 202-965-2300

🖰 www.watergatehotel.com

This has always been one of the best hotels in Washington, legendary long before the Watergate break-in in the nearby apartment complex and the press hordes that waited for Monica Lewinsky to emerge from her mother's apartment. Its location is one of its many drawing cards, along with the view of the Potomac that it offers. Many of the performers playing at the Kennedy Center right next door have stayed here; other notable guests include Ingrid Bergman, Muhammad Ali, and Gloria Estefan.

Rooms are spacious, and the suites are reported to be some of the largest in the city. Many rooms have balconies. The hotel has an excellent health club and a heated indoor lap pool. In-room amenities include a robe, minibar, hair dryer, toiletries, nightly turndown service, and daily newspaper delivery. The Potomac Lounge serves afternoon tea. The hotel restaurant is Aquarelle, serving inventive American food.

Room rates are $149 to $329 and above, but there are some specials. Major credit cards are accepted. Valet parking is $26.

Doubletree Guest Suites

✉ 801 New Hampshire Ave. NW, at H St.

🚇 Metro: Foggy Bottom (Orange or Blue Line)

📞 1-800-222-TREE (1-800-222-8733)

📞 202-785-2000

🖰 www.washingtondcsuites.doubletree.com

This 105-room hotel offers larger rooms to business travelers and touring families with a fully stocked and equipped kitchen (with free coffee and tea) and an in-season rooftop pool. There is no restaurant on the premises, although room service for breakfast and dinner is available, and the staff will direct you to the many eateries nearby. Room rates are $144 to $300 for a double. There is always a Dream Deal going for families. Valet parking is $25 per day. All major credit cards are accepted.

Washington Suites
✉ 2500 Pennsylvania Ave. NW, at 25th St.
🚊 Metro: Foggy Bottom (Orange or Blue Line)
📞 1-877-736-2500
📞 202-333-8060
🖥 www.washingtonsuitesgeorgetown.com

This two-room-suite hotel is a great location for families traveling to the city—within walking distance to Georgetown. The rooms are comfortably furnished with an apartment feel. All the amenities are here, plus a fully stocked and equipped kitchen with free coffee and tea (finally, you can take leftovers "home" and reheat later). There are many freebies, too: breakfast every morning, a reception Tuesday at 6 P.M., newspaper, exercise room, and cookies at check-in. Pets are allowed. Room rates are $119 to $329, and there are good family deals on the Internet. Parking is $25 per day. All major credit cards are accepted.

Westin Grand Hotel
✉ 2350 M St. NW, at 24th St.
🚊 Metro: Foggy Bottom (Orange or Blue Line)
📞 1-800-228-3000
📞 202-429-0100
🖥 www.westin.com

This 263-room hotel has a number of unique features, such as working fireplaces in some rooms and French doors that open up on terraces overlooking the street. It is within walking distance to

Georgetown and the Kennedy Center. There is a heated outdoor pool, a good on-site restaurant called Café on M, the M Street Grille for breakfast and lunch, and a Starbucks. Good services and amenities abound including the Westin Kids Club. Room rates are $139 to $309 for a double. Parking is $28 a night. All major credit cards are accepted.

Georgetown

Four Seasons Hotel
✉ 2800 Pennsylvania Ave. NW
🚆 Metro: Foggy Bottom (Orange or Blue Line)
📞 1-800-332-3442
📞 202-342-0444
🖥 *www.fourseasons.com/washington*

This is one of Washington's premier hotels and has been the hotel of choice for celebrities for years. It recently burnished its image after a $25 million restoration by interior designer Pierre Yves Rochon made it the only D.C. hotel to be awarded the Mobil Five-Star award and the only North American hotel to be added to the list. The rooms are well appointed, and with plants and art, armchairs and desks, as well as down comforters on the beds. Rooms come stocked with a minibar, CD players, video/DVD/Playstation library, bathrobes, hair dryers, and a toiletry basket. The on-site health club is considered one of the best in the hotel business, with weights, exercise equipment, a two-lane pool, and classes in everything from yoga to tai chi. Other hotel amenities include twice-daily maid service, limousine service, and a morning newspaper.

Room rates are $375 to $1,975. Major credit cards are accepted. Parking is $35 per night. This hotel is five blocks from the Metro.

☂ RAINY DAY FUN

At the Four Seasons Hotel, the kids' amenities are awesome. Inform the hotel you will be traveling with kids, and it will give each kid a welcoming gift and cookies and will provide books and magazines, games, bathrobes, toiletries, and healthy menus—all age-appropriate down to infants.

The Latham Hotel

✉ 3000 M St. NW
🚇 Metro: Foggy Bottom (Orange or Blue Line)
✆ 1-800-368-5922
✆ 202-726-5000
🖅 www.thelatham.com

Set in the center of Georgetown, this hotel is conveniently located near all the good restaurants and nightlife, but it is quiet because it is set back from the street. The rooms have a comfortable, French country flair. In-room amenities of interest to families include: cable/satellite/Web TV, videogames (fee charged), coffeemaker, iron and board, hair dryers, and robes. The hotel has an outdoor pool and a fitness center. There are two excellent French restaurants on the premises—Citronelle, which is one of the more talked-about D.C. eateries, and one of the La Madeleine chain. Room rates are $159 to $259. There are excellent deals offered, especially in the summer. Valet parking is an additional $24. Major credit cards are accepted. There is about a six-block walk to the Metro.

CHAPTER 19

Day Trips from D.C.

THE SURROUNDING TOWNS AND suburbs of Washington D.C. are as old (if not older) than the city itself. They offer a host of fascinating and interesting things to see and do, from visiting our first president's "gentleman farm" in Mount Vernon (now with its spectacular new visitors' center and museum) to enjoying more modern forms of entertainment like amusement parks and outlet shopping malls. If you have the time you should try to see Mount Vernon and the spectacular Pope-Leighey house designed by Frank Lloyd Wright on the grounds of the neighboring Woodlawn Plantation. They are both worth the trip.

Mount Vernon

✉ George Washington Memorial Parkway (Rt. 1 South)
✆ 703-780-2000
✑ *www.mountvernon.org*

Washington lived at Mount Vernon for forty-five years, from the time he was twenty-two until his death. He and Martha are buried on the premises. He loved this place, and over the years he tripled the size of the mansion, redesigned the grounds and outbuildings, and bought neighboring lands. The present site was purchased by the Mount Vernon Ladies Association in 1858 from Washington's descendants for $200,000 and is almost unchanged in its appearance from 1799, when Washington died.

Today the estate is a mere 500 acres of the former president's holdings, but even at one-sixteenth of its original size, Mount Vernon is at least a half-day's touring experience. Visitors can now enjoy the fruits of a multiyear, $95 million campaign to revitalize the historic property and promote the legacy of George Washington, including two new and spectacular theater and museum buildings that give the George Washington experience a new dimension. Also, there's a wonderful gift shop and a Colonial restaurant nearby, so plan on making a day of this trip.

≡FAST FACT

To put visitors face-to-face with George Washington as a real person, three wax heads (with real human hair) were created of him as a nineteen-year-old surveyor, a forty-five-year-old general, and the fifty-seven-year-old president. Since no photographs or paintings exist of his younger years, a team of scientists and artists using cutting-edge techniques re-created his appearance.

The Tour

The Mount Vernon admission includes a tour of the new visitors' center, the new museum, and the mansion, which Washington made the center of his estate. Restoration on the mansion is meticulous, from the color of the paint on the walls to the placement of many of the original furnishings (such as the leather chair in Washington's study that he used for the eight years he was president, and the bed he died in).

The Ford Orientation Center and the Donald W. Reynolds Museum and Education Center opened in late 2006. The new facilities are part of a multiyear, $95 million campaign to revitalize the historic property and promote the legacy of our first president.

The Orientation Center is a light-filled space allowing panoramic views of the estate, and it contains state-of-the-art theaters showing a mini-epic of Washington's life, a working model of the mansion that took $500,000 and five years to make, and a series of bronze sculptures of the Washington family.

The museum and education center houses twenty-three galleries and theaters, with something of interest for everyone in the family. The experience is intensive, using computer imaging, LED maps and displays, surround-sound audio, "immersion" video, and interactive computers to tell the story of Washington's life. With five times the area of the previous space, there is room for hundreds of original objects on display, some never before seen in public. There are furnishings, china and silver, clothing, jewelry, Revolutionary War artifacts, rare books and manuscripts, and personal effects of the family.

≡FAST FACT

Martha Washington had been married before she wed the president, and she was once considered the wealthiest widow in Virginia at twenty-six years old. Martha was also a year older than her husband George and brought two children from her previous marriage to her union with George (she and George never had children of their own).

There is also a replica of Washington's presidential office. His last will and testament and the famous bust of Washington by Houdon are also on view. An interesting display on the archaeology and restoration of the site shows how work was done and what has been found on the site over the years.

The property includes a new forest trail so you can walk through Washington's wilderness grounds, see his cobblestone quarry, cross a footbridge, and learn about wildlife on the estate. Washington himself loved to ride around his grounds on horseback.

Washington considered himself quite a scientific farmer, and he oversaw all the plantings on his estate. (Some of his original tree plantings are still growing at the Bowling Green entrance to the estate.) At the new Pioneer Farmer site, horses tread wheat outside the restored sixteen-sided barn, and costumed workers participate in hands-on Colonial farming activities and farm animal demonstrations.

TRAVEL TIP

There are a number of activities and experiences geared toward children at Mount Vernon. Kids can learn to build a Colonial fence, play a variety of eighteenth-century games, and harness a fiberglass mule. There's also a special "treasure hunt" for kids as well as an opportunity to have the kids dress up in Colonial garb for a picture.

Mount Vernon is also the site of the Washington Tombs (where memorial services are held on Washington's birthday and a daily wreath-laying takes place at 10 A.M., April through October), along with four gardens, a slave memorial (Washington freed his slaves upon his death), a greenhouse, stables, slave quarters, and the original outbuildings throughout the estate.

The gift shop is large and offers a great selection of Washington-related memorabilia, from a porcelain bust of Washington (a copy of the Houdon) to plates depicting Washington crossing the Delaware. The shop offers great gifts to take home, such as Mount Vernon wine (Virginia Blush), mulled cider, Martha's cake, and Colonial toys for kids.

Where to Eat

No food is allowed on the grounds, but there is a snack bar right outside the entrance that offers a fair selection of fast food. Next door to the gift shop is The Mount Vernon Inn (703-780-0011, *www.mountvernon.org*), which serves both lunch and dinner in a Colonial setting with costumed wait staff. The food is moderately priced and features a Colonial menu. Also nearby is the Cedar Knoll Inn, which also serves lunch and dinner. The dinner menu offers a Colonial meal at a prix fixe for dinner for two.

Seasonal Events at Mount Vernon

Special events are held on the estate throughout the year. These are subject to change, so call ahead to check:

February. Weekends in February include musical presentations and storytelling. On the weekend of Washington's birthday, there are always special events, and Mount Vernon is open free to the public.

April. A new event celebrates the coming of spring with a festive Spring Garden Party, music, activities, and a free packet of seeds as a party favor.

July. Independence Day weekend admission is only $1 at the Gristmill.

September. The annual 18th-Century Craft Fair features dozens of premier craftspeople and family activities. Colonial-costumed artisans demonstrate and sell traditional wares.

October. This is also the month for the Fall Wine Festival and Sunset Tour. Celebrate the history of the Virginia wine industry on the east lawn with this popular event. A $25 fee includes admission to the mansion, Washington's wine vaults (rarely opened), wine, live blues, and a meeting with "George Washington." A food basket for two is $22, advance purchase only. No outside food is allowed. Get tickets early from Ticketmaster at 202-397-7328 or *www.ticketmaster.com*.

December. Holidays at Mount Vernon are commemorated with a special tour that includes costumed characters and a visit to the rarely opened third floor of the mansion. Hot cider, cookies, and caroling around a bonfire are also on the program.

Location and Hours

The best way to get from D.C. to Mount Vernon is by car. The drive is simple. Cross any of the memorial bridges and then take the George Washington Memorial Parkway (Rte. 1) going south; the road will end at Mount Vernon.

Another option is to take the Gray Line bus (202-289-1999 or 1-800-862-1400), which leaves for Mount Vernon at 8:30 A.M. from Union Station and returns at 6 P.M. Adult fare is $37; it's $18 per child. The bus will drop you off at your hotel when the four-hour tour is over. There are also evening tours in the summer.

Another option is to take a boat. *The Spirit of Washington II* (202-554-8000) leaves from the Washington waterfront and offers a five-hour cruise at $38 for adults, $36 for seniors, and $31 for children age six to eleven (under six free), which includes the price of admission to the estate but not lunch on board, but this tour is operated only from March through October.

Mount Vernon is open to visitors from 8 A.M. until 5 P.M. April through August. In March, September, and October, hours are 9 A.M. to 5 P.M. From November through February, Mount Vernon is open from 9 A.M. to 4 P.M. Admission is $13 for adults and $6 for children (under six free); seniors are charged $8.50.

Woodlawn Plantation

✉ 9000 Richmond Highway, Mount Vernon, VA
✆ 703-780-4000
✐ *www.woodlawn1805.org*

Woodlawn Plantation was the home of Washington's nephew, who married Washington's adopted granddaughter. Washington gave the couple the property to build their home from his holdings at Mount Vernon. William Thornton, one of the first architects of the U.S. Capitol building, designed the Georgian-style house. You can see the Potomac from the back porch.

The house has much Washington-related memorabilia on its two floors, as well as many early American works of art (two Rembrandt

Peales and a Hiram Powers bust). One of the most intriguing items on display is a mourning embroidery by Anna Austin that features a woman crying over a large memorial urn; the woman disappears and reappears as an angel when you change perspective.

Pope-Leighey House

The grounds of the Woodlawn Plantation are also home to the Pope-Leighey house, one of Frank Lloyd Wright's earliest Usonian houses (designed for middle-income families), and one whose construction he personally oversaw. It was commissioned by newspaperman Loren Pope, who was so taken with a *Life* magazine profile on Wright that he wrote Wright a letter requesting he design a house.

The small three-bedroom house was built in 1939 in Falls Church, Virginia (it has been moved twice by the National Trust, which now runs it), and has many of the signature Wright elements: a small utility center where the kitchen and bathroom are housed (the size of those in a small one-bedroom apartment), a cantilevered roof, horizontal lines, a repeating fret stencil pattern on the windows, and next to no closets.

Although Pope loved the house, his family outgrew it, and it was sold to the Leighey family, who lived there until the 1980s and opened it to the public in 1996. Much of the original furniture and color scheme is preserved. When the house was commissioned, its purchase price of between $6,000 and $7,000 included the furniture. During the month of December, a 1940s Christmas is on display at the house.

The Woodlawn Plantation Gift Shop

There is a gift shop in the basement that offers many wonderful Early American gifts and T-shirts (and you can see the old well, which was one of the first successful attempts at indoor plumbing). There is also a gift store in the Pope-Leighey House, so you can buy many Frank Lloyd Wright knickknacks as well, such as cups, a mouse pad, and canvas bags, with the decorative fret design from the house's windows.

☰ FAST FACT

Most architects consider Frank Lloyd Wright the greatest and most influential American architect. His designs, which spanned nearly fifty years, influenced American homes to such an extent that we might not have the ranch house with its open living-room space connected to the kitchen and the carport if it were not for his vision of the American home.

Location and Hours

Woodlawn Plantation is adjacent to Mount Vernon. You can actually walk from Mount Vernon to Woodlawn, but take your car if you have one. The estate is open daily March through December, closed January and February, but it is open on Presidents' Day for ninety-nine cents admission. Guided docent-led tours are offered on the half hour for $7.50 per person and $3 for students. You can buy a joint tour ticket to see the Pope-Leighey house as well for $13 ($5 for students). High tea is offered at the Woodlawn Plantation at noon and 2 P.M. for $25, which also includes a tour; $30 for an additional tour of Pope-Leighey.

Alexandria, Virginia

Only about a ten-minute drive or a Metro ride from downtown D.C., Alexandria is as charming as Georgetown, but with more history. It still has a lot of Colonial character, such as its brick sidewalks, cobblestone streets, and many historic homes. Washingtonians refer to it simply as Old Town.

Alexandria is a small town and is easy to walk around in. The center of the grid is the intersection of Washington and King Streets. Many of the streets retain their original Colonial names. For information on special events and celebrations, call the Alexandria Convention and Visitors' Association at 1-888-738-2764 or 703-838-5005, or visit its Web site, *http://oha.alexandriava.gov*. You can also drop in at its headquarters situated in the historic William Ramsay House at 211 King Street, (and South Fairfax Street), where you can obtain a free map for a self-guided tour, brochures, and knowing advice.

A Little History

Alexandria was named after a Scottish tobacco merchant who purchased the land in 1669. The town was founded in 1749, and one of the surveyors who helped plan the streets was seventeen-year-old George Washington.

Since its founding, Alexandria has always been a country retreat for prominent Washington families. George Washington had a townhouse here, and many of the upper-crust Colonial families worshipped at the English-style Christ Church (Cameron and North Washington Streets, 703-549-1450, *www.historicchristchurch.org*), where Washington was a vestryman and had his own pew; Robert E. Lee was also confirmed here.

Washington is also said to have held his last birthday party at Gadsby's Tavern (134 N. Royal St., at Cameron Street, 703-838-4242, *http://oha.alexandriava.gov/gadsby*), which features a museum and is still a restaurant where costumed wait staff serve homemade Colonial fare. Jefferson, Madison, and the Marquis de Lafayette are also said to have dined here.

Robert E. Lee's Boyhood Home at 607 Oronoco Street at North Street is another historic home in Alexandria. Lee lived here until he enrolled at West Point in 1825. He married one of Washington's great-granddaughters and lived in Arlington House, whose grounds eventually became Arlington National Cemetery.

On the south side of Oronoco Street (No. 614) is the Lee-Fendall House (703-548-1789, *www.leefendallhouse.org*), where more Lee descendants lived (a total of thirty-seven over 118 years), and where there is an extensive display of Lee memorabilia. Phillip Richard Fendall bought the property from his cousin, Revolutionary War hero "Light Horse Harry" Lee, father of Robert E. Lee.

🧳 TRAVEL TIP

Three historic homes in Alexandria—Carlyle, Lee-Fendall, and Gads-by's—charge a $4 tour price. However, you can buy a multi-admission ticket and save money. The Tricorn ticket costs $9 for adults and $5 for children at the Visitors' Center or any of the homes. A two-building ticket is also available.

Other historic homes in Alexandria include the Carlyle House (121 N. Fairfax Street at Cameron St., 703-549-2997, *www.carlylehouse .org*), where in 1755 Major General Edward Braddock met with five Colonial governors to begin taxing the colonies in order to defend themselves from the French and the Indians. The colonists were not happy with this proposal and eventually drove him out.

City Hall and Market Square (bounded by King, N. Royal, Cameron, and N. Fairfax Sts.) is the site of a weekly outdoor market, Saturday, 6:30 to 10:30 A.M. Across the street on the south side of King Street is the newly restored Stabler-Leadbeater Apothecary Museum (703-838-3852, *www.apothecarymuseum.org*) which was the second oldest drugstore in the nation until it closed in 1933. A Quaker family ran it for five generations. It is now a museum and gift shop.

The Lyceum (201 S. Washington St., off Prince St., 703-838-4994) is a museum that features changing exhibits on the history of Alexandria from the seventeenth century to the present.

The Torpedo Factory Art Center (105 N. Union St. between King and Cameron Sts., on the waterfront, 703-838-4565) is the shell of a former torpedo factory. Two hundred artists now show their works on the premises; an exhibition of Alexandria archeology lets visitors see archaeologists at work in their lab. Open seven days a week, 10 A.M. to 5 P.M.

The Alexandria Black History Museum (703-838-4356, *www .alexblackhistory.org*) is housed in the former Robinson Library, once a segregated library for Alexandria's black community. America's first sit-in against segregation was staged in Alexandria in 1939 to protest the exclusion of blacks from Alexandria's public libraries, which led to the creation of the Robinson Library in 1940. The center, located at 902 Wyeth Street, displays objects and records of African-American history in the region, as well as special exhibits. There is also a research library on the premises. The center is open Tuesday through Saturday from 10 A.M. to 4 P.M.; Sunday, 1 to 5 P.M. Free admission.

☂ RAINY DAY FUN

Visit Fredericksburg, Virginia, where you can find Kenmore Plantation and Gardens, the former home of George Washington's sister and brother-in-law, Betty Washington and Colonel Fielding Lewis. This stately mansion, built in 1755, is open to visitors daily 10 A.M. to 5 P.M.; closed January, February, Thanksgiving, and December 24, 25, and 31. Call 540-373-3381, or visit *www.kenmore.org*.

Getting There

By car take the Arlington Memorial or 14th Street Bridge to the George Washington Memorial Parkway south, which becomes Washington Street in Old Town Alexandria. If you go to the Visitors' Bureau, it will give you an all-day parking pass, or you can park in metered spaces on the street.

Alexandria is also surprisingly easy to reach by Metro (whereas Georgetown is not). Take the Yellow line to the King Street station, and catch an eastbound AT2 or AT5 bus to the Visitors' Bureau.

Fort Ward Museum and Historic Site

✉ 4301 W. Braddock Rd., Alexandria, Virginia
✆ 703-838-4848
✎ *www.fortward.org*

Fort Ward was taken under the wing of the City of Alexandria in 1961, and it has since been both restored and preserved as befits an important Civil War site. Today, this fifth largest of 162 forts built by Union forces features a completely restored northwest bastion and over 95 percent of its original walls. Both the fort and accompanying museum occupy a 45-acre park setting just east of Route 395.

The museum is open to visitors from 9 A.M. to 5 P.M. on Tuesday through Saturday and from noon to 5 P.M. on Sunday. You can browse through artifacts, a research library, and a range of educational programs here. One recent exhibition covered "Medical Care for the Civil War Soldier," full of the expected horrors of battlefield treatment; a gentler exhibit, "Off the Pages of *Godey's*: A Guide to the 'Domestic Sciences,'" here featured items from *Godey's*, an influential magazine that set the standards for mid-nineteenth-century fashion, housekeeping, and deportment.

The historic site itself is open from 9 A.M. to sunset daily. A path runs along the earthwork walls and can take as long as forty-five minutes to walk. Admission to the fort and the museum is free.

The College Park Aviation Museum

✉ 1985 Cpl. Frank Scott Dr., College Park, MD
✆ 301-864-6029
🖝 *www.collegeparkaviationmuseum.com*

The Museum is located on the grounds of College Park Airport, the world's oldest continuously operating airport. The state-of-the-art facility uses animatronics and interactive exhibits, memorabilia, photographs, aviation-related books and manuscripts, oral histories, and information kiosks to tell the story of College Park Airport's significance in aviation history. The facility has a curved roofline reminiscent of an early Wright aeroplane that houses an open, one-and-a-half-story exhibit area for full-size aircraft, as well as display and exhibition areas. The deck off the second-floor gallery offers a clear view of the airfield. You can get some unusual souvenirs at the Prop Shop Gift Shop. The museum is open to the public for self-guided tours from 10 A.M. to 5 P.M. daily, except holidays. Admission is $4 for adults, $3 for seniors, and $2 for children.

You can maintain the theme by dining nearby at the 94th Aero Squadron Restaurant (5240 Paint Branch Pkwy., College Park, 301-699-9400). It is designed to look like a 1919 French farmhouse and serves lunch and dinner daily.

The NASA/Goddard Space Flight Center

✉ Soil Conservation Rd., Greenbelt, Maryland

✆ 301-286-8981

⌨ *www.nasa.gov/goddard*

Named for the "Father of Modern Rocketry," the Goddard Space Flight Center was built by NASA back in 1959. Along with displays of rockets and spacecraft, the lab's visitors center has lots of fun hands-on stuff. The new "Science on a Sphere" uses an enormous white sphere to project animated data and graphics. Some other attractions are the Rocket Garden, with full-size rockets, space artifacts, and a real Apollo spacecraft module, and the new Hubble space telescope exhibit. Special events include model rocket launches, stargazing groups, lectures by scientists, and videos of new NASA projects. The visitors' center is open daily, call for hours and a schedule of special events. Visits are self-guided and free.

🧳 TRAVEL TIP

In addition to seeing the exhibits at the Goddard Space Flight Center, you can tour some of the actual laboratories—including stops at the Test and Evaluation Facility, NASA Communications Network, Flight Dynamics Facility, and satellite control centers for such spacecraft as the Hubble Space Telescope. Tours are offered Monday through Saturday.

Amusement Parks

If your kids are a little tired of art, history, and "old houses," you might be able to bribe them into touring through the Hirshhorn, Corcoran, or Phillips collections with the promise of a trip to one of the three amusement parks in neighboring Virginia and Maryland.

Six Flags America

✉ P.O. Box 4210, Largo, MD

✆ 301-249-1500

🖰 www.sixflags.com

This family theme park offers more than 100 rides, shows, and attractions. There are eight roller coasters, including the Batwing, the Superman, and the ever popular Mind Eraser. There's also a variety of children's rides in Looney Tunes Movie Town; the Hurricane Harbor water park; live shows, games, gift shops, restaurants, and more. Six Flags is open from April through October (in April, May, September, and October the hours are limited to weekends and certain holidays, so check the schedule before you plan to visit), and hours vary. Admission for adults is $49.99 (discount on the Internet); for children and disabled, $34.99, and you'll pay $15 for parking, $25 for preferred parking.

King's Dominion

✉ P.O. Box 2000, Doswell, VA

✆ 804-876-5000

🖰 www.kingsdominion.com

King's Dominion is 400 acres of fun for everyone in the family, from the youngest up. It has over a dozen roller coasters and a 19-acre water park, with Big Wave Bay, a 650,000-gallon wave pool; Surf City Splash, which has fifty water attractions; and many water slides. There are special attractions for the little ones, who can meet their favorite cartoon characters and enjoy safe rides just like the big kids.

King's Dominion is open from April through early November (in April, May, September, October, and November the hours are limited

DAY TRIPS FROM D.C.

to weekends and certain holidays, so check the schedule before you plan to visit), and hours vary. There are concerts and special events; call for information. King's Dominion is located 75 miles south of Washington D.C. Adult admission is $49.99; seniors fifty-five and older, $39.99; for children ages three to six it's $34.99. There are two-day tickets available, and Internet discounts. Parking is an additional $10 per vehicle. Take Interstate 95 south to exit 98 and follow the signs.

Busch Gardens Europe
✉ One Busch Gardens Blvd. Williamsburg, VA
✆ 1-800-343-7946
✑ www.buschgardens.com

A European-theme park with seventeenth-century flair, Busch Gardens boasts more than forty thrilling rides, dazzling shows, a wildlife preserve, quaint shops, European cuisine, and a separate water park. There are also more than a score of younger kid–friendly rides and shows. The park is open March through October. It is located in Williamsburg, VA, 150 miles south of Washington D.C. Single tickets are $51.95 for adults, $44.95 for children. There are special deals for seniors, and multiday and meal plan deals are available. Parking is $8.

CHAPTER 20

Suggested Itineraries

WASHINGTON D.C. COULD KEEP you and your family entertained for weeks. There is so much to see and do that you'll never feel you've seen it all, even if you spend a month there. This may be why Washington D.C. is one of the leading family travel destinations in the country.

When you're traveling with children, you have to plan your trip and cater your activities to their ages and interests—and your own interests as well. That means reading up ahead, going online to check schedules and timing, and making sure you have as many tickets in advance as possible so as not to waste a lot of time waiting in lines or disappointing your kids.

If You Have Only One Day

One day is barely enough to get a feel for the city and see what it has to offer, but if you are in town only for one day, head straight to the National Mall and visit the Smithsonian museums that interest you and your family the most. Plan on eating in one of the cafeterias or museum food courts, and preorder a ticket for the Washington Monument online, so you can make sure to see the city from this vantage point and experience this grand architectural and historical monument.

JUST FOR PARENTS

Washington's art galleries have banded together to hold mutual openings so that you may see several new works in one night. In the Dupont Circle area, on the first Friday of every month, the galleries along Connecticut Avenue hold opening-night receptions. The galleries along Georgetown's main drag hold their opening night on the third Friday of every month.

If you have some time in the evening, race down to Union Station, or check with your hotel concierge to find out if you can take a nighttime tour of the city's monuments (by bus, Tourmobile, trolley, or van), which should include the Lincoln, Jefferson, Vietnam Veterans, Korean War, and Franklin Delano Roosevelt Memorials.

A Weekend in D.C.

If you and your family are in town for a weekend and have a full Saturday and Sunday, check the museum and federal building schedules to make sure that they are open on the weekends—most museums are. If you have White House tickets, they would be for early Saturday morning, and that would be your first stop.

TRAVEL TIP

The only weekend day White House tours are given is Saturday from 7:30 A.M. until 12:30 P.M. Do not be late, and don't forget to eat before the tour, because no food or drinks are allowed inside the White House. Also make sure you and your family have all gone to the bathroom because there are no bathrooms open to the public inside the White House.

If possible, try to find a hotel downtown or near the National Mall (L'Enfant Plaza Hotel, Holiday Inn Downtown, Red Roof Inn, or the Hotel Monaco), so you can do as much as possible in a short amount of time, and if your kids get tired, you can race back to the hotel for a nap.

Saturday

Once you check into your hotel, either head toward Union Station and take the D.C. Ducks or Old Town Trolley tour of the city, or head to the Mall and hop on the Tourmobile. Sit with the kids and let the wise and entertaining tour operators give you and your family a grand overview of the sites. Then you can get your kids to help you decide what you'll see over the rest of the weekend. You may not be able to fit everything into the schedule, but it's nice to see what's out there and how close some of the places are to each other.

If you take the Tourmobile or Old Town Trolley, you can hop on and off, and you might want to make that your day, visiting some of the museums on the Mall and some of the sites. D.C. Ducks is a three-hour tour that goes on both land and sea in those wonderful amphibious vehicles from World War II. It hands out duck noisemakers, which are charmers for kids, and the kids can keep them as mementos (and annoy you in the car on your way back home).

🧳 TRAVEL TIP

After a hard day of sightseeing the monuments and the museums, your kids may not be ready to call it a night, but you might be tired. An easy dinner and a movie can be found at Union Station, where there's a nine-theater multiplex and a food court that offers everything from 1950s-style diner burgers to quiche Lorraine to cannolis for dessert.

If you have not elected to hop on and off, you might want to spend an afternoon in one of the Mall museums until it closes. You can have dinner at Red Sage (café and chili bar), at ESPN Zone, the Hard Rock Cafe, or TGI Friday's.

Then either go on a nighttime exploration of the Washington Monument (if you have a ticket and it's summertime) or catch a movie at Union Station—there are nine theaters—or even in your hotel room on pay-per-view.

Sunday

Eat breakfast in your hotel, and then head to the National Zoo. It is a must-see for families with children. Get there early so you can catch a museum later in the afternoon. If it is Sunday, and you are so inclined, you might want to catch a morning service at the National Cathedral, which is close to the zoo, where you can see the Darth Vader gargoyle and the moon-rock stained-glass window (or just pop in there to take a look).

The zoo will take about three or four hours to see. Plan on eating lunch there. Then you can take a cab downtown and do a late afternoon walk-through of the International Spy Museum. If there's some time left, you can quickly pop into Ford's Theatre (where President Lincoln was shot) and then cross the street to look at the Petersen House, where Lincoln died. You can have dinner at Zola or Zaytinya, or even Poste in the nearby Hotel Monaco, or try one of the fabulous restaurants in nearby Chinatown.

In the evening, check with your hotel concierge or head to Union Station, and take a bus tour of the memorials at night—Lincoln and Jefferson are spectacular all lit up, and the Vietnam Wall has a unique power after dark.

The Three-Day Weekend in the Capital

If you're visiting D.C. over a Monday-holiday weekend, expect many other families to do the same. Book hotels early, and do make reservations at the restaurants you and your family really want to go to.

Day One

If it's not a federal holiday, and you've opted for a Friday-Saturday-Sunday visit, try to get the White House tour for Friday morning. It should be a little easier to get and less hectic and crowded. Eat a quick lunch at Old Ebbitt Grill or Ollie's Trolley, which has great burgers and hotdogs.

Then head to the Bureau of Engraving and Printing to see paper money being printed and shredded. You can catch a tour in the early afternoon—the last one is at 2 P.M., but they sometimes add later, tours in the summer. They're closed on the weekend, but you could visit Monday morning, if you have a Saturday-Sunday-Monday visit.

⚲ RAINY DAY FUN

If you are traveling with toddlers, make sure you include the D.C. Ducks Tour, the National Zoo, the new National Children's Museum (if it is open), the Smithsonian Carousel at the Mall, and the Orkin Insect Zoo at the Museum of Natural History.

If you have energy left, head to the Mall and do as much of the Museum of American History as you can, if renovations are completed. Pause for an ice cream in the re-created old ice cream parlor in the museum, and let the younger kids take a ride on the carousel outside the museum. If the museum is not yet open, go to the new National Museum of the American Indian instead. In the evening, take one of the night bus tours.

Day Two

After a quick breakfast in your hotel, head straight to the Mall, and finish Air and Space and Natural History. Eat lunch in either Wright Court in Air & Space, where you can choose burgers, pizza, or a chicken meal, or the restaurant in Natural History, which features soups and sandwiches. If you've got time, stop in at the National Aquarium around 2 P.M., when you can catch them feeding the sharks, piranhas, or alligators—always a kid-pleaser.

🧳 TRAVEL TIP

D.C. is a tourist town, and many visitors are too exhausted to go out at night. This means you often can get into a good theater performance at night. Many Broadway shows make their way to Washington, and you can often see some excellent theater on tour, often for half price by calling TICKETplace (202-842-5387), which offers half-price tickets the day of the show.

If you're planning on heading to the Kennedy Center for the free daily 6 P.M. concert, you can have dinner in or around the Center and then enjoy the show. Be sure to arrive early.

Day Three

Start with one of those terrific D.C. Sunday brunches (see Chapter 15), then visit the zoo and the International Spy Museum. If you get hungry, the Waffle Shop right next to the Petersen House is an authentic D.C. lunch counter, where you can get crab cakes or steak sandwiches with great onion rings for about $10.

In the evening, visit Verizon Center for a sporting event. Tickets are pretty easy to come by.

A Five-Day Getaway

Follow the three-day weekend plan, and add the following activities. Unless your kids are very young (and therefore don't have the attention span for this), you can dedicate a day to learning about how our government works and touring government sites (see Chapter 8). This is best done during the week, when you might be able to catch the U.S. Supreme Court and/or Congress in session. Write ahead of time, and see if it's possible to meet with your representative or senator while you're in town. It will be a memorable family event, and one that you should definitely bring the camera to record (even if you didn't vote for him or her).

Day Four

Begin with a hearty breakfast at Eastern Market. Perhaps one of the adults can run over to the line for free tickets to the Capitol while the other waits with the kids for a seat for a breakfast of blueberry buckwheat pancakes or the breakfast "brick"—eggs, sausage, and a roll. If there's time, explore the marketplace.

Try to get a morning tour of the Capitol, the legislative seat of our government. The guided tour will take forty-five minutes, and you'll probably want to walk around a bit. Make sure you let the kids try the whisper that can be heard across the room. Then tour the U.S. Supreme Court.

You might want to head to Union Station for lunch at either the food court (with forty kiosks to choose from, there's bound to be something for everyone), or a sit-down meal at Uno Chicago Grill or America. If the kids are feeling rambunctious, let them run through the National Postal Museum across the street from Union Station. It will take less than an hour and will be surprisingly entertaining for everyone.

TRAVEL TIP

If you want to just walk through the streets of the city and window shop (or even buy something), Georgetown is Washington's late-night shopping area, where many of the stores are open until 11 P.M. From college gear to fun youth-oriented clothing and housewares, Georgetown has an eclectic mix of stores and late-night eateries, too.

Then head to the Library of Congress, the world's largest library with 26 million items, and follow it up with a trip to the National Archives, where the kids will see the Declaration of Independence and the Bill of Rights.

Everyone will be pretty tired, so a nice leisurely dinner is probably in order. You can head to Georgetown and eat in a historic restaurant like 1789 (pricey, but memorable). Benihana is always a hit,

Clyde's has a great hamburger, or enjoy a relaxing dinner at Firefly downtown in the Hotel Madera.

Day Five

If you've brought the car, drive out to the new Udvar-Hazy Center near Dulles, where you can see even more aviation artifacts and specimens. The museum has the *Enola Gay*, the plane that dropped the bomb on Hiroshima, as well as the space shuttle *Enterprise* and an Air France Concorde. You can have lunch at the center or drive to the nearby Westfields Marriott, where you can have a spectacular Sunday brunch or a delightful afternoon tea. In the afternoon, drive to Tyson's Corner, one of the outlet staples of the city, and shop until you drop. You can have dinner at one of the many restaurants in the outlet center or neighboring malls, or head back to the city for a meal at one of the many Ethiopian restaurants, where kids get to eat with their hands.

Make It a Full Week

You should plan on spending a full day at Mount Vernon/Woodlawn Plantation (make sure you explore the Pope-Leighey House, designed by Frank Lloyd Wright, which is also on the grounds) and then have dinner in Alexandria, Virginia. It's a delightful way to explore the past and present, and there's so much for both kids and adults.

RAINY DAY FUN

Preteens and teens might be interested in the Washington Segway tours, shopping at Georgetown and the outlets, and visiting the National Museum of Health and Medicine, which has some of the grossest medical exhibits in the country. If your kids are over twelve and mature enough, the Holocaust Museum is a good family event, though very difficult to experience.

You might also want to consider spending a day at one of the nearby amusement parks—Six Flags America in Largo, MD, is closest. Take Metro's Blue Line toward Largo Town Center and exit at Addison Road. Transfer to the C21 bus and exit in front of Six Flags. Further afield are Paramount's Kings Dominion, 75 miles south in Doswell, VA, and Busch Gardens, in Williamsburg, VA, 150 miles south. It's a great way to let your hair down after an educational vacation.

Washington's Annual Events

January

Restaurant Week

This occurs one week, twice a year, in January and August. During Restaurant Week, the city's finest restaurants offer patrons a three-course prix fixe lunch for the price of the year, such as $20.06 for 2006. Dinner is usually $10 more. This is a wonderful opportunity to sample the very best cuisine the city has to offer at a fraction of the price. Visit *www.washington.org/restaurantwk* for more information.

Martin Luther King Jr. Day

Every third Monday of January, the city hosts a variety of activities, such as speeches by civil rights leaders, lectures, readings, theatrical performances, and concerts. There's also the laying of a wreath at the Lincoln Memorial and the playing of King's "I Have a Dream" speech. The Martin Luther King Jr. Memorial Library usually hosts some commemorative events. Call 202-727-1186 for more information.

Presidential Inauguration

January 20 after a presidential election is the day of presidential inauguration. This is always a major production in D.C. The swearing-in ceremony takes place in front of the Capitol, and crowds line the sidewalks. Afterwards, the new president and his entourage head toward the White House on Pennsylvania Avenue. The entire day features free public events, such as concerts and parades, as well as many semi-private parties.

Washington Auto Show

D.C.'s premier automobile show is held at the Washington Convention Center. Check out the newest models and dream cars. It's fun for the entire family. Adults, $10; children six to twelve, $5; under five, free. Visit *www.washingtonautoshow.com*.

February

Chinese New Year Celebrations

The Chinese follow a lunar calendar, so the exact dates vary from year to year; generally, the Chinese New Year falls in late January or early February. D.C.'s Chinese neighborhood is centered in the area around 7th Street and H, marked by the brightly colored arch given by its sister city of Beijing. From the day of the Chinese New Year through the ten days following, there are parades, fireworks, and celebrations. Area restaurants feature special menus. Check *The Washington Post* for listings.

Holiday Homecoming

Throughout February and citywide. Look for special discounts, events, and promotions at D.C.'s hotels, restaurants, and attractions. Call 1-800-422-8644, or visit *www.washington.org*.

Come Out and Play

Throughout February and citywide. Enjoy theater, pre-show dining, and post-show discussions with writers and cast. Many special hotel packages. Call 1-800-422-8644, or visit *www.comeouttoplay.org*.

Warm Up to a Museum

February is museum month with seasonal extras, free hot beverages, and special concerts, tours, and film series. Visit *www.cultural tourismdc.com.*

Black History Month

The city offers a wealth of special exhibits, concerts, and performances all month long. Call the Smithsonian's Anacostia Museum for its events (202-633-4820) as well as the Frederick Douglass Historic Site (202-426-5960), the Mary McLeod Bethune House (202-673-2402), and the Martin Luther King Jr. Memorial Library (202-727-0321). Also check *The Washington Post* listings. February 12 marks the birthday of Frederick Douglass. A wreath-laying ceremony, performances, and activities are held all day long at his historic home.

Lincoln's Birthday

Every February 12, there is an annual laying-of-a-wreath ceremony at the Lincoln Memorial and a reading of the Gettysburg Address at noon in commemoration of Lincoln's birthday. Call 202-619-7222 for more information.

Washington's Birthday

George Washington was born on February 22, and his birthday is marked with a celebration similar to other birthday events, plus a parade. Mount Vernon celebrates Washington's birthday with free admission all day, as well as activities and fanfare on the bowling green. Call 703-780-2000 for more information.

March

St. Patrick's Day Parade

The nation's St. Patrick's Day parade is held noon to 3 P.M. on the Sunday before March 17 on Constitution Avenue, from 7th to 17th Streets. Free grandstand tickets are $15. *www.dcstpatsparade.com.*

Ringling Brothers and Barnum & Bailey Circus

The circus comes to town at the D.C. Armory, 2001 E. Capitol Street, and Verizon Center. Call 202-397-7328 for tickets and dates (generally March and April).

National Cherry Blossom Festival

Late March and early April is when more than 6,000 Japanese cherry trees along the Tidal Basin are in bloom. National news media monitor the cherry trees' budding, and the festivities are timed to coincide with the two weeks of blooming. Activities include a parade, kite festival, concert, and fireworks. For parade information or tickets for seats along the parade route ($15 plus tax and fee), contact Ticketmaster *www.ticketmaster.com*, or call 202-397-7328 or 202-547-1500. The National Park Service offers guided tours of the trees in bloom, leaving from the Jefferson Memorial. For more information, call 202-661-7584 or visit *www.nationalcherryblossomfestival.org*.

North American Wildlife Celebration (formerly Seal Days)

In mid-March, the National Zoo (3001 Connecticut Avenue) hosts animal demonstrations, encounters, arts and crafts, and educational displays. Free. Call 202-633-4800 or visit *www.nationalzoo.si.edu* or *www.fonz.org* for more information.

Smithsonian Kite Festival

Held during March, the festival allows kite flyers and makers from all over the country to come to the parkland around the Washington Monument to show their stuff and compete for juried prizes and ribbons. For more information and rules call 202-633-1000.

April

Easter

Easter in the capital is a special time. Events include sunrise services at Arlington National Cemetery at the Memorial Amphitheater (703-607-8000) as well as various services at the National Cathedral (202-537-6200).

White House Easter-Egg Roll

This fantastic hunt for more than 1,000 wooden Easter eggs for kids between the ages of three and six takes place on the Monday after Easter Sunday. Entertainment is also provided for the parents and siblings who accompany them. The hunt and entertainment takes place between 8 A.M. and 2 P.M., but entry is by timed tickets, which are issued at the National Park Service Ellipse Visitors' Center (just behind the White House at 15th and E Streets), beginning at 7 A.M., two days earlier. If you're planning on attending, you might want to ask your representative or senator about getting tickets way ahead of time. There is also an Easter celebration at the Ellipse, which includes entertainment, music, storytelling, and food giveaways for the whole family. For additional information, call 202-456-7041 or visit *www.whitehouse.gov/easter.*

African-American Family Celebration

This annual festival of music, dance, Easter Egg hunts, live storytelling, art and more is held every Easter Monday at the National Zoo, at 3001 Connecticut Avenue NW. Free. For more information, call 202-633-4800.

Thomas Jefferson's Birthday

April 13, Jefferson's birthday, is celebrated with wreath-laying, speeches, and a military ceremony, all of which take place at the Jefferson Memorial. Call 202-619-7222.

White House Garden Tours

Every year, for two afternoons in mid-April, the White House opens its beautiful gardens and terrific outdoor sculpture to the public. Call 202-456-2200 for more information. Because of security, arrangements may change, but free timed tickets may be distributed by the National Park Service, or you might ask your representative or senator to see about getting tickets. Visit *www.whitehouse.gov.*

Shakespeare's Birthday

In middle to late April, the Folger Shakespeare Library hosts an afternoon party in honor of the Bard's birthday. The free party includes performances for kids and adults, music, and food. Call 202-544-7077.

Washington International Film Festival

The festival is held for two weeks in middle or late April. Films are screened at various locations, including historic theaters and the National Gallery of Art. For full schedule and location, visit the Web site at *www.filmfestdc.org.* Tickets can be purchased in advance through Tickets.com or by calling 703-218-6500.

Taste of the Nation

As part of a national fundraiser to feed the hungry, nearly 100 D.C. restaurants offer tastings of their cuisines at Union Station on the Taste of the Nation Day, held in late April. Tickets run about $75, and there is an auction afterwards. Visit *www.tasteofthenation.org* for information and tickets.

Smithsonian Craft Festival

A juried craft fair in the National Building Museum at 401 F Street, about a ten- to fifteen-minute walk from the Mall, held in late April, features about 100 artists and artisans offering beautiful one-of-a-kind crafts. Admission is $15, children under 12 free. Call 1-888-832-9554, or log on to *www.smithsoniancraftshow.org* for more information.

May

National Cathedral Annual Flower Mart

This May festival and flower sale takes place on the first Friday and Saturday in May. There are activities for children and adults, as well as food. Call 202-537-6200 or visit *www.nationalcathedral.org* for more information.

Georgetown Garden Tour

The annual tour, sponsored by the Georgetown Garden Club, which takes place on the second Saturday in May, offers a glimpse into the private gardens of D.C.'s oldest homes. Light fare is provided with the cost of the ticket ($25 two weeks in advance, $30 after). Information and tickets are available at *www.georgetowngardentour.com.*

Candlelight Vigil

This memorial service, held in mid-May as part of Police Week, honors the nation's law enforcement personnel who have died in the line of duty. Services begin at 8 P.M. at the National Law Enforcement Officers Memorial, at 4th and E Streets. Call 202-737-3400 for more information.

Annual Mount Vernon Wine Festival

Wines of Virginia and modern-day versions of those made at the Washington estate are presented at this festival; arts and crafts of the Colonial period are on sale as well. The festival takes place in mid-May. See more in Mount Vernon listing, Chapter 19. Call 703-799-8608 for more information and tickets.

Andrews Air Force Base Annual Air Show

Another option for travelers to D.C. in mid-May is the Andrews Air Force Base Annual Air Show, your opportunity to watch the flying feats and parachute jumps and attend an open house at the Andrews Air Force base, at Route 5 and Allentown Road. This is a crowded event, so get there early. Attendance is free of charge. Call 301-981-1110 for more information.

Rolling Thunder Motorcycle Rally

This annual, end-of-May bike rally pays homage to the nation's veterans, particularly those missing in action and prisoners of war. Information at 908-369-5439, or *www.rollingthunder.com*

Welcome Summer Concert

The National Symphony Orchestra performs a free concert to welcome summer on the West Lawn of the Capitol. The event is held on the Sunday before Memorial Day. Call 202-619-7222 for more information.

Memorial Day

The last Monday in May is Memorial Day. In D.C., this national holiday is celebrated with a wreath-laying ceremony at the Tomb of the Unknown Soldier in Arlington National Cemetery, followed by a service and speeches by officials (sometimes the president), as well as a performance by a military band. Log on to *www.fmmc.army.mil* for more information.

Wreath-laying ceremony, speeches, and the playing of taps takes place at the Vietnam Veterans Memorial at 1 P.M. The U.S. Navy Memorial (701 Pennsylvania Avenue NW) commemorates the navy veterans with performances and speeches all day. Call 202-619-7222 for more information.

The National Memorial Day Parade starts at 10:30 A.M. in front of the Capitol and moves down Constitution Avenue toward the White House. It was recently revived after a sixty-year hiatus.

June

Capital Pride

Held in the first week of June, Capital Pride is the fourth largest gay-pride event in the country and is a nine-day diversity festival with varied events and an annual parade and street festival. For more information, visit *www.capitalpride.org*.

Annual Dupont-Kalorama Museum Walk

An all-day event held in early June along Dupont Circle and the Kalorama district, this walk includes open houses of six museums and historic sites featuring food and performances. See *www.dkmuseums.com* for more information.

Shakespeare Theater Free-for-All

In mid-June, a two-week run of evening performances of a free Shakespeare play are offered at the outdoor Carter Barton Amphitheater. Call 202-547-3230 or *www.shakespearedc.org* for information and dates.

Barbecue Battle

For the past fifteen years, the annual barbecue battle has seen the nation's leading barbecue chefs and restaurants compete for over $25,000 in cash and prizes. The event features lots of free food and interactive cooking demonstrations, as well as children's activities. The battle takes place on the third weekend in June. For more information, call 202-828-3099 or visit *www.barbecuebattle.com*.

D.C. Caribbean Carnival

One of the fastest growing carnivals in North America. In the last week of June there is a weeklong celebration of Caribbean culture and food, culminating in a six-hour parade with over 5,000 masqueradees strung along the Georgia Avenue corridor starting at Missouri Avenue and ending at the International Marketplace at "De Savanah" Banneker Recreation Park. It features crafts, food, and entertainment for the general public. For more information, visit *www.dccaribbeancarnival.com*.

Smithsonian Folklife Festival

This annual festival on the National Mall spans about ten days from late June to early July. Sponsored by the Center for Folklife and Cultural Heritage, it celebrates national and international contemporary living conditions and features crafts, performances, music, and food from all fifty states, highlighting one region or state in particular. Most performances and demonstrations are free, and food is available for purchase. Call 202-275-1150 or visit *www.folklife.si.edu* for dates and featured events.

July

Fourth of July Weekend

Millions of tourists visit D.C. for the Fourth of July, and the city hosts a number of free family activities. There is a huge Independence Day parade down Constitution Avenue at noon, with floats and 100 marching bands. At the National Archives, there is a morning reading of the Declaration of Independence, as well as performances by military bands. There is free entertainment at the Sylvan Theater on the grounds of the Washington Monument all day long.

In the evening, the National Symphony holds an annual free concert on the west steps of the Capitol building at 8 P.M. Fireworks over the Washington Monument begin at sunset (around 9:20 P.M.).

Annual Soapbox Derby

On July 10, homemade and professional soapbox cars drive down Constitution Avenue, between New Jersey and Louisiana Avenues, from 10 A.M. to 6 P.M. Call 330-733-8723 for more information and entry rules.

Bastille Day

Hosted by the French restaurant Les Halles (1201 Pennsylvania Avenue) on July 14, this celebration of French Independence Day features live entertainment, a waiter's race, a children's race, a customers' race, an obstacle course on Pennsylvania Avenue, a special menu, and affordable outside treats. It's from 11:30 A.M. to 4 P.M., but there's also an indoor party that runs all day until midnight. Call 202-347-6848 for more information. This is part of a ten-day Liberty Festival that begins on July 4.

Latino Festival
In late July, Latino bands from all over the United States play music on Pennsylvania Avenue between 9th and 14th Streets. Food is available for purchase.

Water Lily Festival
This is held on the fourth Saturday of July at the Kenilworth Aquatic Gardens on the east bank of the Anacostia River. It's a beautiful 14-acre oasis of gardens and aquatic plants and animals. Free admission. 202-426-6905, *www.nps.gov/kepa*

Legg Mason Tennis Classic
Tennis champions including Andre Agassi are present for this prestigious tournament at the William H. G. FitzGerald Center, 16th and Kennedy Sts. NW, held in the last week of July and the first week of August. For more information, call the tournament hotline at 202-721-9500, or visit *www.leggmasontennisclassic.com*.

Screen on the Green Film Festival
On Monday nights during July and August, you and your family can attend free showings of American movie classics on a 20 × 40 foot screen on the grounds of the National Mall. Past films include *The Wizard of Oz* and *Rocky*. Bring a blanket to sit on, and get there early to stake your claim on the lawn. Films start at sunset. Call 877-262-5866 for schedule.

September

National Book Festival
This is held each September on the National Mall between 7th and 14th Sts. and is hosted by the Library of Congress, whose pavilion features interactive family-centered activities. You can meet over 70 award-winning authors, illustrators, and poets. Info is available at 1-888-714-4696 or *www.loc.gov/bookfest*.

Kennedy Center Prelude Festival

Each September, the Kennedy Center gears up for its fall season with a monthlong festival of discounted performances and events designed to celebrate the performing arts in D.C. In the past, the festival has included performances by the KC Jazz Club and the National Symphony Orchestra. There is also a free daylong Open House Arts Festival.

For more information, visit *www.kennedy-center.org*.

Labor Day Concert by the National Symphony Orchestra

On the first Monday of September, Labor Day, the National Symphony Orchestra offers a free concert that begins at 8 P.M. on the West Lawn of the Capitol. Call 202-416-8000.

National Black Family Reunion

This two-day cultural celebration of African-American families in America, held in mid-September, features performances, food, education, and entertainment on the grounds of the Washington Monument. All events are free, except for the opening day VIP reception. Call 202-737-0120 for more information or visit *www.ncnw.org*.

Adams Morgan Day Festival

Held the second Sunday in September, this celebration of regional diversity showcases the Adams Morgan neighborhood of eclectic and ethnic retail, entertainment, and dining establishments, with live outdoor music. Information is available at 202-232-1960 or *www.AMMainStreet.org*.

Kalorama House and Embassy Tour

Every second Sunday in September from noon to 5 P.M., take a walking tour of the historic homes and embassies of D.C. Maps are supplied. The cost is about $25. Call 202-387-4062 for more information.

Annual Children's Festival at the Wolf Trap Theater in Vienna

The festival is held in mid-September. Featured are paid performances, as well as clowns and puppet shows. Call 703-642-0862 or see Web site *www.artsfairfax.org* for information on performers.

Fiesta Musical

This annual Hispanic Heritage Month event is held in mid-September at the National Zoo (3001 Connecticut Avenue NW) from 11 A.M. to 5 P.M. The free family event features crafts for kids, music, dancing, special animal encounters, and a Latin American food court. For more information, call 202-633-1000, or visit *www.fonz.org*.

National Cathedral Open House

In late September, there are demonstrations by master stonecarvers, activities, and food from 10 a.m. to 5 P.M. *The Washington Post* claims that this is the only opportunity to climb the central tower stairway and see the bells and a spectacular view. Call 202-537-6200 or visit *www.nationalcathedral.org* for more information.

October

Dupont Circle Historic Homes Tour

The tour is offered sometime in mid-October, from noon to 5 P.M. Call 202-265-3222 or log on to *www.dupont-circle.com* for tickets and information.

Family Day in the National Garden

Create a butterfly, listen to music, or explore the wetlands. On the last Saturday of September from 10 A.M. to 4:30 P.M. at the new National Garden of the U.S. Botanic Gardens, across from the Capitol along First Street SW, on the National Mall. Free. 202-225-8333. *www.usbg.gov*.

White House Fall Garden Tours

In mid-October, the White House opens its private gardens to visitors for two days, with musical entertainment. Call 202-456-2200 for more information.

Marine Corps Marathon

In late October, thousands of runners race from the Iwo Jima Memorial in Arlington through the city and end at the Mall, a 26.2-mile run that passes by most of the city's most famous attractions and has been nicknamed "Marathon of the Monuments." The race starts at 8:30 a.m. Call 703-784-2225 or visit *www.marinemarathon. com* for more information.

The Annual Boo at the Zoo

Over the weekend before Halloween, the National Zoo stays open late and offers night tours of the bat cave, haunted trails, and trick-or-treat stations for kids where costumed volunteers hand out treats. There's also a goodie bag for all grownups, from 5:30 P.M. to 8:30 P.M. Children under two get in free, members pay $13, nonmembers pay $23. Call 202-633-1000 or *www.fonz.org* for more information. For tickets, call Friends of the National Zoo at 202-633-4470 early—it usually sells out weeks in advance.

November

Veterans Day

Memorial ceremonies are held at Arlington National Cemetery at the Tomb of the Unknown Soldier at 11 a.m. and at the Vietnam Veterans Memorial at 1 P.M.

Kennedy Center Holiday Performances

Holiday concerts and free performances run at the Kennedy Center from late November through New Year's Eve. Call 202-467-4600 for more information.

December

Lighting the National Christmas Tree and the Pageant of Peace

Each night in December, through January 1, myriad groups entertain visitors at the Ellipse, the grassy area south of the White House. The opening ceremony is at 5 P.M., December 1, when the official White House Christmas Tree is lit. Also illuminated from dusk until 11 P.M. are fifty-six smaller decorated trees representing all fifty states, five territories, and the District of Columbia. Visit *www.pag eantofpeace.org* for more information.

Charles Dickens's *A Christmas Carol*

The play has a two-week run at Ford's Theatre in late December. For tickets and information, call 202-347-4833 or visit *www.ford theatre.com*.

White House Candlelight Tours

Evening viewing of the decorated interior of the White House by candlelight is available from 5 P.M. to 7 P.M. on December 26 through 28. Lines are long for this special holiday event, so get there early or ask your representative or senator to put you on the list. Check 202-456-2200 or *www.whitehouse.gov* to make sure that the tour is offered this year.

A Frank Lloyd Wright Christmas

All December long, the Pope-Leighey House on the grounds of Woodlawn Plantation near Mount Vernon offers a Frank Lloyd Wright Christmas event. Decorations from the 1940s, when the house was built, adorn the Christmas tree. Call 703-780-4000 for more information.

Trees of Christmas Exhibition

Another monthlong event, the exhibition takes place at the Smithsonian's National Museum of Natural History. A number of Christmas trees and their decorations are on view in the museum. A different state sponsors the event each year with ornaments themed to that state. Call 202-633-1000.

Lighting of the National Menorah

One of the world's largest menorahs is lit by Rabbi Levi Shemtov to mark the eight-day Jewish festival of Chanukah, followed by complimentary holiday treats of latkes (potato pancakes) and doughnuts, along with festive music and children's activities. Exact dates can vary from year to year; this event can be held in late November some years. The lighting takes place on the Ellipse, 1600 Constitution Ave. NW. The midwinter event is free, but advance tickets are required. Call 202-332-5600.

Additional Resources

Web Sites

Washington D.C. Convention and Tourism Corporation

✑*www.washington.org*

This is the essential Web address for planning your trip. This site will give you hotel and restaurant suggestions and discounts, a local calendar of events, suggested itineraries, and ways to plan and save money.

The Washington Post

✑*www.washingtonpost.com*

If you can tear yourself away from the news, this Web site will have you hitting the ground running when you get into town. The site offers a trip planner: Type in the days you will be visiting, and it gives you a listing of what will be taking place while you're there. Other resources include a kids' guide, a weather forecast, tours of the town, Metro maps, restaurant listings, Weekend Best Bets, and an archive.

The Washingtonian

✑*www.washingtonian.com*

The Washingtonian is the city's grumpy regional magazine, sold on newsstands. Its Web site will give you enough to make it worthwhile to peruse, but it doesn't make money giving out freebies. The various listings and reviews will steer you in the right direction, but be warned, the taste is not middle America.

DC Pages
✐*www.dcpages.com*
It's mainly for the locals, but you might find an event that the other Web sites missed.

Washington Free Weekly
✐*www.washingtoncitypaper.com*
This is the great Web site for the capital's alternative newspaper, which is published on Wednesdays and is available free of charge at most coffee shops and bookstores. There are lots of good things here—a lively and opinionated listing of events, interactive search windows, and fun articles.

AlexandriaCity.com
✐*www.alexandriacity.com*
It's aimed at residents and heavily commercial, but some listings are valuable if you visit the historic neighboring town of Alexandria, Virginia.

Suggested Reading

The following is a brief list of books you might want to read before or after your visit, if you found any history or lore of the capital particularly fascinating:

Alexander, John. *Ghosts: Washington Revisited.* (1998, Schiffer Publishers Ltd.). This is a great guide to capital-city hauntings.

Berman, Richard, and McBride, Deborah. *Natural Washington: A Nature Lover's Guide to Parks, Wildlife Refuges, Trails, Gardens, Zoos, Forests, Aquariums, and Arboretums Within a Day's Trip of the Nation's Capital.* (1998, Howell Press, 4th Edition). The sub-title tells it all—the great outdoors within 50 miles of the Washington Monument.

Luria, Sarah. *Capital Speculations: Writing and Building Washington D.C.* (2005, University Press of New England). The connection of architecture, politics, and literature in designing Washington D.C. as America's grand new capital city.

Svrluga, Barry. *National Pastime: Sports, Politics and the Return of Baseball to Washington D.C.* (2006, Bantam Dell). The fascinating story of the Washington Nationals and the Cinderella return of baseball to Washington D.C. after more than thirty years.

Carey, Francine Curro. *Washington Odyssey: A Multi-Cultural History of the Nation's Capital.* (2003, HarperCollins). Check out this wonderful history of D.C.'s immigrant communities.

Graham, Katherine. *Personal History.* (1998, Random House). You'll find this memoir by the former owner of *The Washington Post* both interesting and informative.

Moore, John L. *Speaking of Washington: Facts, Firsts and Folklore.* (1993, CQ Press). You'll enjoy this fun book of facts and trivia about people, places, and things "inside the Beltway."

Whitman, William B. *Washington D.C.: Off the Beaten Path: A Guide to Unique Places.* (2007, Globe Pequot, 4th Edition). This great guide points out hidden treasures and unique places of interest.

APPENDIX C
Maps

The Mall

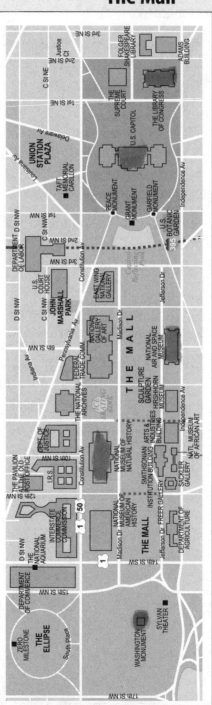

Washington D.C. Downtown

D.C. Neighborhood Map

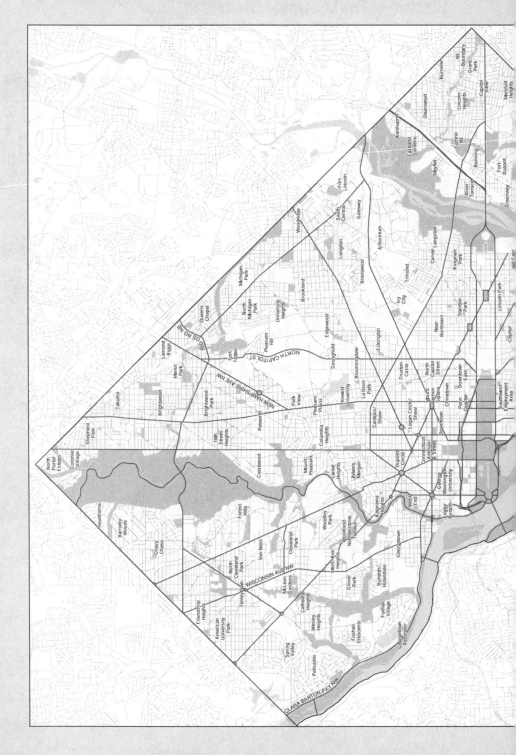

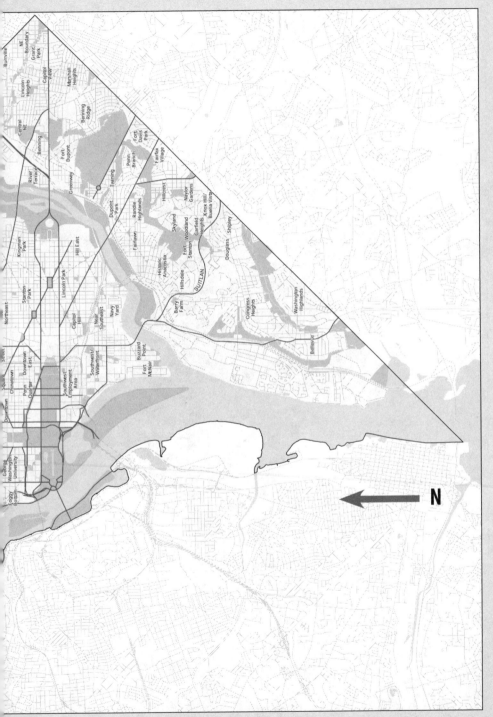

D.C. neighborhood map used with permission of the D.C. Office of Planning, the National Park Service, the D.C. Department of Parks and Recreation, and the District Department of Transportation.

Washington D.C. City Bus Routes

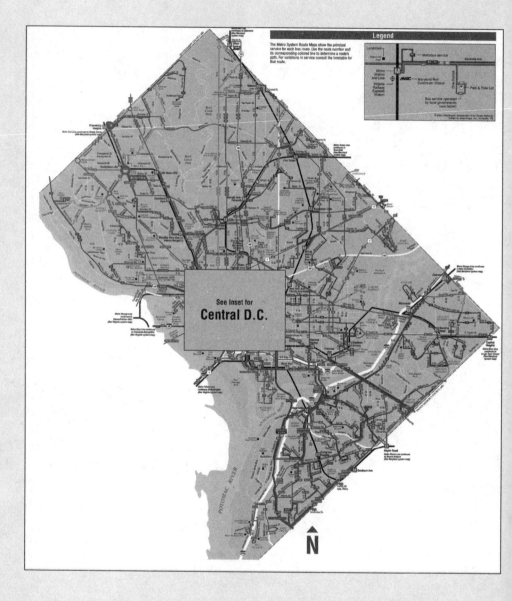

Washington D.C. Metro map

Metrorail System map used with permission of the Washington Metropolitan Area Transit Authority (WMATA).

Index

Everything® You Need for a Family Vacation to Remember

The Everything® Family Guide to the Caribbean
ISBN 10: 1-59337-427-5
ISBN 13: 978-1-59337-427-3
$14.95

The Everything® Family Guide to Coastal Florida
ISBN 10: 1-59869-157-0
ISBN 13: 978-1-59869-157-3
$14.95

The Everything® Family Guide to Cruise Vacations
ISBN 10: 1-59337-428-3
ISBN 13: 978-1-59337-428-0
$14.95

The Everything® Family Guide to Hawaii
ISBN 10: 1-59337-054-7
ISBN 13: 978-1-59337-054-1
$14.95

The Everything® Family Guide to Las Vegas, 2nd Ed.
ISBN 10: 1-59337-359-7
ISBN 13: 978-1-59337-359-7
$14.95

The Everything® Family Guide to Mexico
ISBN 10: 1-59337-658-8
ISBN 13: 978-1-59337-658-
$14.95

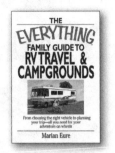